KT-437-320

Hybrid Cloud
FOR
DUMMIES®

by Judith Hurwitz, Marcia Kaufman,
Dr. Fern Halper, Daniel Kirsch

WILEY

John Wiley & Sons, Inc.

Hybrid Cloud For Dummies®

Published by
John Wiley & Sons, Inc.
111 River Street
Hoboken, NJ 07030-5774

www.wiley.com

Copyright © 2012 by John Wiley & Sons, Inc., Hoboken, New Jersey

Published by John Wiley & Sons, Inc., Hoboken, New Jersey

Published simultaneously in Canada

No part of this publication may be reproduced, stored in a retrieval system or transmitted in any form or by any means, electronic, mechanical, photocopying, recording, scanning or otherwise, except as permitted under Sections 107 or 108 of the 1976 United States Copyright Act, without either the prior written permission of the Publisher, or authorization through payment of the appropriate per-copy fee to the Copyright Clearance Center, 222 Rosewood Drive, Danvers, MA 01923, (978) 750-8400, fax (978) 646-8600. Requests to the Publisher for permission should be addressed to the Permissions Department, John Wiley & Sons, Inc., 111 River Street, Hoboken, NJ 07030, (201) 748-6011, fax (201) 748-6008, or online at http://www.wiley.com/go/permissions.

Trademarks: Wiley, the Wiley logo, For Dummies, the Dummies Man logo, A Reference for the Rest of Us!, The Dummies Way, Dummies Daily, The Fun and Easy Way, Dummies.com, Making Everything Easier, and related trade dress are trademarks or registered trademarks of John Wiley & Sons, Inc. and/or its affiliates in the United States and other countries, and may not be used without written permission. All other trademarks are the property of their respective owners. John Wiley & Sons, Inc. is not associated with any product or vendor mentioned in this book.

LIMIT OF LIABILITY/DISCLAIMER OF WARRANTY: THE PUBLISHER AND THE AUTHOR MAKE NO REPRESENTATIONS OR WARRANTIES WITH RESPECT TO THE ACCURACY OR COMPLETENESS OF THE CONTENTS OF THIS WORK AND SPECIFICALLY DISCLAIM ALL WARRANTIES, INCLUDING WITHOUT LIMITATION WARRANTIES OF FITNESS FOR A PARTICULAR PURPOSE. NO WARRANTY MAY BE CREATED OR EXTENDED BY SALES OR PROMOTIONAL MATERIALS. THE ADVICE AND STRATEGIES CONTAINED HEREIN MAY NOT BE SUITABLE FOR EVERY SITUATION. THIS WORK IS SOLD WITH THE UNDERSTANDING THAT THE PUBLISHER IS NOT ENGAGED IN RENDERING LEGAL, ACCOUNTING, OR OTHER PROFESSIONAL SERVICES. IF PROFESSIONAL ASSISTANCE IS REQUIRED, THE SERVICES OF A COMPETENT PROFESSIONAL PERSON SHOULD BE SOUGHT. NEITHER THE PUBLISHER NOR THE AUTHOR SHALL BE LIABLE FOR DAMAGES ARISING HEREFROM. THE FACT THAT AN ORGANIZATION OR WEBSITE IS REFERRED TO IN THIS WORK AS A CITATION AND/OR A POTENTIAL SOURCE OF FURTHER INFORMATION DOES NOT MEAN THAT THE AUTHOR OR THE PUBLISHER ENDORSES THE INFORMATION THE ORGANIZATION OR WEBSITE MAY PROVIDE OR RECOMMENDATIONS IT MAY MAKE. FURTHER, READERS SHOULD BE AWARE THAT INTERNET WEBSITES LISTED IN THIS WORK MAY HAVE CHANGED OR DISAPPEARED BETWEEN WHEN THIS WORK WAS WRITTEN AND WHEN IT IS READ.

For general information on our other products and services, please contact our Customer Care Department within the U.S. at 877-762-2974, outside the U.S. at 317-572-3993, or fax 317-572-4002.

For technical support, please visit www.wiley.com/techsupport.

Wiley publishes in a variety of print and electronic formats and by print-on-demand. Some material included with standard print versions of this book may not be included in e-books or in print-on-demand. If this book refers to media such as a CD or DVD that is not included in the version you purchased, you may download this material at http://booksupport.wiley.com. For more information about Wiley products, visit www.wiley.com.

Library of Congress Control Number: 2012937957

ISBN 978-1-118-12719-3 (pbk); ISBN 978-1-118-23500-3 (ebk); ISBN 978-1-118-22487-8 (ebk); ISBN 978-1-118-26292-4 (ebk)

Manufactured in the United States of America

10 9 8 7 6 5 4 3 2 1

WILEY

Lambeth
Libraries

STREATHAM LIBRARY
63 STREATHAM HIGH ROAD
LONDON SW16 1PL
TEL: 020 7926 6768

Items must be returned on
or before the last date
stamped below, or over
due charges will be made.

Renewals may be made by
personal application, by
post or by telephone.

08/13

9112

9 MAR 2013

18 SEP 2013

10 JAN 2015.

LM 1314849   4

About the Authors

Judith Hurwitz is President and CEO of Hurwitz & Associates, a research and consulting firm focused on emerging technology, including cloud computing, big data, analytics, software development, service management, and security and governance. She is a technology strategist, thought leader, and author. A pioneer in anticipating technology innovation and adoption, she has served as a trusted advisor to many industry leaders over the years. Judith has helped these companies make the transition to a new business model focused on the business value of emerging platforms. She is the founder of Hurwitz Group. She has worked in various corporations, including Apollo Computer and John Hancock. She has written extensively about all aspects of distributed software. In 2011 she authored *Smart or Lucky? How Technology Leaders Turn Chance into Success* (Jossey Bass, 2011). Judith is a co-author on five retail For Dummies titles including *Cloud Computing For Dummies* (John Wiley & Sons, Inc., 2010), *Service Management For Dummies*, and *Service Oriented Architecture For Dummies*, 2nd Edition (both John Wiley & Sons, Inc., 2009). She is also a co-author on many custom published For Dummies titles including *Platform as a Service For Dummies*, CloudBees Special Edition (John Wiley & Sons, Inc., 2012), *Cloud For Dummies,* IBM Midsize Company Limited Edition (John Wiley & Sons, Inc., 2011), *Private Cloud For Dummies*, IBM Limited Edition (2011), and *Information on Demand For Dummies*, IBM Limited Edition (2008) (both John Wiley & Sons, Inc.).

Judith holds BS and MS degrees from Boston University, serves on several advisory boards of emerging companies, and was named a distinguished alumnus of Boston University's College of Arts & Sciences in 2005. She is also a recipient of the 2005 Massachusetts Technology Leadership Council award.

Marcia Kaufman is a founding Partner and COO of Hurwitz & Associates, a research and consulting firm focused on emerging technology, including cloud computing, big data, analytics, software development, service management, and security and governance. She has written extensively on the business value of virtualization and cloud computing, with an emphasis on evolving cloud infrastructure and business models, data-encryption and end-point security, and online transaction processing in cloud environments. Marcia has more than 20 years of experience in business strategy, industry research, distributed software, software quality, information management, and analytics. Marcia has worked within the financial services, manufacturing, and services industries. During her tenure at Data Resources, Inc. (DRI), she developed sophisticated industry models and forecasts. She holds an AB from Connecticut College in mathematics and economics and an MBA from Boston University.

Marcia is a co-author on five retail For Dummies titles including *Cloud Computing For Dummies* (John Wiley & Sons, Inc., 2010), *Service Oriented Architecture For Dummies*, 2nd Edition, and *Service Management For Dummies* (both John Wiley & Sons, Inc., 2009). She is also a co-author on many custom published For Dummies titles including *Platform as a Service For Dummies*, CloudBees Special Edition (John Wiley & Sons, Inc., 2012), *Cloud For Dummies*, IBM Midsize Company Limited Edition (John Wiley & Sons, Inc., 2011), *Private Cloud For Dummies*, IBM Limited Edition (2011) and *Information on Demand For Dummies* (2008) (both John Wiley & Sons, Inc.).

Fern Halper, PhD, a partner in Hurwitz & Associates, has more than 20 years of experience in data analysis, business analysis, and strategy development. Fern has published numerous articles on data analysis and advanced analytics. She has done extensive research, writing, and speaking on the topic of predictive analytics and text analytics. Fern publishes a regular technology blog. She has held key positions at AT&T Bell Laboratories and Lucent Technologies, where she was responsible for developing innovative data analysis systems as well as developing strategy and product-line plans for Internet businesses. Fern has taught courses in information technology at several universities. She received her BA from Colgate University and her PhD from Texas A&M University.

Fern is a co-author on four retail For Dummies titles including *Cloud Computing For Dummies* (John Wiley & Sons, Inc., 2010), *Service Oriented Architecture For Dummies*, 2nd Edition, and *Service Management For Dummies* (both John Wiley & Sons, Inc., 2009). She is also a co-author on many custom published For Dummies titles including, *Cloud For Dummies*, IBM Midsize Company Limited Edition (John Wiley & Sons, Inc., 2011) *Platform as a Service For Dummies*, CloudBees Special Edition (John Wiley & Sons, Inc., 2012), and *Information on Demand For Dummies*, IBM Limited Edition (John Wiley & Sons, Inc., 2008).

Daniel Kirsch, JD, an analyst with Hurwitz & Associates, focuses his research primarily in the areas of compliance, governance, security, and privacy. Dan earned his legal degree from Boston College Law School where he focused on business law issues. Having a legal background, Dan brings a unique perspective on customer issues, strategy, and potential hazards. Dan's research focuses on how compliance, governance, security, and privacy are affecting the software industry and customer requirements. Increasingly, these issues are gaining more currency with the growth of cloud computing and the growth of big data. His work looks at how these issues are being automated as well as the best practices that companies are putting in place. Additionally, Dan graduated magna cum laude from Union College in Schenectady, NY.

Dedication

Judith dedicates this book to her husband, Warren, her children, Sara and David, and her mother, Elaine. She also dedicates this book in memory of her father, David.

Marcia dedicates this book to her husband, Matthew, her children, Sara and Emily, and her parents, Gloria and Larry.

Fern dedicates this book to her husband, Clay, and daughters, Katie and Lindsay.

Daniel dedicates this book to Sara; his grandmother, Dorothy; parents, Michael and Margery; and siblings, Jonathan and Rebecca.

Authors' Acknowledgments

We heartily thank our friends at Wiley, most especially Katie Feltman and Nicole Sholly. In addition, we would like to thank our technical editor, Amy Wohl, for her insightful contributions.

The authors would like to acknowledge the contribution of the following technology industry thought leaders who graciously offered their time to share their technical and business knowledge on a wide range of issues related to hybrid cloud. Their assistance was provided in many ways, including technology briefings, sharing of research, case study examples, and reviewing content. We thank the following people and their organizations for their valuable assistance:

Alert Logic: Urvish Vashi
BMC: Lilac Schoenbeck
Cloud Security Alliance: General acknowledgment
CloudBees: Steven Harris, Sacha Labourey, and Andre Pino
CloudPassage: Rand Wacker
CloudScaling: Randy Bias
CloudTrigger: Lonnie Willis
Corent Technology: Scott Chate and Feyzi Fetehi
Dome9 Security: Dave Meizlik
Dynamic OPS: Rich Bourdeau, Chad Jones, and Candyce Plante
Egnyte: Vineet Jain
EMC: Chuck Hollis
Equinix: Sam Johnston
HP: Terence Ngai
IBM: Snehal Antani, Angel Luis Diaz, Robin Hernandez, Shawn Jaques, Dave Lindquist, and Kristin Lovejoy
Linux Foundation: Jim Zemlin
Liquidhub: Rob Kelley
National Institute of Standards and Technology (NIST): Tim Grance and Peter Mell
OpenStack: Jonathan Bryce
Orchestratus: Shlomo Swidler
Porticor: Gilad Parann-Nissany
Redhat: Gordon Haff and Jim Totton
Rightscale: Michael Crandell
Salesforce: Steve Gillmor, Arti Narayanan, Anshu Sharma, and John Taschek
SoftLayer: Andre Fuoch, Duke Skarda, and Simon West
SUSE: Patrick Quariroli
The Open Group: Dr. Chris Harding
Vistaprint: Clay Bogusky

Publisher's Acknowledgments

We're proud of this book; please send us your comments at http://dummies.custhelp.com. For other comments, please contact our Customer Care Department within the U.S. at 877-762-2974, outside the U.S. at 317-572-3993, or fax 317-572-4002.

Some of the people who helped bring this book to market include the following:

Acquisitions and Editorial

Senior Project Editor: Nicole Sholly

Senior Acquisitions Editor: Katie Feltman

Copy Editor: Melba Hopper

Technical Editor: Amy Wohl

Editorial Manager: Kevin Kirschner

Editorial Assistants: Amanda Graham, Leslie Saxman

Sr. Editorial Assistant: Cherie Case

Cover Photo: ©iStockphoto.com / ranplett

Cartoons: Rich Tennant (www.the5thwave.com)

Composition Services

Project Coordinator: Sheree Montgomery

Layout and Graphics: Jennifer Creasey, Cheryl Grubbs, Joyce Haughey, Lavonne Roberts

Proofreaders: Rebecca Denoncour, Christine Sabooni

Indexer: Steve Rath

Special Help
Amanda Graham, Jennifer Riggs

Publishing and Editorial for Technology Dummies

    Richard Swadley, Vice President and Executive Group Publisher

    Andy Cummings, Vice President and Publisher

    Mary Bednarek, Executive Acquisitions Director

    Mary C. Corder, Editorial Director

Publishing for Consumer Dummies

    Kathleen Nebenhaus, Vice President and Executive Publisher

Composition Services

    Debbie Stailey, Director of Composition Services

Contents at a Glance

Table of Contents

Introduction

● ●

*W*elcome to *Hybrid Cloud For Dummies*. Cloud computing has become ubiquitous these days. It's impossible to look at the current implementations of technology and not be consumed by references to cloud. But much has changed since Hurwitz & Associates wrote *Cloud Computing For Dummies* in 2009. Cloud computing has indeed evolved. Now, we're looking at the new world of the *hybrid cloud,* an environment that employs both private and public cloud services.

The hybrid cloud, however, is more than just a collection of disconnected services running on different platforms. It's a pragmatic way in which companies are starting to look at the best platform to provide the types of services that internal and external constituents need. Therefore, computing is increasingly becoming a set of business services that are architected based on need. As this happens, the very nature of what a data center is will change. Increasingly, IT and business management are working collaboratively to find new ways to streamline their computing infrastructure through a hybrid cloud model to make it more flexible and adaptive to change. Likewise, companies are finding that the ability to create highly optimized services for everything from compute to storage and e-mail is changing the economics of computing. Thus, the hybrid cloud begins to use new business models. Suddenly, software ecosystems are emerging that allow businesses to create their own cloud services as profit centers. Small companies can leverage a hybrid of services that enables even a tiny company to offer the most sophisticated business services.

It's clear that the ability to combine public clouds with private cloud services is having a dramatic impact on computing for small and large companies as well as service providers and cloud application builders. In fact, the growing importance of hybrid cloud environments is transforming the entire computing industry as well as the way businesses are able to leverage technology to innovate. Economics and speed are the two greatest issues driving this market change.

No matter what type of cloud services will be best at meeting your business needs, the cloud is the foundation for the future of computing. Even for organizations that will use only minimal cloud services, the requirements to optimize computing will dramatically change how computing is delivered to internal and external customers.

As you can see, for many reasons, we think that it's important to understand what the hybrid cloud is all about and what services are available to you. We wrote this book to provide a perspective on what the hybrid cloud is and how it's changing the data center and the world of applications and infrastructure. We think this book will give you the context to make informed decisions.

About This Book

The hybrid cloud is new to many people and, therefore, it requires some investigation and understanding of both the technical and business requirements. Many different people need knowledge about the hybrid. Some of you want to delve into the technical details, while others will want to understand the economic implications of using the hybrid cloud. Other executives need to know enough to be able to understand how the hybrid cloud can affect business decisions. Implementing a hybrid cloud environment requires both an architectural and a business approach — and lots of planning.

No matter your goal in reading this book, we address the following issues to help you understand the hybrid cloud environment and the impact it can have on your business:

- ✔ Whether you should keep your data center just the way it is today or evolve it to support only certain types of applications and workloads
- ✔ When it's a good idea to use a public cloud service and how to use private cloud services
- ✔ How a move to a public cloud service affects security and governance requirements
- ✔ What it means to really have a private cloud computing utility behind a firewall
- ✔ Whether the IT organization can become a service provider to the business
- ✔ What cloud management means in a hybrid environment
- ✔ The best approaches to cloud storage
- ✔ What it means to have the right service agreement across different vendors and services
- ✔ What you need to know about the economics of the hybrid cloud

Foolish Assumptions

Try as we might to be all things to all people, when it came to writing this book, we had to pick who we thought would be most interested in *Hybrid Cloud For Dummies*. Here's who we think you are:

- ✔ **You're smart.** You're no dummy, yet the topic of hybrid cloud gives you an uneasy feeling; you can't quite get your head around it, and if you're pressed for a definition, you might try to change the subject.

✔ **You're a businessperson who wants little or nothing to do with technology.** But you live in the twenty-first century, so you can't escape it. Everybody's saying, "It's all about moving to the hybrid cloud," so you think that you better find out what they're talking about.

✔ **You're an IT person who knows a heck of a lot about technology.** The thing is, you're new to this cloud stuff. Everybody says it's something different. Once and for all, you want the whole picture.

Whoever you are, welcome. We're here to help.

How This Book Is Organized

We divided our book into seven parts for easy reading. Feel free to skip about.

Part I: Understanding Concepts and Construction

In this part, we explain the basic concepts you need for a full understanding of the hybrid cloud, from both a technical and a business perspective. We also introduce you to the major concepts and components so you can hold your own in any meaningful cloud conversation.

Part II: Examining Cloud Service Delivery Models

Part II is for both technical and business professionals who need to understand the different models of cloud computing that make up the hybrid cloud. In this section, we dive deeper into the actual foundational elements of the cloud.

Part III: Evaluating the Business Value of the Hybrid Cloud

What is the purpose of the hybrid cloud, and how does it support business objectives? This part of the book gives you a perspective on how to evaluate the hybrid cloud based on your objectives. This part helps you think about the hybrid cloud's effect on businesses.

Part IV: Creating a Unified Hybrid Environment

This part gets to the nitty-gritty of what it means to create a computing environment that brings elements of a data center together with public and private cloud services. This section gives you plenty to think about in this critical area.

Part V: Operationalizing Hybrid Clouds

At the end of the day, the value of the hybrid cloud is only as good as how well you operationalize these services to support all your constituents. Therefore, look to this section to understand how IT needs to make this new architectural approach work on a day-to-day basis.

Part VI: Getting Set for the Hybrid Cloud Journey

This part helps you think about what it takes to get started on your hybrid cloud journey. It takes lots of planning — not just for the precise service you're considering, but also the way you apply service orientation and service management to completing the picture.

Part VII: The Part of Tens

If you're new to the *For Dummies* treasure trove, you're no doubt unfamiliar with "The Part of Tens." In "The Part of Tens," Wiley editors torture *For Dummies* authors into creating useful bits of information easily accessible in lists containing ten (or more) elucidating elements. We started these chapters kicking and screaming but are ultimately very glad they're here. After you read through the hybrid cloud resources, best practices, and do's and don'ts we provide in the "Part of Tens," we think you'll be glad, too.

Glossary

We include a glossary of terms frequently used when people discuss the cloud. Although we strive to define terms as we introduce them in this book, we think you'll find the glossary a useful resource.

Icons Used in This Book

What's a *For Dummies* book without icons pointing out useful tips, interesting facts, and potentially dangerous pitfalls? Familiarize yourself with these icons to help ensure you don't miss a thing.

Pay attention. The bother you save may be your own.

You may be sorry if this little tidbit slips your mind.

With this icon, we mark particularly useful points to pay attention to.

Tidbits for the more technically inclined.

Where to Go from Here

We've created an overview of the hybrid cloud and introduced you to all of its significant components. We recommend that you read the first three chapters to give you context for what the cloud is about and how it changes the way services will be delivered in the future. The next five chapters break down the different types of cloud services and how they're relevant to your organization.

You can read from cover to cover, but if you're not that kind of person, we've tried to adhere to the *For Dummies* style of keeping chapters self-contained so you can go straight to the topics that interest you most. Wherever you start, we wish you well.

Many of these chapters could be expanded into full-length books of their own. The hybrid cloud and the emerging technology landscape is a big focus for us at Hurwitz & Associates, and we invite you to visit our site and read our blogs and insights at www.hurwitz.com.

Part I
Understanding Concepts and Construction

The 5th Wave   By Rich Tennant

"We're still working out the kinks in our cloud computing environment."

In this part . . .

The phrase *hybrid computing* is made up of many different parts. In this part, we introduce the concept and provide some guidelines to help you understand the foundational elements and key components. We use this section to put the idea of the hybrid cloud into the context for your organization.

Chapter 1

Discovering the Fundamentals of Your Computing Environment

*H*ow quickly things change. Cloud computing has evolved from a risky and confusing concept to a strategy that organizations large and small are beginning to adopt as part of their overall computing strategy. A few years ago when Hurwitz & Associates wrote *Cloud Computing For Dummies,* there was plenty of skepticism. Would businesses really be willing to adopt cloud computing? What exactly is cloud computing, and how does it help businesses be more effective?

The market has come a long way in a short amount of time. Today more companies — large and small — are doing everything from prototyping a new application with public clouds to implementing a complex private cloud as a utility to support customers and partners. Indeed, we have moved out of the first phase of this new market. We are now at the stage when customers are starting to ask not whether they should think about cloud computing but what types of cloud computing are best able to meet their business problems. Companies are realizing that they need many different types of cloud services in order to meet a variety of customer needs. Therefore, the idea of combining all forms of cloud models in conjunction with data center services as an amalgam or hybrid is the direction computing is headed. An organization deploys a hybrid cloud when it utilizes public and private clouds together with its data center(s) and there are touch points between at least one or more of the deployment models. For example, it shares data between a public and private cloud.

In this chapter, we provide an overview of the hybrid cloud computing environment, including the basics you need to understand in order to move forward in the world of hybrid clouds. First, it's important to understand that an ecosystem of participants define the market. This ecosystem consists of three categories of players: consumers of services, providers of services, and designers of services. In addition, a fourth type of player is a combination of the other three: systems integrators can be consumers of cloud services, they can become a service provider themselves, or they can design services. Here are the characteristics of each:

- **Consumers:** There are different types of consumers. A cloud services consumer might be an individual, or a small business team. Departments in large companies can be cloud services consumers. The IT department can use cloud services either to supplement existing data center services, or to provide specific cloud-based applications such as customer relationship management (CRM) to the sales team. Likewise, even a company that provides cloud services to consumers may use third-party cloud services to supplement their capacity.

- **Service providers:** Cloud service providers are companies that offer packaged services to consumers. Many different types of providers range from those who offer services to individuals and those that serve a broad set of constituents. Many service providers focus on certain markets or certain types of workloads so they can optimize their offerings inexpensively. Thousands of cloud service providers provide public cloud services. Other service providers offer private clouds to support specialized services. A service provider can also be the consumer of a service they acquire to support their customers. Some traditional businesses have taken on the role of becoming a service provider to their customers and partners. These companies are discovering that like professional service providers, they can create a private cloud and offer their own set of services to their customers, which is viewed as a new source of revenue.

- **Service designers:** Companies that can create sophisticated services, tools, and applications to support a variety of cloud models have a huge opportunity. These designers typically build everything from a full Software as a Service (SaaS) platform to tools needed for developers or deployers of cloud services. For example, there is an emerging market for companies that design security and governance offerings to support a variety of cloud models.

- **Systems integrators as cloud service providers:** Systems integrators are getting into the act. Systems integrators are helping customers integrate their data center with public cloud services and private cloud environments. These companies are helping to define best practices and implementation road maps. These integrators can provide private clouds that they host and manage for customers.

Deconstructing Cloud Concepts

Cloud computing is a method of providing a set of shared computing resources that includes applications, computing, storage, networking, development, and deployment platforms as well as business processes. Cloud computing turns traditional siloed computing assets into shared pools of resources that are based on an underlying Internet foundation. Cloud computing makes these resources easier to use by providing standardization and automation. *Standardization* is the implementation of services using a consistent approach supported by a set of consistent interfaces. Likewise, a cloud requires that processes are implemented through the use of automation. *Automation* is a process that's triggered based on business rules, resource availability, and security demands. Automation is required to support a self-service provisioning model. To promote efficiency, automation can ensure that after a provisioned service is no longer needed, it can be returned to the resource pool. This type of automation based on rules can help with capacity planning and overall workload management.

Equally important is that the cloud provides a new economic model of computing. Instead of purchasing, managing, and maintaining a self-contained, traditional *data center* — a specialized environment where a variety of different computing resources are managed — a business is able to transform computing into a more streamlined computing environment that better serves changing computing requirements. If a company has already invested in a data center to support a line of business applications, it can transform that data center into a more targeted environment. If the company wants to provide a flexible self-service resource environment on its premises, it can create what's called a private cloud. Likewise, a company can use sophisticated services available from a third-party public cloud provider (either applications or platforms) to extend and enhance the environment.

Most businesses today are already using some kind of cloud service — even if they don't think of it as a cloud. For example, any company that uses ADP for payroll service is using a cloud-based service. A company may use online data backup or storage services that live in a commercial cloud. If employees use Google's Gmail service, they are using a cloud service. Many companies are discovering that having customer relationship management (CRM) available as a service is a better way to support the sales team than the traditional on-premises software options.

You should be getting the idea that cloud computing means that everything — from compute power to computing infrastructure, and from applications and business processes to personal collaboration — can be delivered to you as a service. To be operational in the real world, the cloud must be implemented with common standardized processes and automation.

Clouds come in different versions, depending on your needs. There are two primary deployment models of cloud: public and private. Most organizations will use a combination of private computing resources (data centers and private clouds) and public services, where some of the services existing in these environments touch each other — which is what we call a *hybrid cloud environment*.

The public cloud

The *public cloud* is a set of hardware, networking, storage, services, applications, and interfaces owned and operated by a third party for use by other companies or individuals. These commercial providers create a highly scalable data center that hides the details of the underlying infrastructure from the consumer. Public clouds are viable because they typically manage relatively repetitive or straightforward workloads. For example, electronic mail is a very simple application. Therefore, a cloud provider can optimize the environment so that it is best suited to support a large number of customers, even if they save many messages. Likewise, public cloud providers offering storage or computing services will optimize their computing hardware and software to support these specific types of workloads. In contrast, the typical data center supports so many different applications and so many different workloads that it cannot be optimized easily.

The private cloud

A *private cloud* is a set of hardware, networking, storage, services, applications, and interfaces owned and operated by an organization for the use of its employees, partners, and customers. A private cloud can be created and managed by a third party for the exclusive use of one enterprise. The private cloud is a highly controlled environment not open for public consumption. Thus, a private cloud sits behind a firewall. The private cloud is highly automated with a focus on governance, security, and compliance. Automation replaces more manual processes of managing IT services to support customers. In this way, business rules and processes can be implemented inside software so that the environment becomes more predictable and manageable.

The hybrid cloud

A *hybrid cloud* is a combination of a private cloud combined with the use of public cloud services where one or several touch points are between the environments. The goal is to create a well-managed hybrid cloud management environment that can combine services and data from a variety of cloud models to create a unified, automated, and well-managed computing environment. In reality, it will be a number of years before the full range of services becomes the norm. Components of this hybrid management approach are available today, but these are the early days. For a good understanding of this management model, we recommend you read Chapter 4 about hybrid cloud management. Many companies in the market are working on this model because it will solve critical problems. Why is this necessary? A company might use the private cloud as a way to support changing needs of the application development team within various departments where developers need to constantly build new experimental applications or create new value to meet emerging business needs. A private cloud provides a flexible environment with a higher level of security than would be available in a public cloud. The same company might also use public services ranging from compute, storage, platform, and application services to augment and strengthen their changing business needs.

Combining public services with private clouds and the data center as a hybrid is the new definition of *corporate computing*. Not all companies that use some public and some private cloud services have a hybrid cloud. Rather, a hybrid cloud is an environment where the private and public services are used together to create value. In the following circumstances, a cloud is not hybrid:

- ✔ If a few developers in a company use a public cloud service to prototype a new application that is completely disconnected from the private cloud or the data center, the company does not have a hybrid environment.
- ✔ If a company is using a SaaS application for a project but there is no movement of data from that application into the company's data center, the environment is not hybrid.

A cloud is hybrid in the following situations:

- ✔ If a company uses a public development platform that sends data to a private cloud or a data center–based application, the cloud is hybrid.
- ✔ When a company leverages a number of SaaS applications and moves data between private or data center resources, the cloud is hybrid.
- ✔ When a business process is designed as a service so that it can connect with environments as though they were a single environment, the cloud is hybrid.

Cloud Computing Elements: Resource Pools/Cloud Models and Services

Now that you have a context for the types of cloud environments, it's important to understand the common elements required to make clouds functional. In this section, we give you the basics of what you need to know. Figure 1-1 illustrates the related elements that come together to create clouds. On the bottom of the diagram is a set of *resource pools* that feed a set of cloud delivery services. On the top of the diagram are the common service elements needed to support these delivery models.

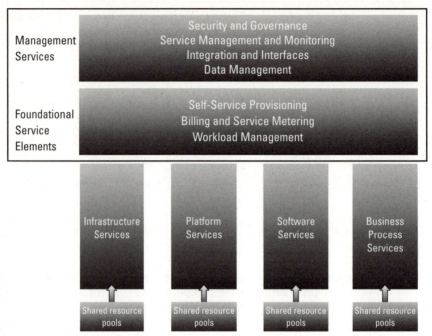

Figure 1-1:
How the
cloud
elements fit
together.

One of the fundamental differences between cloud computing and traditional computing is the way a cloud is designed to manage workload resources. Managing workloads is foundational to the cloud. For more details on workload management, you may want to read Chapter 12. Whereas a data center is designed to manage applications, a cloud is intended to manage a pool of resources, which is precisely what it sounds like — a set of shared, configured services that are independent of a physical location. In many situations, cloud service providers create a multi-tenant environment to support the deployment of these resources. Multi-tenancy enables the sharing of a service while keeping the data and configurations of individual customers separate.

For example, say that you are a cloud provider. You don't want your customers to have to select one specific server or one storage system for their workloads or data. Instead, you want the customers to be abstracted from that idea so that they can simply say, "I need some more storage" and those storage resources are pooled together from various physical systems to create a set of resources. In other words, customers don't need to know which storage system they're accessing. These shared resource pools are shown at the bottom of Figure 1-1.

To make resource pooling work, each pooled element needs to be written with service-oriented constructs in mind. Consequently, each resource is written as an independent service without dependencies and with well-defined interfaces. For more details on service orientation, turn to Chapter 3.

Understanding the foundations of cloud computing calls for an understanding of the four different cloud delivery models:

✔ Software as a Service

✔ Platform as a Service

✔ Infrastructure as a Service

✔ Business Process as a Service

Part II has a chapter on each of these models, but here we cover the basics on the different cloud computing delivery models. These are illustrated as infrastructure services, platform services, and software services in Figure 1-1.

Infrastructure as a Service

Infrastructure as a Service (IaaS) is the delivery of services such as hardware, storage, networking, data center space, and various utility software elements on a request basis. There are both public and private versions of IaaS. In the public IaaS, the user simply needs a credit card to acquire these resources. When that user stops paying, the resource disappears. In a private IaaS service, it is usually the IT organization or an integrator who creates an infrastructure designed to provide resources on demand to internal users and sometimes business partners. Whereas criteria for a public cloud are based primarily on the ability to pay for a service, a private service applies company policy to a service request. IaaS is the fundamental element used by other cloud models. Some customers will bring their own tools and software to create applications. For more details on IaaS, turn to Chapter 5.

Platform as a Service

Platform as a Service (PaaS) is a mechanism for combining IaaS with an abstracted set of middleware services, software development, and deployment tools that allow the organization to have a consistent way to create and deploy applications on a cloud or on-premises environment. A PaaS offers a consistent set of programming and middleware services that ensure developers have a well-tested and well-integrated way to create applications in a cloud environment. A PaaS environment brings together development and deployment together to create a more manageable way to build and deploy applications. A PaaS requires an Infrastructure service. For more on PaaS, see Chapter 7.

Software as a Service

Software as a Service (SaaS) is a business application created and hosted by a provider in a multi-tenant model. Customers pay for the service either per user on a monthly or yearly contract model. The SaaS application sits on top of both a Platform as a Service and foundational Infrastructure services. Typically, these underlying services aren't visible to end users of a SaaS application. To read more details on SaaS, turn to Chapter 6.

Business Process as a Service

In traditional computing environments, business processes are often built into the application. For example, there may be a payment service or a service that sets up a delivery service request. However, one of the benefits of the movement to cloud computing is that organizations can use cloud-based business process services across the organization. Standardizing on business process services reduces the chance of error and makes it easier for an organization to ensure that the right services are used for the right purpose. If your company is using only a few cloud services, you may wonder why you need to worry about business process services. However, because organizations will use more cloud services over time, business leaders will want the ability to move data among various cloud applications and data center services. So, having a plan for thinking about business process services from a cross-environment perspective will help streamline your organization's movement toward cloud services. These BPaaS can become a revenue source for both cloud consumers and service providers.

Foundational services supporting cloud resource models

No matter what type of resource pool is involved, some core capabilities are essential in the cloud environment, including the following:

- ✔ Elasticity and self-service provisioning
- ✔ Billing and meters of service usage
- ✔ Workload management

These are referred to as foundational service elements in Figure 1-1.

Elasticity and self-service provisioning

One benefit of the cloud is that customers have the potential to access as much of a service as they need when they need it. If they need computing services for a month, they can rent that service for that time period. They don't have to buy a system to handle the need. Although this potential clearly benefits customers, it makes life more complicated for providers of services. In the cloud, the service provider can't know in advance what a customer might need at any given time. So, service providers (whether a public provider or a private cloud provider) must create an environment that can scale to support a diverse set of customer requirements. A provider of cloud services needs to design a platform architecture that is optimized for the service the company is providing. The platform must be designed so that the users/customers provision resources such as computing or storage resources that they pay for on a per-unit basis. When the user no longer needs that resource and stops paying, the resource is released back into the pool of resources.

There are situations when a service provider can't anticipate the needs of a customer. Therefore, it is common for a service provider to add additional capacity from a third-party service provider. Typically, the consumer is unaware that they are dealing with an additional cloud service provider.

Self-service is one of the most important capabilities of cloud computing. With self-service, the developer of an application, for example, is able to use a browser or portal interface to acquire the resources needed to build an application, which is dramatically different than how a developer works in a data center. In the traditional data center model, a developer must request resources from IT operations, which might require IT to acquire more servers and storage and to purchase the required software. At this point, the system has to be configured to meet the development project requirements. Assuming that the cloud service is designed to meet the required goal, the developer can avoid these complicated steps. We go into more detail about how cloud computing helps with software development in Chapter 7, which focuses on Platform as a Service.

Billing and metering services

A cloud service has to provide a way to measure and meter a service. Consequently, a cloud environment includes a built-in service that tracks how many resources a customer is using. Customers consuming public cloud resources will be charged for a unit of usage — whether that is a CPU hour or an amount of storage. Customers using software as a service will be charged for each registered user on a per-year basis. In a private cloud, employees probably won't be charged directly, but usage will be tracked. In many companies, a department's budget will be tied directly to the amount and type of services it uses.

Managing workloads

As we mention earlier in this chapter, a cloud isn't a single unified environment; rather, it's a combination of resources that could be spread across systems and geographies. The cloud is a federated environment that brings together resources so that they can work together. To make this happen in an organized manner requires an organization of workloads. A *workload* is an independent service or collection of code that can be executed. So, you need to think about the cloud as a group of workloads that are managed as though they were a single cohesive environment. It is important in a cloud environment that workloads be designed to support the right task with the right cloud services. For example, some workloads will need to be placed in a private cloud because they require fast transaction management and a high level of security. Other workloads may not be so mission critical and can be placed in a public cloud.

When organizations begin thinking about cloud computing as a strategy, they must do more than simply go to a public or private resource and leverage those services. Like any computing environment, cloud computing requires that workloads be balanced and managed, regardless of the resource pool they're based on. Within a well-designed cloud environment, workloads can move among resource pools in different cloud environments. Because, in the real world, you will use a combination of services, it's important to think not just about an individual workload but also about a combination of workloads and how they interact with each other and with collaborators.

Management services

Many other management services are mandatory for ensuring that cloud computing is a well-managed platform that supports customer needs, including ensuring that a variety of workloads are supported in the right way. This is the case no matter what the cloud deployment and delivery model. Some core services are illustrated at the top of Figure 1-1. Security and governance are key services to ensure that your applications and data are protected. Data management in a hybrid environment is also critical since data will be moving between cloud environments. Moreover, the right level of service must be provided to meet consumer requirements. This is the case regardless of whether you're dealing with a public, private, or hybrid model. That's why hybrid cloud management and monitoring is so important. Finally, since various services will need to be integrated in a hybrid cloud, the interfaces between clouds are also important.

Examining the Role of the Data Center

What happens to the data center when companies begin to implement hybrid clouds? First, the data center does not go away. After all, almost all medium-size and large companies run their own data center — which is how many companies operate their systems of record, including accounting systems, payroll, human resources applications, and line of business applications, to name a few. Many data centers have grown in an unplanned manner over many decades. The typical data center supports different hardware architectures, operating systems, applications, and hundreds, if not thousands, of different tools. To make matters worse, a lot of the money spent in supporting a data center is used for maintenance of existing systems, heating, air conditioning, floor space, and labor.

So, it's not surprising that many companies have taken the time to streamline their data centers through technologies such as server virtualization. In essence, virtualization decouples the software from the hardware. In decoupling, the software is put into a separate container so that it's isolated from the underlying operating system. (See Chapter 16 for more details on how virtualization works.) With the use of virtualization, data center management can more easily and efficiently manage the way applications are placed on servers.

However, even though IT has made the data center more efficient, cloud computing has made it apparent that more can be done to transform computing. Organizations are beginning to take a hard look at what the centralized data center is well suited for and at the changes required to create a computing environment that truly serves the needs of their business.

Companies are beginning to discover that they can have the best of all worlds by finding the tasks that are most appropriate for a highly controlled data center and which workloads are best suited to either a private or a public cloud.

Although a well-designed and well-tuned data center provides essential services to a company, it is often best suited for a complex line of business applications. These are often transaction-intensive applications that need to confirm and track the movement of financial transactions among customers, suppliers, and partners. Additionally, large, often highly customized systems of record are and will continue to be data center–based. These applications are typically tightly monitored for corporate governance and compliance.

The key difference between the traditional role of the data center and the new role of the data center is just beginning to be clear: The traditional data center is changing from a general-purpose repository for all applications to a highly tuned corporate asset for a class of applications. This is explained in Tables 1-1 and 1-2.

Table 1-1	Traditional Data Center
Type of Data Center	**Description**
Traditional Data Center	Data center with all applications and data centrally managed
Consolidated Data Center	Virtualization applied to enable server consolidation supporting existing model

Table 1-2	Next Generation Data Center
Type of Data Center	**Description**
Purpose-Built Data Center	Highly tuned data center for enterprise systems of record
Purpose-Built Private Cloud	Self-service resource available for developers and partners

Traditional data center

One way to think about where we are today with data centers is to think about the car garage in the typical suburban home. When the home is first built, the homeowners use the garage for its intended use — storing two cars. For the first year or so everything works well, but over time the garage is used to store the lawn mower, boxes of books, and random things that are no longer used. Soon there is little room in the garage for even a single car. Figure 1-2 illustrates this concept. The built for purpose garage is no longer efficient and no longer serves its purpose, but the family still needs to store cars and still needs room for everything else. The solution could be to build a shed in the backyard to store yard tools and other stuff. What is the point of this example? It mirrors what has happened to the data center over time.

For the past 30 years, organizations have had traditional data that has been in a centrally managed environment for a huge variety of applications and company requirements. Consequently, the typical data center has become more complicated, expensive, and cumbersome to manage. This situation has resulted in data center consolidation, where IT management has taken a hard look first at what applications are actually needed.

Rethinking the data center

IT management has begun to pare down the number of applications being used, and to use virtualization to consolidate workloads and remove superfluous hardware. Traditionally, it was complicated to determine how much physical space an application would require in the data center. Rather than take the risk that an application would not have enough room to support customer requirements, companies simply bought additional capacity in order to ensure performance. However, this approach to applications management became unsustainable. In essence, through virtualization technology, IT has been able to add a software layer that allows applications to be more easily consolidated onto specific servers. But even these moves have not been enough.

The purpose-built data center

Just as the homeowners reclaimed the garage, IT is beginning to make the transition to purpose-built data centers. These new generation data centers are tuned to support the key systems that manage a business. In some situations, key applications are simply maintained in their current state because of the way they're used for stable, mission critical business processes. In other cases, the IT organization has taken the time to rearchitect these applications into a set of modular services that can be used to support many different business initiatives. For example, a company might create a service as the authorized way to pay a supplier for a service. By creating a single service that is used across many business units, the data center becomes a more efficient environment. In addition, the emerging purpose-built data center doesn't try to provide all services for all needs. It becomes the source of the business services and data services that apply to the cross-organizational needs.

A garage built for purpose: like the original data center

Garage with lots of stuff added: the data center over time

Figure 1-2:
The original data center evolved over time just like the typical home garage. The cloud brings back the idea of a fit for purpose environment.

Shed = private cloud

Getting the garage reconfigured for its purpose by adding a shed: a data center with a private cloud in a separate environment

Purpose-built private cloud

IT organizations have discovered that it's much more efficient and effective to create private cloud services for developers to create new applications and services. Therefore, companies are setting up a highly automated computing environment enabled with a self-service portal. This portal is often designed with business process rules that dictate what services a developer or an authorized partner can use. For example, a developer beginning to develop a new application may be permitted to use the Java language, specific types of middleware, and a specified amount of computing capacity and storage. Once the project is completed, there may be a rule that automatically returns the capacity back to the pool of resources. The private cloud service is intended to support an organization's need for speed and agility based on fast-changing company requirements. Having a private cloud available for projects allows a company to easily experiment with new ideas and new applications without having to request funding for a project that might not become a reality.

Seeing how the public cloud fits

Say that your company is a retailer with a vibrant and well-used transactional portal for selling products online. The biggest event for the company is its yearly 50 percent–off sale. During a two-week period, the company has an agreement with a public cloud company to supplement its capacity so that performance is always consistent. Your company has a contract with the public cloud provider to provide capacity services during the sale as well as other times when additional resources are required. Because your company can rely on the public cloud provider, it doesn't have to buy additional servers for incremental usage, thus saving time and money.

Your company has selected two different software applications from service providers to replace existing on-premises applications. One application is a customer relationship management (CRM) that allows the sales force to easily get access to prospective and current customer information from a cloud-based public service. In addition, your company uses a human resources management platform as a service. The company has implemented integration software that allows data to be managed among the data center and the two SaaS environments. Both of these SaaS applications have enabled your company to avoid purchasing additional hardware and software that would require IT management. In addition, because the sales team can access their data much faster from any device they're using, from a business perspective, the sales team's performance is much more effective.

Your company is in a new market where getting a series of new services operational quickly has the potential to leapfrog the competition. Your company hasn't been in business very long. Because the company can use a public service, it can make services available before more established companies can act. At the same time, the company can use its data center to monitor the effectiveness of services, manage data privately, and combine with other services that aren't visible to customers.

Knowing when the private cloud shines

Now, say that your company's products and services are offered in a portal to your business partners. These products are key to a company's revenue. For example, you might be part of a financial services company that offers a key business service that is purchased by various banks around the globe. Because this service is a revenue source and because the company is a well-run and orchestrated computing environment, it makes sense for the company to establish a private cloud to support this business model. An architected private cloud that supports this business initiative is ideal for the financial services company. Using a public service where the company is charged on a time or usage basis wouldn't be cost-effective.

Your company has a large team of developers spread across the world. You decide to create a private cloud that allows any authorized developer to gain access to data, tools, and processes required to create applications. You have set up rules to ensure that developers can access only the tools and data they're supposed to use. The private cloud makes the process of managing a distributed development team more productive and more cost-effective.

What might your cloud deployment look like in the future?

Let's imagine that the year is 2020 and you have implemented a next generation computing environment based on re-envisioning the data center and how you use cloud resources. What might your computing environment look like? Let's say your company is a retailer with stores in 20 different countries and has a healthy online commerce business. In the past you supported three very large data centers in different geographies. You also used a smattering of SaaS applications for sales automation, marketing services, commerce services, human resources, and package tracking. You also used some public cloud storage services to handle transactions during peak holiday seasons.

Inside the data center you implemented server virtualization to reduce the energy and space you required. You also took some time to get rid of applications that weren't used anymore but somehow were still running in the data center.

While all of these changes helped make the computing environment better, none of the changes gave the company the competitive edge that management wanted to see. Management wanted to go further by having the IT organization become a service provider to its customers and business partners. This new business model was intended to help the company become more proactive in responding to opportunities before competitors.

So, the CIO in consultation with the CEO decided to make some radical changes. The first change was to rethink the data center itself. The company transformed the data center into a streamlined environment to manage a line of business applications. Therefore, the data center now included the ERP system, and customized commerce systems that were tailored specifically to the type of retail business. In addition, a specialized system that was used to manage the manufacturing process of

(continued)

(continued)

special-order merchandise was also managed in the data center. Finally, there were four other specialized systems that had been built 15 years ago that were necessary but used only sporadically. With fewer systems, it was possible to optimize the data center to support these workloads much more efficiently. The company was able to purchase new hardware designed specifically for these types of workloads. They were more efficient systems. Networking, storage, and even power, cooling, and floor space were redesigned. More automation was implemented throughout the environment.

To support the needs of the development organization, the company established a private cloud environment. The private cloud was designed specifically to support the development of new applications and prototypes of new innovative ideas that might become products in the future. The private cloud also provided storage, networking resources to support new business services created as a profit center for new business services. Business subsidiaries were able to procure computing services from a self-service portal. IT set up clear business rules that defined what services each business unit was allowed to procure based on the project definitions.

The company also selected some public cloud services to support the business. To support the sales and marketing team, the company continued to use SaaS applications. In addition, the company decided that selecting a public cloud service for e-mail was quite economical, so the company got rid of its internal e-mail system. At the same time, a number of innovative SaaS collaboration services made the process of working with partners a streamlined environment.

The IT team spent the bulk of its time on integration and architectural issues. The team discovered that it was just as easy to create silos with SaaS applications as it was in the data center. This was a difficult lesson to learn. Therefore, the team continues to spend its time on ensuring that the new data center environment includes data and process integration across the data center, the private cloud, and the public cloud services. To manage the environment, the organization invested in service management, security, and governance.

The process of transforming computing was complicated. There were mistakes because either technology was immature or the organization did not consider how all the components of IT needed to be orchestrated. But the IT management team was able to take a step back and create a road map and implementation strategy that took a holistic view of how the next generation of IT would help the company grow in new directions supported by a highly effective and flexible computing environment that was becoming the engine for innovation and business growth.

Chapter 2

The Hybrid Cloud Continuum

*I*n the real world, there's no one method of implementing a computing environment, and the same rule applies to cloud computing. The reality is that most companies use a combination of public and private hybrid cloud services in conjunction with their data center. Companies will use different methods, depending on their business requirements, to link and sometimes integrate these services. In this chapter, you take a closer look at what *hybrid* really means and the types of cloud services that are best suited for which business goals.

Explaining the Hybrid Cloud

A public cloud environment is open to anyone with an Internet connection. In contrast, a private cloud environment is available only to the owners of that service environment and other entities they choose to share it with, such as business partners or customers. A hybrid cloud, on the other hand, offers the ability to integrate and connect to services across public and private clouds and data centers to create a *virtual computing environment* — a fluid mix of on-premises physical infrastructure and virtualized infrastructure that may be located on- or off-premises. However, before getting into more detail about how this environment actually works, you need to understand the continuum from public to private clouds.

Obviously, all cloud environments aren't the same. In fact, because the computing needs of a business aren't static, but change frequently, the best way to determine the type of environment that meets your needs is to think of a cloud as a continuum. It might be straightforward to assume that all public clouds are the same and all private clouds work in the same way. But in reality there are shades of gray. For example, you might have a public cloud service that is only available to customers who sign a long-term agreement. You might have a public SaaS service that offers a private version of the same application. You might have a private cloud that is actually part of the data center. Some public clouds might offer a sophisticated level of security offerings while other public clouds have virtually no security at all.

The bottom line is this: Meeting the needs of business requires that IT provide a variety of different types of cloud services. Understanding the characteristics of a continuum of cloud services will help you understand what's required to meet specific business goals. Ultimately, you need to select the type of cloud service that will provide use of the right resources at the right time with the right level of security and governance.

Open community clouds

The most open type of cloud environment is an *open community cloud*, a cloud environment that doesn't require any criteria for joining, other than signing up and creating a password. In fact, you can create an account under an alias. There are two primary types of open community clouds:

- ✔ Commercial sites with a strong advertising model. These clouds may be private or publically owned and include social networking environments such as Facebook, LinkedIn, and Twitter. These sites rarely charge a fee to users and use the size and scope of their user base to sell advertising. Some sites such as LinkedIn have professional, fee-based services that offer access to more in-depth services and information. Although these sites do not have an explicit guarantee of service to users, they do have an obligation to advertisers.

- ✔ Open community sites enable individuals with a common interest to participate in online discussions. There might be a community of professionals in a certain industry, such as manufacturing or retail, that want to share ideas. There are many communities based on individuals who share a passion for a hobby, such as biking or chess. There is typically very little security and no guarantee that the site will remain active over time. Open community sites frequently disappear when the most active members move on.

All of these community sites have some characteristics in common, including the following:

✔ **A relatively simple sign-up process:** The only criterion is that you have a login name and password and an e-mail account.

✔ **Requests for additional information:** Some more sophisticated sites may ask you to provide information about yourself, whereas others don't ask users for any information at all.

✔ **Low-level security:** The level of security is very low for these sites. With little effort, someone without authorization to do so can gain access to an account. Most of these sites include disclaimers about how they will or will not use data. They explain their responsibilities in managing the site and warn users not to use copyrighted material and the like.

✔ **No service-level guarantee to the user:** This doesn't mean that these community sites perform poorly. How well they perform is based on the engagement of the community and how important that site is to those managing the site. For example, the consumer products manufacturer in the previous example might spend a lot of time and money maintaining a site that provides important product information to customers and generates goodwill and loyalty. In addition, the site may become a valuable source of consumer sentiment and market research on new and existing products. Members of the site may enjoy the benefit of a well-managed and useful site.

If the company changes its business focus or determines the community is no longer worth the expense, it can shut down the community at will. There are no guarantees made to users that content generated and stored on the community cloud will be accessible for a specific amount of time.

In such a case, there is nothing that community members who have become dependent on that site can do. There is no contract or guarantee that the service will continue. Abandoned community sites are a common occurrence with open community clouds. For example, Google and LinkedIn both allow users to create their own online communities on any topic on the planet. Some of these sites are well moderated and well managed and, therefore, have hundreds or thousands of visitors. Others become phantom sites and disappear.

Some of these community sites are very sophisticated. Sites with a strong revenue model based on selling advertising to users have a compelling incentive to ensure a minimum amount of downtime because it can definitely have an impact on revenue. Some of these communities may actually be private clouds that are open only to qualified customers. Some governments have created private community clouds to provide services to businesses that they support.

Commercial public clouds

An open community site is only one type of public cloud. Some sites are designed for professional use and, therefore, charge a fee for services provided. *Commercial public clouds* are those environments that are open for use by anyone at any time, but these clouds are based on a pay-per-use model. A variety of cost models exist. For example, most Infrastructure as a Service (IaaS) vendors charge a per-hour fee for use of a measured service. A Software as a Service (SaaS) vendor typically charges a per-user-per-month (or per-year) fee.

Companies like Amazon.com, Joyent, Rackspace HP, and hundreds of start-ups offer a public cloud capability that's open to anyone with a credit card. Logically, because these companies are offering a commercial service, they provide a higher level of security and protection than the open community sites. This increase is related to the combination of the cost charged for the service and the requirement to have a solid reputation in order to maintain customer loyalty.

Unlike open community clouds, commercial public clouds have a written *service level agreement* (SLA) — an agreement outlining the obligation of the provider to the consumer of a service. An SLA is typically designed to protect the vendor rather than the customer. However, these vendors have an unwritten obligation to maintain the level of security and service required to protect their business relationships.

Packaged public cloud services

A group of public cloud vendors has productized its offerings, often as Software as a Service (SaaS), Platform as a Service (PaaS), or Business Process as a Service (BPaaS). With these *packaged public clouds,* a user cannot simply create login credentials, provide a credit card, and start using the service. Instead, in most situations, the user actually signs a contract for service. For example, if you want to use customer relationship management (CRM) SaaS applications, such as salesforce.com or SugarCRM, you actually have to sign a contract for a term of service. The term might be as short as a month or, more typically, a year. With a BPaaS vendor, such as PayPal, you sign a contract, even though you pay only when you use the service.

PaaS vendors that offer a packaged software development and deployment environment may offer customers a variety of options from a free but limited service to a fully fledged yearly contract. The vendor has the option of rejecting a potential customer with poor credit. The vendor also collects specific data about the company and the specific users. In this type of public cloud environment, the expectation is for a high level of security, privacy, and governance.

Thus, these vendors will provide a written SLA (generally designed to protect the vendor, not the customer). Nevertheless, there is an implied service level because of customer expectations.

In a SaaS environment, customers can cease being customers because they don't purchase the software directly. This is especially true at the early stage of the relationship. Typically, a customer will sign on for a month-long trial subscription to a service. If service is poor, the customer will inevitably look elsewhere for a service. Of course, the ability to easily sever a relationship will depend on how much integration and customization the customer has done. Because of the need to keep customers and prospects trusting the company, the level of security and SLA is much higher for public cloud companies in this category.

In addition to the requirement to provide an acceptable level of service and security, the packaged public service also typically manages customer data, which adds to the level of responsibility for securing and protecting information. In these public environments, it's important to have a clear understanding that the vendor manages the data but that the data is owned by the customer. Likewise, customers who rely on a SaaS or PaaS environment will own the software intellectual property that they've created. Therefore, it is important that customers maintain a copy of their proprietary business process logic as well as their own data. Be sure to read the fine print; there are environments where vendors claim the rights to customers' intellectual property.

Private clouds

In some situations, a company will want to create an environment that sits behind a firewall. Unlike a data center, a *private cloud* is a pool of common resources optimized for the use of the IT organization. When an organization is building and deploying complex applications, creating a highly automated private cloud that supports internal needs is practical. Unlike a public cloud, a private cloud adheres to the company's security, governance, and compliance requirements. Whatever service level is required for the company applies to the private cloud.

There are two different types of private clouds:

✔ A private cloud owned and managed by a company for benefit of its employees and partners

✔ A commercial private cloud operated by a vendor to support a company that doesn't want to build or operate its own private cloud

Privately owned and managed cloud

Organizations with a business model that requires the company to provide commercial technology services within an ecosystem often will build a *private partner cloud*, in which case, these companies effectively become a cloud provider. Instead of hiring a public cloud vendor to take full responsibility for creating, managing, monitoring, and updating the software, the private cloud provider assumes those responsibilities.

Like commercial public cloud providers, a private partner cloud provider creates an optimized environment to support the workloads needed to support its customers. The main difference is that in a private partner cloud scenario, a company isn't hiring a third party to operate the cloud. For example, a financial services company that provides individual banks with sophisticated payment services can create a sophisticated service that is automated and streamlined to support its customers.

Because of the security and compliance demands of its customers, the private cloud provided by the financial services company is based on a stringent SLA and even indemnifies customers against lawsuits. Likewise, because the financial services company already acts like an IT vendor to its customers, it has the economies of scale to make creating and managing such a service cost-effective.

Commercial private cloud

Although many companies see the benefits of creating their own private clouds, others want to have the security and governance of a private cloud but want to obtain that service from a third party. Therefore, vendors have created public clouds that are based on a contracted service model. Unlike a commercial public cloud where anyone with a credit card can sign up, a *private customer contractual cloud* requires that customers sign a formal contract with the vendor. In exchange, the vendor, such as IBM and HP, will provide strict governance and security capabilities and even indemnify customers from lawsuits related to the use of the service. In addition, vendors of commercial open clouds also offer customers private cloud options, including virtual private networks and mirrored sites so that if one data center is offline, a second data center can support customers.

As a result of these types of offerings, customers receive a more explicit SLA. This is different from hosting because, in the private contractual cloud, the service is designed with a self-service portal interface so that customers can add and subtract services based on demand.

Examining the continuum

The continuum of services, which is depicted in Figure 2-1, encompasses a variety of different types of public services that meet different needs within organizations. Open public clouds are often great resources for sharing ideas, while commercial public clouds are more tuned to the needs of businesses in terms of providing oversight and accountability. On the other hand, companies are increasingly using private clouds for their own internal uses. Some companies with sophisticated IT organizations may build and manage their own private clouds for employees and partners. These companies may actually become service providers in their own right. Other companies needing a private cloud for security and governance requirements may decide to have a third party manage a private cloud on their behalf.

Figure 2-1:
Companies and individuals will typically use a combination of services to meet a variety of business needs.

Model	Open Community	Controlled Open Mode	Contractual Open	Public/Private Hybrid	Private Closed
Examples	Facebook Twitter LinkedIn MyFitnessPal Google Groups	Amazon Web Services Rackspace OpSour	Salesforce.com Workday MailChimp QuickBooks Online	IBM SmartCloud HP Cloud Service Microsoft Azure	Internal but can be implemented by a third-party vendor
Characteristics	No SLA No Contract	Simple SLA Transactional pricing	SLA with no indemnification Contract	SLA guaranteeing uptime Contract	Explicit SLA Capital expense with ongoing maintenance
	Simple Password Protection No governance model	More security No explicit governance	High security provided Governance in place	Highest level of security Explicit governance	Secure platform Explicit governance

Combining Services to Create a Hybrid Cloud Environment

In most situations, companies large and small use a combination of public and private cloud services. A retail company may have a private cloud to support its highly distributed development organization, and it may also use a SaaS Human Resources public cloud application. In addition, to support its online commerce system, the company may leverage public commercial cloud services to ensure that customer service remains satisfactory during times of peak use, such as holidays. The same company might also create a private cloud application that it makes available to partners linking to its online sites.

This type of hybrid environment will become the standard way companies run IT in the future. A company will typically use public cloud services such as SaaS and various data services in conjunction with the private cloud. This development makes sense because increasingly companies are looking for a cost-effective, flexible, and optimized environment to support customers, partners, and suppliers.

When a company selects a hybrid path, the company takes on the responsibility for integration, security, manageability, and governance of the composite environment — including the public services that are included. If a problem arises with the public cloud provider, the responsibility lies with the private cloud provider — not the public service provider.

The Integration Imperative

Now that you have a sense of the different types of cloud services, it's time to think about how you bring services together — essentially, to integrate those services — to create a hybrid next-generation computing environment that offers the flexibility and cost control organizations are beginning to demand. Standards will have to emerge so that there is a consistent approach to integration across a hybrid computing environment. Foundational requirements necessary to make this type of integration work include

- ✔ **A service-oriented approach:** Creating an environment that allows services to be linked together requires modular components with well-defined interfaces. A service-oriented approach facilitates integration at the process level.
- ✔ **Well-defined data:** Organizations need to combine data from different cloud environments. This data must be designed to support common definitions.
- ✔ **Service-level integration:** When creating a hybrid environment, services need to be managed in a way that allows them to perform according to customer expectations.

Service-oriented integration

An important element of a flexible hybrid computing environment is the ability to easily link services together to create a virtual environment. Of course, not every element of a computing environment needs to be combined. There are clearly situations where the integration takes place only at the data level so that a data record can be moved from a SaaS environment to a system of record, such as an Enterprise Resource Planning (ERP) system. However, often organizations want to use a set of modular services from public and private services that, when combined, add a new and more flexible value to the company — without having to do massive programming whenever something changes.

One of the most important aspects of this service-oriented approach happens at the process level. The systems that have the data you value include business logic and processes that control the way that data is managed. So, you can't simply connect data elements or business logic together without a deep understanding of how these systems behave from a business process perspective.

It's helpful, for example, if you can graphically define the flow of data between source and target applications. In this context, you can graphically define all the steps needed to extract purchase order data from your ERP-specific system and send it to a different system (that is, a specific CRM system).

Unless your business is standing still, you can expect to see the SaaS vendor improve the underlying application. It may find a more efficient way to manage a certain business process that affects how you connect the logic among various systems. However, the typical SaaS vendor doesn't make arbitrary changes. The typical vendor bases its approach to integration on best practices in integration patterns and often reuses these common patterns. By understanding these patterns and watching for changes, your organization is better able to withstand changes in the implementation details.

Data integration

The most common way organizations create hybrid environments is through integration at the data level. To get a better idea of what this looks like, consider the example of a manufacturing company that has embraced cloud computing. The company set up a private cloud for its developers across three continents and established a private exchange to support its parts suppliers. At the same time, to support the global sales team, the company selected a cloud-based CRM system. To support the Human Resources department, it selected a SaaS-based HR platform. The company continues to manage its own ERP system in its data center.

Integrating information across multiple public- and private-based siloed data sources can be challenging, even if all your information assets are tightly controlled in an internal data center. However, when you begin to incorporate data from public cloud sources — such as a SaaS application or with data stored in a private cloud, such as a commerce system — the complexity of the integration process increases. Maintaining the integrity of your information is at great risk unless you're able to consistently integrate across your hybrid environment.

Information is the heart of how companies differentiate themselves from competitors. Companies must approach cloud integration with these fundamental concepts of information management in mind:

✔ To truly innovate, you need a complete understanding of all the information about your customers, partners, and suppliers.

✔ You need a full understanding of all aspects of your relationship with your value chain. This information has to be accurate, timely, and in the right context.

✔ You need to gain an understanding of what your customers are buying or the status of orders.

✔ You must understand what your customers and partners are saying and how satisfied they are with your products and services.

In addition, your customers and partners need to trust the shared information. These collective information assets must be secured and managed according to business, governmental, and industry rules and regulations.

In many ways, the need for integration remains the same as it has been for decades — providing an organization with a clear understanding of the transactions, services, and other critical information about the business. Departments such as finance, operations, human resources, and sales all typically use applications designed specifically to support their unique business processes. These applications are likely to have unique and independent sources of data.

Regardless of the technical means used to integrate data across these systems — whether in the data center or in private or public clouds — business and IT must collaborate to identify inconsistencies in data definitions and apply best practices to maintaining the quality of its data. For example, prior to integrating data across internal data sources, IT may need to account for variability in data definitions, data formats, and data lineage (like a family tree for the data element), how that data is derived, and its relationship to other data elements.

What has changed? In addition to integrating data across legacy applications in the data center, you may need to integrate data managed in multiple private and public cloud platforms. For example, say that a manufacturing company implemented salesforce.com to provide CRM support to over 500 customer sales representatives across the globe. Initially, the sales team found that its productivity decreased under this new system because they spent a lot of time manually comparing sales order and invoice information from SAP, the company's internal ERP system, against prospect and customer information in salesforce.com. Without timely insight into the company's orders, shipments, and invoices managed in SAP, the sales team couldn't perform up to expectations.

The company also recognized that other internal systems managing billing and inventory were dependent on some of the same data that needed to be reconciled between SAP and salesforce.com. The solution is for the IT organization to leverage technology that provides consistent connectors between its internal ERP system and its cloud-based CRM system in a way that will allow for consistency and repeatability across multiple systems.

Looking at the Requirements for Cloud Integration

Many companies initially underestimate the challenges of integrating data across hybrid computing environments. (For more details on data integration you will want to refer to Chapter 11.) Most of the integration issues between public and private clouds will focus on SaaS applications. This may be a new experience for many IT organizations that are used to controlling the data sources they are integrating. They assume they already have the tools and expertise required to manage the integration process because of their prior experiences with integration in the data center. Traditionally, most organizations used a consistent process for moving data within a computing environment. This approach, known as *Extraction, Transform, Load* (ETL), is most appropriate for transferring and processing large volumes of data in fast, high-throughput transactional environments within an enterprise data center. However, ETL is inadequate for integrating across multiple delivery platforms of the cloud.

A major complexity with trying to make ETL work in a hybrid environment is the varied structure of the data. The IT staff typically doesn't have the same level of insight into the data elements, data structures, data configurations, and database in SaaS platforms as compared to the applications managed and controlled in the data center. Therefore, it is important for IT management to spend the effort to gain as much understanding as possible into how the SaaS platform manages data to avoid confusion. This may require advanced training provided by the SaaS provider.

Accommodating SaaS platforms with information managed in the data center requires a lot of work on the part of the IT organization. With enough time and programming staff, companies can create custom-coded connections between internal and cloud applications. However, keeping a custom solution up-to-date can take significant, ongoing maintenance.

One of the characteristics of a SaaS environment is that the developer of that application often makes changes to the structure of the application without notifying customers. A SaaS vendor may suddenly change a data format that the customer is unaware of. These changes could potentially impact the integration process. In some situations, companies may facilitate the integration process between data in the public cloud and data in internal systems by creating an additional data repository. This causes unwanted delay and complexity.

You need an integration process that's adaptable based on unexpected changes.

To maintain the benefit of using SaaS environments in concert with your line of business applications requires that you establish an effective and repeatable integration process. By leveraging new sets of integration platforms and best practices, you can overcome these integration challenges. Overall, you need a common and standardized way to link your applications wherever they're managed — the five main requirements for creating this standardized approach to integrating data across internal data center applications and public and private clouds. These elements are covered in this section.

Connectivity

You need to be able to connect many different types of applications and data — SaaS applications, custom web applications, on-premise applications, private cloud applications, databases, flat-files — quickly and easily without requiring a lot of ongoing maintenance. You also need to consider different types of integration, including data migration, process integration, or some unique new type of integration, including taking data from an internal application, such as SAP, and then displaying the data in a SaaS application, such as salesforce.com.

You may need to make connections between two applications, or you may need to connect one application to many application endpoints. Even more important is the ability to scale quickly from a one-to-one integration to a one-to-many integration. In addition, different connectivity protocols or techniques may work better in different situations, so you must be prepared to choose different options for different business requirements.

Transformation

In a typical business, you often have to map the data about customers in your line-of-business application (such as accounting) with data about those same customers in your SaaS application. If you're lucky, the formats of both these data sources will be the same. However, many times, these applications are designed or managed by different groups that never communicate with each other. For example, the IT organization manages the data in the ERP system, whereas the sales department has its own staff to manage the data in the SaaS CRM system.

Business management needs to ensure that the accounting system is consistent with the sales management system. Your IT staff is most likely familiar with the data format specifications in your legacy applications but doesn't have the same level of understanding of the specifics of the data in your SaaS applications. One of the major advantages of SaaS applications is that business process owners can leverage these applications without any support from IT. All the data-management complexity is hidden from the user. However, in order to create these necessary mappings, you need to understand, for example, whether a customer identification (ID) number is numeric or if it includes alpha characters. After you understand the specific characteristics, you can graphically transform the ID number in both applications so they can be recognized and understood as the same information.

Service level integration

In a hybrid environment, you are asked to bring services together from different environments as though they are one unified environment. This type of service management is critical to the use of a hybrid environment. The goal is not simply to create combined value of public and private cloud services, but also there needs to be a way to create an overall SLA to support the combined environment. This service level must be planned to ensure the right overall security, governance, performance, monitoring, and management of this new virtual cloud world.

Business logic

The systems that have the data you value include business logic and processes that control the way that data is managed. You can't simply connect data elements without a deep understanding of how these systems behave from a business process perspective. It is helpful, for example, if you can graphically define the flow of data between source and target applications. In this context, you can graphically define all the steps needed to extract purchase order data from your ERP specific system and send it to a different system (that is, a specific CRM system).

Unless your business is standing still, you can expect to see the SaaS vendor improve the underlying application. It may find a more efficient way to manage a certain business process that impacts how you connect the logic between various systems. However, the typical SaaS vendor doesn't make arbitrary changes. The typical vendor bases its approach to integration on best practices in integration patterns and often reuses these common patterns. By understanding these patterns and watching for changes, your organization is better able to withstand changes in the implementation details.

One way to increase the speed of integration is to use an integration provider who's studied metadata structure of SaaS applications. These vendors can provide a preconfigured integration pattern or template that jump-starts the effort of integration between data sources. One of the benefits of working with a standardized template is that the same template can be reused for other integration projects. The template is typically designed to cover about 60 percent of the requirements for a particular integration.

Management

Data doesn't live in isolation. No matter what type of data you're working with, it lives on specific hardware platforms, leverages specific storage environments, and connects with third-party services (payment services, credit verification, partner commerce systems, and so on). All these elements become part of the way you manage the flow of data between your applications in the data center and in the cloud.

From a management perspective, you must be able to monitor and manage these workloads. The approach you take largely depends on how you manage your business. For example, ask yourself these questions:

- ✔ How many third-party services do I use?

- ✔ Have SaaS applications, such as CRM, workforce planning services, and the like, become part of my IT strategy?

- ✔ Does my business require seamless integration across these business services?

- ✔ How much do my business partners and customers depend on the smooth and accurate integration across information sources and business services?

If you don't have a well-planned way to manage these resources and services, the lack of planning can dramatically impact the overall efficiency of your hybrid environment. To be successful in breaking down data and processing silos, you have to focus on overall management of business workloads. This is especially true because these workloads are becoming increasingly fluid and mobile.

Chapter 3

Service Orientation in the Cloud

*T*he increasing adoption of hybrid cloud environments can be directly linked to the success enterprises have made in moving to a service-oriented approach to IT. *Service orientation* is a way to modularize key business services and to establish well-defined interfaces designed to ensure that these services work in many different situations. This move to service orientation has been an evolving process and not an easy one at that. In fact, organizations have worked very hard to separate traditional components of computing so that application code can function independent of the underlying operating system and hardware. This separation is required to develop the modular and repeatable development process that makes service orientation an important prerequisite for the cloud. Of course, not every organization that is using cloud computing has adopted service orientation, but it certainly makes it easier to create a well-functioning cloud if you are planning and managing services. As companies add more and more cloud services, the service-oriented approach becomes a more important underpinning for success.

As organizations begin to manage integrated environments comprised of private and public cloud services along with traditional data center services, service orientation is being viewed as the glue that keeps everything working as intended. In this chapter, we define service orientation and describe its role in cloud computing.

Defining Service Orientation

Service orientation is an architectural approach based on implementing business processes as software services. These business services consist of a set of loosely coupled components — designed to minimize dependencies — assembled to support a well-defined business task. Designing systems with modular business services results in more efficient and flexible IT systems. Systems designed to incorporate service orientation allow organizations to leverage existing assets and easily accommodate the inevitable changes experienced by a dynamic business. In addition, there are situations when a set of services needs to be combined. This ensures that these combined workloads will be able to execute with less latency than would be possible with loosely coupled components.

Service orientation is also a *business* approach and methodology. Using a service-oriented approach helps businesses adapt to change and makes the scalability of cloud computing possible.

Business services play an essential role in systems designed with a focus on service orientation. These business services cross a number of different IT systems, effectively breaking down the organizational silos that formed around conventional IT systems. We define a business service as the self-contained and reusable software components that you create to carry out your important business processes. Some of these business services may have additional component services. Each service provides a function. Basically, we mean that you wrap up everything you have to do to make a particular business function happen and give that rolled-up something a name and call it a business service. These business services can then be used as building blocks to create other more complicated business services.

Figure 3-1 illustrates how a credit-checking business service is incorporated into an order-processing application. Its service is called on when a new customer places an order to determine whether the customer is credit-worthy. In the figure, we don't show or even care about how the credit checking is done. For the sake of simplicity, say that the credit-checking business service — software component — is run by an external company and simply provides a service. The company using this credit-checking software is confident that the service conducts a credit check properly.

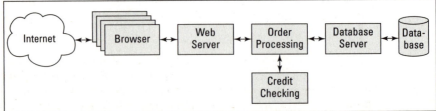

Figure 3-1:
Adding a
service-
oriented
component.

The order-processing application simply requests the credit-checking service and passes along the necessary information (a person's name and Social Security number). The credit-checking service consults its information sources, does some calculations, and passes back a credit rating. The credit-checking service may connect to many computers, consult many different data sources, and use a very sophisticated algorithm to calculate the credit rating, but the details of how the algorithm works are of no concern to the order-processing application. As far as the order-processing application is concerned, credit checking is called on to accomplish a specific business process, and that's all.

Also, we need to emphasize that the credit-checking component *does only credit checking*. It doesn't offer a wide range of services. It's precisely because the components have a narrowly defined scope — that is, they do just one thing — that they can be used and reused as building blocks.

Using a service-oriented approach makes it easier to build new applications as well as change existing applications. Using well-tested and proven components makes testing new applications more efficient.

Why Service Orientation Matters in the Cloud

Hybrid cloud environments are becoming important because organizations are constantly reinventing themselves to respond to change and to become more competitive. These organizations recognize that IT must be at the forefront of a business strategy based on innovation and transformation. They also understand that it's hard to find one IT computing approach that is the best one for all types of workloads. Therefore, the most practical approach is to implement a hybrid cloud environment. (See Chapter 9 for more on the business value of hybrid cloud.)

To make a cloud infrastructure work in the real world requires a high level of flexibility and modularity. A cloud must be designed to support a variety of workloads and business services. No one can anticipate when a service needs to be scaled up and when it will be scaled down. Specifically, it is this service-oriented approach to architectural design that supports the key cloud characteristics of elasticity, self-service provisioning, standards-based interfaces, and pay-as-you-go flexibility. The combination of a service-oriented approach and cloud services enables companies to lower costs and improve business flexibility.

Utilizing reusable and loosely coupled components makes scalability and elasticity a reality for public and private cloud environments. Consider what might happen in a cloud environment if the principles of service orientation aren't applied. Say, for example, that you've built a private cloud that deals with some of your company's applications and data, but you're using a public cloud for some other applications. You don't want these applications to be stove-piped. They need to act together. If there are well-defined interfaces that enable you to share data, for example, among these applications (no matter where they are), you will be well served. If you're working with vendors where the platform has lots of dependencies that will lock you in, you will not be able to gain the business advantages you expect.

One of the key benefits of a service-oriented approach is that software is designed to reflect best practices and business processes, instead of making the business operate according to the rigid structure of a technical environment. Service orientation lets companies leverage existing assets and create new business services that are consistent, controlled, and more easily changed and managed. As a result, a service-oriented approach leads to business goals consistent with the demands of cloud computing environments. Here are some of the potential benefits:

- Improve flexibility of IT
- Improve responsiveness
- Improve performance
- Reduce cost of building and testing software
- Improve accuracy
- Decrease complexity
- Improve customer service
- Align with the business
- Increase interoperability
- Increase federation

Characteristics of Service Orientation

Modularity, reusability, and flexibility are among the key characteristics of service orientation. Each of these concepts is clarified here:

- **Modularity:** Organizations need to begin their move to service orientation by rethinking the large, complex, and unmanageable applications of the past. The route to modularity begins with the following:

  - Identifying the components of business applications
  - Configuring reusable services to meet business demands

✔ **Reusability:** Knowing which services are best suited for reuse depends on how you classify the service. Basically, the components of an application can be classified in one of two ways:

- *Reusable:* These services are common to various business processes important to the organization. You need to encapsulate the rules and logic of a common business process to create a reusable business service. A service designed to check a customer's credit is an example of a service that can easily be reused in lots of different situations.

- *Application-specific:* These services are unique to a particular business process and include logic or instructions that are likely to be used in the specific context of the application at hand. Such services are not likely to be reused.

Using a tested and proven component speeds development enables a higher level of security and trust and saves money.

✔ **Flexibility:** The flexibility derived from service orientation is a function of the modularity and reuse of business services. The efficiency, manageability, and flexibility of service-oriented IT environments don't happen by magic. A fair amount of oversight on the part of the IT team to maintain the desired flexibility is needed over the long run. Here is a list of some of the responsibilities required to make sure savings and benefits of service orientation are achieved:

- Maintain a catalog of business services to make it easy for developers to identify which services are tested and approved and should be reused. The more these services are used in different applications, the lower the cost of using them. However, it's important to remember that the benefit of reusable services is much more than just the savings from reusing the same software code.

- Make service management a top priority by building in a way to identify root causes of problems early in the development process and by continuously monitoring and fixing sources of errors.

- Seek continuous improvement with ongoing measurement of performance and accuracy of business services.

This responsibility for quality becomes increasingly important in hybrid cloud environments. The provider of cloud services shoulders much of the responsibility for oversight because the consumer of a cloud service sees only the end result. The consumer of a cloud service needs to operate under the assumption that the business service will work as intended.

In a business service that is reused 500 times, a single error in your applications quickly becomes 500 errors or more. By adding a greater level of control and management to IT, you will be able to improve the security and governance of your business processes. To avoid this type of problem, make sure that a service is well tested before deploying it throughout your organization.

Building reusable components

Building reusable components can be very challenging. You need to identify which components are best suited for reuse. To accomplish this goal, you need to keep business logic separate from plumbing — technical infrastructure.

To build a software application, you must tell the computer how to do what you want on two levels:

> In human terms: *the business logic*
>
> In computer terms: *the plumbing*

Business applications comprise lines of program code that tell computers what actions to take. Some of these instructions are written as business logic — "Add an item line to the order," for example. Some are simply plumbing at the infrastructure level — computer-level directives, such as "Check that the printer is available." Both are necessary. If you don't describe the application's activity in simple business logic (purchase orders, products, customers, accounts, and so on), you quickly lose sight of what you're trying to achieve. If you don't describe in computer terms exactly how the computer should carry out its task, the software simply won't work.

Business logic needs to be as free of plumbing dependencies as possible if you intend to follow a service-oriented approach. You need to keep them separate so you maintain flexibility when things change. For example, if you want to change the order in which particular business functions happen, and you've kept your business logic separate from your plumbing, making these changes is no big deal. But if your business logic and your plumbing are one giant application, changes are costly and complicated, take time, require extensive testing, and are a very big deal, indeed.

Figure 3-2 introduces the idea of a business layer and a plumbing layer, also introducing the idea of specific services (for simplicity's sake, we left out the web server and browser). The combination of business and technical layers works like this:

- ✔ **The Business Service layer** consists of software components that provide and carry out specific business functions. In this example, the business services that will be delivered to users are *order processing* and *credit checking*.

- ✔ **The Plumbing layer** consists of components that support the aforementioned business services by marshaling and managing actual computer resources. In this example, the components needed to handle the plumbing are the web server and the database server.

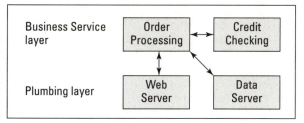

Figure 3-2:
A service-
oriented
view.

The diagram in Figure 3-2 illustrates the concept of dividing software applications into components that carry out business functions — business services — and components that support the use and management of computer resources — plumbing. With this breakdown, you are in a better position to reuse the narrowly defined business services in multiple ways.

Service orientation compared to traditional architecture

In traditional software architecture, various software components are often highly dependent on each other. These software component dependencies make the application change management process time-consuming and complex. A change made to one software component may affect lots of other dependent software components, and if you don't make all the right changes, your application (or related applications) may fail. One small change to an application can make its way through the whole application, wreaking havoc and leading to massive revision of software code.

How do you achieve flexibility? By implementing an approach that removes dependencies between components and services. An architectural approach based on service orientation helps to change the rules by avoiding the complex layers of software components all dependent on each other. Developers need to embrace a new way of thinking to take advantage of modular and reusable components. As a result, they have more freedom to change quickly and accurately. Table 3-1 summarizes some of these key differences between traditional and service-oriented computing.

Table 3-1   Traditional versus Service-Oriented Computing

Traditional Computing	Service-Oriented Computing
Siloed applications	Breaking down of silos
Dependent components	Loosely coupled composite components
Complex change management	Efficient change management
Many different software architectures	More standardized architecture

The Open Group developed and approved a standard for service-oriented computing infrastructure for a cloud called Technical Standard for the Service-Oriented Cloud Computing Infrastructure (SOCCI) Framework. This standard recognizes that IT infrastructure and the management of IT infrastructure need to change to adequately support cloud computing. This evolved infrastructure — SOCCI — is defined by the Open Group as follows (reference SOCCI Framework Technical Standard by Open Group — `www.opengroup.org/soa/source-book/socci/index.htm`):

> SOCCI is a "service-oriented, utility-based, manageable, scalable on-demand infrastructure that supports essential cloud characteristics, service, and deployment models. In other words, SOCCI describes the essentials for implementing and managing an Infrastructure as a Service (IaaS) environment."

For more information on the Open Group standards, refer to Chapter 18.

Avoiding and eliminating the many layers and intertwined software dependencies that bog down the change management process in traditional computing is a requirement for moving to service orientation. The goal of service orientation is to ensure that each component is responsible for a single, easily understood function, and nothing else. To accomplish this goal, business and IT need to work together so that the software components represent essential business processes. You will not be able to reuse a component if it tries to do too much at once.

On the other hand, in some situations, business requirements call for certain dependencies to be maintained. This is to be expected. However, it's important to make sure the components are linked together in an organized and structured way so they can be easily located and changed when necessary.

Avoiding dependencies also applies when writing completely new applications. Initially, more discipline and more time to write software without dependencies are required, but eventually writing software without dependencies becomes the norm for many developers. In the long run, the reality of dependencies in traditional applications slows development, thwarts easy business change, and chokes the manageability of hybrid cloud environments. So, investing in the creation of modular and reusable software components makes sense.

Cataloging Services

If you want to create, use, change, or manage a business service, you need access to documentation — that is, a *catalog* — about that service. These services may include business services that represent a company's important business processes, and they may include a range of IT services, such as software services, networking services, communications services, and data services. Because a cloud needs to be able to use a service that might originate from many different places, a catalog is essential in both locating a service and understanding its characteristics.

The catalog should help users locate the right service, understand how services are being used, and identify who is using the services. However, assembling all the key components and creating a central reference point for your services aren't enough. You need to plan for managing those services; otherwise, your IT implementations won't meet your expectations.

Many organizations are creating catalogs of business and IT services. They're doing so because service catalogs provide a foundation for good service management by helping companies standardize the approach to delivering and managing services across all units. Some organizations have merged catalogs of different types of services to improve their ability to manage and govern *all* the services delivered to the business.

If cloud is going to act as a truly distributed environment, you will need a catalog. In a distributed computing environment, it is critical to provide services that tell you where the services are located that you might want to use. In other words, you have to create the services in a distributed environment that would be a part of an integrated environment.

A service catalog should be dynamic and capable of managing constantly changing services in order to handle the changing needs of the business. A service catalog is needed because programmers will no longer write as much original code themselves. Rather, they will be expected to use these business services as part of creating new applications for the business. So, the catalog needs to give the developer all the information she needs to make good use of these services. She needs to know how and when to use a service. Here's a sample of the information included in a service catalog:

- ✔ Whom to contact about a service
- ✔ How to find and access a service
- ✔ Who has authority to change the service
- ✔ Which critical applications are related to the service
- ✔ Outages or other incidents related to the service
- ✔ Information about the relationships among services
- ✔ Documentation of all agreements between IT and the customer or user of the service

A banking institution's service catalog, for example, may have information about its online banking service, the key performance indicators — measurement indicating the effectiveness of a process — for that service, and the service-level agreements between IT and the online banking business. If an outage occurs, the bank's IT service management team can read the service catalog to locate the root cause of problems with the service.

Why Service Orientation Is Important to Each of the Cloud Models

When you have some of the background on what it means to take a service-oriented approach to architecting technology systems, you can begin to see the relationship between this approach and cloud computing. Services are important for cloud computing from both an infrastructure and an application perspective.

Service orientation permeates the cloud, and the cloud serves as an environment that can host other services (either at a technical or a business level). Therefore, cloud vendors need to think about the architecture of their platforms so they can support different business models. Here are two different scenarios that a cloud provider may have to deal with:

- ✔ On the one hand, cloud providers built the cloud infrastructure on well-designed services with clearly defined black-box interfaces. These black-box services allow the cloud to scale. In order to execute this approach, the cloud infrastructure needs to be service-oriented.

- ✔ On the other hand, companies building applications designed for the cloud tend to build them out as services, which makes it easier for customers and partners to use them. For example, SaaS providers need an ecosystem of partners that provides either complementary components or full applications that are important to sustaining and growing their businesses. Following a service-oriented approach is a prerequisite for partners desiring to build economically on these platforms.

In Part II of this book, we delve into each of the different cloud models — *Infrastructure as a Service (IaaS), Platform as a Service (PaaS), Software as a Service (SaaS)*, and *Business Process as a Service (BPaaS)*. We illustrate how each of these models exhibits some important characteristics, such as elasticity and self-service provisioning.

This section shows how a services approach is critical to the development of each of these cloud models. Check out Part II for more information on the various ways that cloud services are created and deployed.

Infrastructure as a Service

The IaaS layer offers storage and compute resources that developers and IT organizations can use to deliver custom business solutions. A cloud provider wants the provisioning capability associated with the IaaS to be designed as a modular service with published interfaces so it can be used for many different situations.

Say that you have a group of applications that you want to run in a public cloud because you want capacity on demand. You sign up with an IaaS provider. Via your web browser, you can buy this capacity and start running your applications on the service. The service is provisioning the capacity. While you're running the application, the service provisions hardware to run it and then de-provisions the virtualized servers when you're done.

As a user of this capacity provisioning service, you don't need to know how the provider is making the service happen; it's a black box to you. If the cloud weren't service oriented, you'd have to figure out how to provision your application to the environment. With the cloud, you can use a single provisioning service.

Platform as a Service

The PaaS layer offers development environments for IT organizations to use to create cloud-ready business applications. This model is offered as a set of black-box services that enables developers to build applications on top of the compute infrastructure. This might include developer tools that are offered as a service to build services, or even data access and database services, or even billing services.

In these situations, the principles of service orientation (such as loose coupling and reusability) are applied to IT infrastructure components that are delivered as cloud services to PaaS users. Developers in your organization may locate the platform services they need by referring to a service catalog.

Software as a Service

With SaaS, the provider hosts the software for you so that you don't need to install it, manage it, or buy hardware for it. All you have to do is connect to it and use it.

For example, you might make use of CRM as a service or accounting as a service. Many of these providers have created their services in a modular way to enable scalability (because you're using these services along with perhaps thousands of other clients). A services-oriented approach allows the provider, for example, to swap out functionality easily.

In all these models, companies will use a set of well-defined services that they can access through interfaces. Companies can leverage these services in many different ways, depending on the problems they're trying to resolve.

Companies benefit from service orientation and the cloud because both of these approaches place a priority on understanding what the business needs, when it needs it, and how efficiently and cost-effectively the business can be served.

Business Process as a Service

With BPaaS, the service provider creates a set of commonly used processes that can be connected to other environments including IaaS and SaaS. A service provider or a developer could use a BPaaS to design a business process.

An example of a business process might be a way for a retailer to including a shipping service as part of the e-commerce system. Because these services are written as an independent service, it makes it easier to add new business processes to either serve a different constituent or automate a new business initiate.

Chapter 4

Hybrid Cloud Management

Managing a cloud environment requires an organization to coordinate many different resources owned and operated by many different companies and individuals. So, when you are thinking about leveraging cloud resources to support many different constituents, you have to think about management. Management of clouds is more than simply using a tool to tune a service. Cloud management is the process of orchestrating many different services, so they behave in the right manner and perform as promised. The more hybrid a cloud environment becomes, the more complicated the management.

In this chapter, we give you an understanding of the various players involved in managing a hybrid cloud environment and the type of capabilities you need to consider. Automation and service delivery will be at the heart of cloud management. At the end of the day, you need to be able to operationalize your entire environment so that you are delivering the right service level to those constituents that you are responsible for.

Understanding the Cloud Service Management Ecosystem

Because the hybrid cloud encompasses so many different services from so many different places, cloud management needs lots of attention. Secure, reliable, interoperable, and cost-effective cloud services require an underlying infrastructure that is highly tuned, well monitored, and well managed. Your level of responsibility for managing the delivery and operation of cloud services depends on your role in the cloud ecosystem.

You might be a consumer of cloud services, a provider of cloud services, or an organization that brings a variety of services together (such as a broker of cloud services). In hybrid cloud environments, the roles and responsibilities for management are complicated. An organization consuming Software as a Service (SaaS), Platform as a Service (PaaS), Business Process as a Service (BPaaS), and Infrastructure as a Service (IaaS) from different vendors may need to play multiple roles, including both as a cloud consumer and a cloud provider. Responsibilities for managing and securing these cloud services will overlap and often be shared across different participants.

With so many different players in the hybrid cloud environment, one thing is certain. At the end of the day, organizations are responsible for delivering the right service level for its customers. The primary goal of a well-managed environment is to ensure that end-user experiences are maintained and satisfy expectations. Therefore, it is beneficial to understand the three constituents who are responsible for hybrid cloud management:

- ✔ Cloud providers
- ✔ Cloud consumers
- ✔ The cloud broker

Cloud providers control performance

A cloud provider can be any organization or company that provides a service to cloud consumers. Some cloud providers may focus on a single cloud model such as IaaS, SaaS, PaaS, or BPaaS, Other cloud providers may provide an integrated platform that includes many of these services for a company. Still other cloud providers may be the IT department itself that becomes a cloud provider for its employees and customers.

Cloud providers have responsibility for the architecture of the cloud and for providing cloud resources and services to cloud consumers. These organizations are responsible for monitoring the cloud infrastructure to ensure that service levels for up time, speed of delivery, and other performance characteristics are maintained. In order to bring the right level of management to cloud environments, a cloud provider needs to understand and anticipate the requirements of its customers, provide the right level of security and governance, optimize operating costs, and ensure that cloud services are available to users. Cloud providers also assume the responsibility of quickly finding the root cause of any problems that interfere with the quality of service delivery to maintain compliance with service level agreements.

Cloud consumer focuses on the customer experience

Cloud consumers are the individuals and organizations that use, manage, and pay for services delivered by a cloud service provider. A cloud consumer may be an individual sales manager using the services of a SaaS application, an IT development team consuming PaaS services, or an IT system that provides automated management — such as the provisioning of services based on business policies. In hybrid enterprise environments, there may be many different cloud consumers using services from lots of cloud providers.

The cloud consumer can't be a passive receiver of cloud services. Rather, the cloud consumer must be able to monitor the services the organization uses to make sure that these services deliver as promised. As an important first step to maintaining the right level of oversight, IT needs to begin to recognize that it is a cloud provider to its internal and external customers as well as a cloud consumer. It needs sufficient insight into the performance of each of these services to understand how they individually and collectively impact the overall performance of the business.

Cloud brokers integrate and provide management layer

Cloud management responsibilities may increase exponentially as usage of cloud services expands. As both the quantity and type of cloud services used across your organization increase, it becomes increasingly challenging to maintain a consistent level of visibility and control. A cloud service broker is a vendor or a business unit within a company that provides oversight and management for a variety of cloud providers. The broker can stand between an organization and its cloud services, managing the use, performance, integration, and delivery of such resources. Using a cloud broker can help organizations to gain more control over which cloud services are being used and who is using them. It is so easy to set up a cloud service with a credit card payment or a simple user license for a SaaS application that many IT organizations have no idea how many cloud services are in use across the company. This practice of having too many uncontrolled cloud services can present significant security and governance risks to the company.

One option for cloud broker services is to create a single environment or portal as a central control point for internal users of cloud services. This allows an individual to securely sign on in order to access services they are authorized to use. The advantages of this process from a management perspective are significant. It gives IT more centralized control over which cloud services are being used in the organization and who is using them. The cloud broker can also consolidate many of the business services like billing across various cloud services. For example, business units may independently begin using cloud services like Amazon web services without the knowledge of the IT organization. Therefore, the company may be spending more money than necessary and may lose control of security and governance.

Key Capabilities in Cloud Service Management

All the players in the cloud management ecosystem have a role to play in ensuring consistent delivery and operation of cloud services. The cloud provider has primary responsibility for the management functions of its cloud service offerings. The cloud consumer needs to monitor the operation of these services with a focus on end-user experience. The cloud broker can act as an intermediary between cloud providers and the cloud consumer to ensure that the cloud consumer has a consistent management view across its hybrid cloud environment.

To effectively manage a hybrid environment requires that all elements of the environment be managed in an automated and standardized way. Therefore, the six primary capabilities that any service provider must include are

- ✔ Management of customer accounts
- ✔ Management of provisioning and configuring resources
- ✔ Management of service catalogs
- ✔ Management of performance
- ✔ Management of security
- ✔ Management of interoperability

We describe the key capabilities in hybrid cloud management in this section.

Managing customer accounts

Cloud providers need to ensure that the basic business relationship with its customers runs smoothly. Due to the self-service nature of cloud service delivery, an essential aspect of cloud management deals with automating processes of customer account management. These processes include opening and closing accounts; establishing user accounts and authorizations; establishing, managing, and metering pricing; tracking usage; and managing service levels according to policies.

Provisioning and configuring services

Provisioning automates the process of accessing the right computing resources needed by the service provider or the consumer of services. Provisioning enables pools of resources ranging from compute, storage, networking, or application services, to be instantly available based on assigned business policy rules.

Without this level of automation, the provisioning process can take months since it often requires organizations to acquire, configure, and set up resources manually. By focusing on standardization and automation, cloud providers can make the provisioning process easier, faster, and more cost effective. In order to ensure that the right services are provisioned, it is critical to manage change. Therefore there must be configuration services in place to keep track of changes to everything from actual applications to operating systems, and the like.

Service catalogs

A *service catalog* plays an important role in ensuring that service providers adequately document the characteristics of services so that service consumers know where to look for the offerings they need. The catalog is essentially a list of internal and external services available to an organization. It is more cost efficient and faster for cloud consumers to select a standardized offering from a catalog. Ideally, an enterprise IT organization wants to provide a comprehensive catalog of services that is easily understood and used by its customers.

In some situations, an organization may need to provide different catalogs for line of business users and developers to make sure each group gets what they need from the catalog. Although, if a cloud consumer has multiple service catalogs to manage, this can make the process more cumbersome.

In a hybrid world where cloud consumers need to choose between services offered across the internal data center, private and public clouds, and hosted environments, a service catalog can provide the means to increase the overall agility of the organization. Using a service catalog can help to ensure that cloud consumers select the right set of offerings based on the rules and priorities of the business.

Some of the information available in a service catalog is as follows:

✔ Definition of the service and what it means to business users

✔ Various options for each service and any limitations

✔ The requirements for executing the service

✔ The cost of the service and whether costs vary by service level options

✔ Creator of the service

✔ Who can use the service

✔ How to request a service

✔ Whether there are bundles of services (*service bundles* can protect consumers from ordering groups of services that don't work together, as in unsupported platforms)

✔ The associated service level and how the service performs against this service level

Management of performance

Cloud providers need to monitor cloud services to ensure they meet agreed-upon service levels. This means that the performance of servers, networks, and virtualized images in the cloud providers' environment need to be measured and monitored — both individually and collectively — to ensure the environment is tuned to satisfy all business requirements.

A standardized and automated system needs to be in place to track, trace, and audit all aspects of performance. For example, bandwidth, connectivity, and scalability are performance characteristics that should be monitored. In addition, automated systems should be designed to quickly identify the root cause of the hardware or software failures so performance can be restored.

These systems should answer questions such as:

✔ Is the cloud infrastructure performing as expected?

✔ Are identified performance problems occurring randomly at regular intervals?

✔ Which performance problems are most severe and need to be given top priority to find the root cause and resolve the issue?

✔ How can performance be improved?

Cloud providers vary in how much performance level detail they make available to cloud users. Even when performance statistics are shared at a very granular level, the cloud user can't control the provider's environment. This lack of insight and control of cloud service performance can present significant challenges to the cloud user organization that is also a cloud provider to its customers. For example, a PaaS platform provider might not meet its service level requirements for its customers if its cloud infrastructure provider suffers a service disruption. Additionally, an enterprise IT organization acting as a cloud provider to users of its hybrid cloud needs to guarantee service to its customers without having control over the performance of public cloud services in its environment.

You can put management services in place to monitor performance of your data center and private cloud, but you still need a way to monitor statistics about service performance from your public cloud service providers. There are some vendors that provide monitoring and management products that will help to improve your ability to monitor performance of your public cloud resources and, hence, improve the overall service level of your hybrid cloud.

Security

Cloud providers are responsible for securing the physical and logical aspects of the infrastructure and operation system in the cloud environment. For example, cloud providers need to validate appropriate levels of network, operating system, and middleware security to prevent intrusion and denial-of-service attacks. Comprehensive governance and security strategies are a non-negotiable requirement for a cloud provider to maintain good customer relationships. A proactive approach is required to protect against security threats that change constantly. That being said, each cloud provider will take a different approach to security, and it is the responsibility of the organization consuming the cloud services to ensure that its security requirements are met. Security management must be viewed as a shared responsibility between the cloud provider and the cloud user. (See Chapter 15 for more detail on cloud security.)

Interoperability and portability

In hybrid cloud environments, interoperability and portability refer to how cloud users can move their tools, applications, virtual images, and so on, between the data center and private and public clouds. A high level of *interoperability* means that cloud users can easily move workloads from one environment to another with very few integration issues. Interoperability also means that an application will work the same if it is moved from one cloud environment to another. *Portability* is a related concept that is often used to describe what is involved when a cloud user wants to move a SaaS or PaaS based application from one vendor to another.

There are many reasons why cloud providers and cloud consumers need interoperability. Cloud providers need interoperability in order to quickly add additional resources from another cloud provider if they need to ramp up to meet customer demand. In hybrid environments, cloud consumers want the flexibility to move workloads between traditional and cloud resources based on which environment is best suited for the specifics of that workload. The optimal environment may change over time based on business priorities and the specifics of the resource environment. In addition, consumers want the flexibility to move from one cloud vendor to another if they are dissatisfied with the services of the vendor or their business requirements change. In addition, a cloud provider may want to use more than one cloud provider for failover protection. In addition, a cloud user may contract with one IaaS provider and wants to easily switch to another IaaS for additional capacity.

Achieving interoperability and portability in hybrid clouds can be very complex. What are cloud providers doing to make it easier to move applications between clouds? Cloud providers like IBM, Rackspace, and Amazon are building in templates to help with the integration process. These templates can provide some level of governance over where you should place a workload. However, there is still a lot of work to be done in this area.

There are many groups working to improve standards so that it is easier for organizations to share data and applications across multiple cloud environments. One organization making progress in developing standards for interoperability and portability is the Open Services for Lifecycle Collaboration (OSLC). Linked Data — using the web to connect related data that was not previously linked — is being used to allow for increasing levels of interoperability between applications and workloads in hybrid clouds. The OSLC is working on the specifications for linked data to be used to federate information and capabilities across cloud services and systems. This will become an evolutionary step in cloud management. It will help to eliminate the time-consuming and complex coding required moving applications and components across environments.

How Virtualization Complicates Managing a Hybrid Cloud

One of the most significant challenges of managing hybrid clouds is the need to coordinate the management of both virtual and physical environments. *Virtualization* is the process of separating resources and services from the underlying physical delivery environment. Many virtual systems can be created within one physical system. Although virtualization is not a prerequisite for cloud computing, this technology is in common practice at its foundation and is at the core of cloud service efficiency. While virtualization is the technology supporting many of the benefits of cloud computing, it also increases the complexity of managing cloud environments. In this section, we discuss two issues that add management complexity in hybrid cloud environments.

Lack of control over cloud resource management

SaaS, PaaS, BPaaS, and IaaS providers manage physical cloud resources and deliver cloud services to users through a virtual image. In hybrid environments, cloud users may need to manage the delivery of these virtual environments without the ability to control the performance and manageability of the resources. The following scenario illustrates the management complexities that may arise as a result.

Assume you have implemented a SaaS application to manage your customer sales interactions. You are able to provide these SaaS services to your sales force of 500 people without adding any additional servers to support the application. Your SaaS provider is responsible for managing the physical infrastructure, and you make sure that all members of your sales team have the right level of access to the application. Your sales team sees an immediate improvement to the quality and timeliness of the data they have on customers and prospects. They can easily access information critical to closing deals directly from their mobile devices, leading to productivity improvements. As the IT manager responsible for SaaS implementations, you look pretty good until something goes wrong.

A sales manager can't access the SaaS application to get the customer information he needs, so he contacts your customer service desk. This is when things get complicated. Figuring out the source of the problem is difficult since you have very little information about your SaaS provider's cloud infrastructure and how it is managed. It turns out that your SaaS provider built its solution on a public IaaS platform so there are at least two vendors (and maybe more) that could be the source of the service disruption. Ideally, your SaaS provider will provide you with information about the problem and resolve it quickly, but you are not in control.

Now to make things a little more complex, consider that you need to manage the delivery of multiple cloud services for your company's users. Your company's information needs to remain consistent across different applications in your hybrid environment. A service disruption in one cloud service may have an impact on other services as well. You want to ensure that your customers receive the right level of service, but you have limited insight into the performance of each cloud service provider's infrastructure environment. Ideally, you or your cloud service broker will see that you have a dashboard to monitor the performance health of the various cloud services from your different vendors. This will help you to pinpoint where the problem is coming from, but it is the responsibility of your provider to resolve the issue. The business needs to be assured that policies for security, governance, and scalability are maintained as workloads are managed across hybrid environments.

Lack of control over managing images

Virtual images need to be carefully managed in order for you to achieve the full benefits of virtualization within a hybrid cloud environment. Each new virtual machine image requires memory, disk, and storage resources.

Because it is so easy to create virtual images, many companies find that the number of virtual images they need to manage expands very quickly.

Without proper controls, images often remain after they are no longer needed. When these images are allowed to grow without out proper oversight or management, infrastructure and storage costs will increase. As a result, a company may find that the cost savings from its virtualization and cloud implementation are less than anticipated. In addition, uncontrolled and unmanaged virtual images can lead to critical gaps in security.

The following three scenarios illustrate how lack of control over managing images can create problems in different situations:

- **Virtual image management in private clouds.** Your organization has created a private cloud as part of your hybrid environment. You have a highly distributed software development organization, and there are multiple teams working on several new customer-facing initiatives. These teams have been asked to complete their development projects on a very tight time schedule. The private cloud makes it easy for the developers to provision the virtual environments needed to meet their deadlines. However, you go over budget based on unexpected costs to store and manage these environments.

  What was missing in your strategy? You need to implement an automated approach to manage the lifecycle of virtual images. Your approach should include rules that ensure that if an image hasn't been touched for a period of time, it is either automatically deleted or a warning is sent to the user.

- **Virtual image management by public cloud providers.** You provide IaaS to your customers. In order to deliver secure, efficient, and cost competitive services, you have a sophisticated cloud management system in place. One of the important capabilities of your automated system of controls is the management of virtual images. You need to make sure images are available to a customer while they are under contract for services. However, you keep tight control so that images are deleted when your customer stops paying for the service.

- **Virtual image management by public cloud users.** As a user of public cloud services you share some of the responsibilities for managing images you're your cloud provider. Your software developers are using a PaaS environment for their work. Although your PaaS provider is responsible for the infrastructure and middleware services that your developers need, you also have some responsibilities. You need to manage virtual resources provisioned in the cloud with the same level of attention as you provide in your internal data center. You will end up paying for extra storage costs if you hold on to virtual images after you no longer need them.

The Reality of the Service Desk in Hybrid Clouds

Use of the hybrid cloud requires a process for managing the ongoing performance of public and private cloud services in connection with internal services. One fundamental issue in managing services is that when you do it well, the service management team is like the wizard behind the curtain in the Land of Oz. If your e-mail never goes down and your technical equipment never fails, you won't go looking behind the curtain to understand why it works.

The reality is that services *do* fail and errors *do* occur — and when they do, customers (or service users) want questions answered and problems resolved.

For many businesses, the service desk is the first port of call when an incident or a problem occurs. A service desk provides a single point of contact for IT users and customers to report issues they have with the service. The service desk is generally responsible to receive information when an incident is reported, ensure that the problem is properly diagnosed and evaluated, and then make sure the problem is fixed quickly. However, in hybrid cloud environments, your service desk may find it challenging to integrate service information across the internal data center and public and private clouds.

How can your service desk provide an accurate and timely response to requests from internal users without controlling the management of your public cloud resources? When public cloud services are well managed, your cloud service providers can significantly ease the cloud management burden on your internal IT staff. However, imagine the lost productivity and revenue (and the all-around chaos) that might occur in the cloud if your cloud provider can't manage service delivery and deal with problems effectively. Also, imagine how difficult it is for your service desk to respond to your internal customers without an effective system of communication with your cloud providers. Without insight into the environment of the cloud provider, your service desk cannot predict when a service interruption may occur and may not be able to provide the business user with any useful information regarding when service will be restored.

You simply cannot assume that your cloud providers will give you the support you need. You may have contracts with lots of different cloud providers and you need to do your homework. As we have said before, all cloud providers are not the same. Depending on the contract you have with your cloud providers, they may or may not offer the right level of information. Open source cloud offerings may not provide a way to contact a service desk.

As described in the previous section on the cloud service management eco-system, you may want to enlist the service of a cloud broker to help with the management of services from multiple cloud providers.

Some service providers may provide different levels of support depending on the provisions of your contract. Basic support might mean a 12–48 hour response time via a web-based portal where you ask your question. It might also simply mean access to a web-based community. Cloud providers are beginning to compete on higher cost premium packages with more personalized and timely service. Some premium packages may provide you with an account manager who can route your trouble ticket to the top of the service queue. Your premium package may provide a rapid 15-minute response to the most critical problems.

Coordination between IT and cloud provider service desks

Your internal customers need to trust that IT services will be delivered as expected and fixed promptly when there are problems. You know your organization needs to monitor the entire environment based on service requirements of your business users.

So how can you best manage the coordination required between your enterprise IT and cloud provider service desks? You should establish policies and best practice guidelines for all internal users so they can easily funnel all service requests through your service desk (or your service broker's service desk). It will only add confusion (and possibly go against service provider contract terms) if each user of a cloud service makes independent service calls or e-mails to the cloud provider. You can also set up a triage based on the severity of the problem. In many cases you may be able to resolve simple problems internally without involving the cloud provider service desk.

When you want your cloud providers to support a major set of services in your environment there are several important capabilities you want them to provide, which we describe in this section.

Incident and problem management

Incident and problem management services include recording, routing, and resolving an issue; notifying interested parties on the status of the issue; and reporting on the issue. The following issues may cause serious outages and are among the most important that need attention.

- ✔ **Configuration management:** Someone made an error while changing a configuration.
- ✔ **Network:** The network gets overloaded.

✔ **Database:** A database table needs to be optimized.

✔ **System management:** A server's processors failed, and the failover didn't work.

✔ **IT security:** A denial-of-service attack is in progress.

✔ **Application:** A program has a bug.

Change management

The service desk should support the management of change requests, including information about how system parts interact. Often, the provider will include some support for customization in the contract. This might consist of one-on-one interactions with someone on the cloud staff.

Knowledge base

If service desk personnel don't have the right information to do their jobs, they won't be able to respond and perform appropriately. Knowledge management ensures that people get the information they need to do their jobs correctly. Service management systems often link to a database for past incidents and how they were resolved; this database speeds the resolution of incidents.

Building Your Hybrid Cloud Service Management Plan

One important requirement for cloud service management is putting a plan in place, which involves understanding what cloud services you are introducing into your company and how they need to interact with your data center assets. Now, you have to make the determination about which services you need to control because they could impact the business and how you can effectively manage the combination of those resources.

Establishing objectives

The first priority is to determine what is most important to the consumers of cloud services who you need to support. You need to ask, "What do I really want to achieve?" Remember that your service management plan is based on the service strategy and needs to support changing business conditions and customer expectations.

You have many options for developing your hybrid environment so that it provides your organization with the business flexibility you need to compete. An understanding of both IT and business requirements, including both flexibility and economic goals, will help to ensure that cloud services deliver what the business needs — both short term and long term.

You need to specify what services your business offers and what the company needs to achieve your vision. When you know what your objectives are, you can assess your current service management capability around those particular goals. At this time, you can find the gaps in your service management capability and develop a plan to deal with those gaps. It's important to evaluate what you have if you expect to be able to locate and close the gaps and achieve your strategy.

Getting started with a cloud service management plan

Here are a few questions to get you started as you develop your service management strategy for the hybrid cloud:

✔ Do you have a consistent way to manage assets across your public and private cloud environments as well as your internal environment?

✔ Do you have a process for change and configuration that ensures that all members of the organization have reliable access to the cloud service configuration information they need to perform their responsibilities?

✔ Can you ensure that business services created and maintained by one division are made available in a consistent manner across other areas of your organization?

✔ Have you developed a service catalog to help identify and govern the use of cloud services?

✔ Can you monitor and measure the effect of your strategy on demands for security, storage, and hardware?

These questions should provide you with an understanding of the issues that you have to plan for with cloud management. You should begin by understanding the consumer or customer for your services. Therefore, cloud management's objective is to provide a consistent and predictable level of service across all of the IT services you provide to consumers. If you wait until services are delivered to figure out service levels and other management issues, you've waited too long. If you start with the outcomes rather than how each individual component operates, you will be on your way to understanding how to plan for cloud management.

Keep in mind that how you manage cloud services will depend on what type of service provider you are. For example, service providers of public cloud IaaS will approach cloud service management very differently from an internal service provider of a private cloud. The cloud inside IT will invariably have to interact with public cloud services. However, no matter what type of service provider you might be, you have to make sure that there are consistent processes that ensure that changes in everything from configurations to code are managed consistently.

The cloud provider also has to make sure that it handles performance of the specific service being delivered as well as security, backup, data storage, scalability, speed of processing — just to name a few. This means that the IT organization has to understand the underlying services including what purpose they serve for the consumers within the organization, what the expectations are for performance, security, and scalability. At the end of the day, IT management needs to be armed with a holistic understanding of the elements of the cloud services used by the organization and the level of service required.

Part II
Examining Cloud Service Delivery Models

The 5th Wave   By Rich Tennant

"Great goulash, Stan. That reminds me, are you still in charge of our system architecture?"

In this part . . .

To really comprehend the cloud, you need to understand the four foundational delivery models. In this part, we examine the different models that are available to deliver cloud services — both public and private.

Chapter 5

Understanding Infrastructure as a Service

*I*nfrastructure as a Service (IaaS) is the most straightforward of the four models for delivering cloud services. IaaS is the virtual delivery of computing resources in the form of hardware, networking, and storage services. It may also include the delivery of operating systems and virtualization technology to manage the resources. Rather than buying and installing the required resources in their own data center, companies are renting these required resources on an as-needed basis.

Many companies with a hybrid environment are likely to include IaaS in some form because IaaS is a highly practical solution for companies with various IT resource challenges. Whether a company needs additional resources to support a temporary development project, an on-going dedicated development testing environment, or disaster recovery, paying for infrastructure services on a per-use basis can be highly cost-effective.

In this chapter we explore the two types of IaaS services: public and private. A public cloud IaaS service is designed so consumers in any size business can acquire services in a rental model. In contrast, private IaaS services are provided inside a company's own data center, enabling IT management to provide a self-service portal for employees and partners to easily access approved services. Although these two approaches to IaaS have their commonalities, their business models also have their differences.

Note: Although it would be great to tell you there are neat differences between a public and a private IaaS, the truth is that many offerings in the IaaS market can be used for either a public or a private cloud. A lot of what you see is the positioning of an IaaS by a vendor based on the types of businesses it wants to sell to. For example, OpenStack can be used both as a public or a private IaaS, as can Red Hat. HP's CloudSystem offers both public and private IaaS services. Eucalyptus is intended as an IaaS for private clouds but can be leveraged as the foundation for a public cloud. Additionally, for internal end users of private clouds, the look and feel of the environment is likely very familiar to them if they have experience using public cloud IaaS services.

Understanding the Key Characteristics of IaaS in a Public Cloud

Public IaaS services are very well known, thanks to the work done by Amazon with its Web Services. Business users over the past several years have discovered that they can bypass the IT organization and — for a small amount of money — access compute and storage services with little effort. They simply go to a self-service interface and provide a credit card number, and an image of compute or storage services is provided almost instantly. This rapid provisioning represents a stark contrast to the reality of many IT enterprise environments. The truth is that the traditional methods of acquiring computing resources simply haven't kept pace with business urgency. A company may miss out on the opportunity to win new customers if its hot new offering is delayed for three months because the IT development and test teams can't get the resources they need.

Companies face all sorts of variations in demand for IT resources. As a result, predicting what the demand for these resources will be and justifying the expense of new hardware are often very hard to do. For example, in a six-week period, a development team may need extra compute and storage infrastructure, but purchasing it for temporary needs makes no sense.

Likewise, in some situations an online vendor may need extra computing and networking capabilities during the holiday rush. If an online retailer in this situation relies on a traditional approach of maintaining all infrastructure within the data center, that company will find it hard to make the best economic decision. If sufficient physical system resources are purchased to satisfy expected capacity requirements over a holiday sales period, the retailer will still be paying for those resources when they're no longer needed. Alternatively, if the retailer underestimates the resources needed to support the demand, the company risks damaging relationships with customers and losing sales. The retailer loses out in both scenarios.

Many providers are beginning to expand the services and features of their IaaS offering. Some of these features — such as management and monitoring of users and resources, access-control, and auto-scaling — are more consistent with the characteristics and definition of Platform as a Service (PaaS) services. Please see Chapter 7 for more information on the definition of PaaS.

To help you make sense of the IaaS delivery model (as well as the other delivery models we talk about in the following chapters), we look at some of its key characteristics, including dynamic scaling, agreed-upon service levels, renting, licensing, metering, and self-service. All the characteristics that we include in the following sections are the same whether the environment is a public or a private IaaS environment.

Dynamic scaling

Some level of uncertainty always exists when planning for IT resources. One of the major benefits of IaaS for companies faced with this type of uncertainty is the fact that resources can be automatically scaled up or down based on the requirements of the application. This important characteristic of IaaS is called *dynamic scaling* — if customers wind up needing more resources than expected, they can get them immediately (probably up to a given limit). A provider or creator of IaaS typically optimizes the environment so that the hardware, the operating system, and automation can support a huge number of workloads.

Service levels

Additionally, consumers acquire IaaS services in different ways. Many consumers rent capacity based on an on-demand model with no contract. In other situations, the consumer signs a contract for a specific amount of storage or compute. A typical IaaS contract has some level of service guarantee. At the low end, a provider might simply state that the company will do its best to provide good service. If the consumers are willing to pay a premium price, they might be able to leverage a mirrored service so that there are almost no change of service interruptions. A typical service level agreement states what the provider has agreed to deliver in terms of availability and response to demand. The service level might, for example, specify that the resources will be available 99.999 percent of the time and that more resources will be provided dynamically if greater than 80 percent of any given resource is being used. To learn more about service level agreements, see Chapter 17.

The rental model

When companies use IaaS, it's often said that the servers, storage, or other IT infrastructure components are rented for a fee based on the quantity of resources used and how long they're in use. Although this is true, there are some important differences between this rental arrangement and the traditional rental models you may be familiar with. For example, when you purchase server and storage resources using IaaS services, you gain immediate virtual access to the resources you need. You aren't, however, renting the actual physical servers or other infrastructure. Don't expect a big truck to pull up to your office and deliver the servers you need to complete your project. The physical components stay put in the infrastructure service provider's data center. This concept of renting is an essential element of cloud computing, and it provides the foundation for the cost and scalability benefits of the various cloud models.

Within a private IaaS model, renting takes on a different focus. Although you might not charge each user to access a resource, in the *charge-back* model you can allocate usage fees to an individual department based on usage over a week, month, or year. Because of the flexibility of the IaaS model, you can charge more of the budget to heavy users.

Even at a few cents per CPU hour or megabytes of storage, expenses can add up to significant cash. Even more complicated are issues related to the ability to track IT governance. If a business user creates important content through an IaaS service, there's no accountability. Moreover, almost no public IaaS vendor releases usage logs to its customers. If customers are storing data within a public IaaS platform, they typically have no way to determine where that data is being stored. So, you need to be aware of potential compliance issues before you embark on IaaS. For example, some military or government contracts may require that the data be stored domestically. This doesn't rule out cloud solutions per se but does mean that you have to discuss where the data is located to meet the specific needs of you or your clients.

Licensing

The use of public IaaS has led to innovation in licensing and payment models for software you want to run in these cloud environments. Note that this licensing is for the software you want to run in your cloud environment, not the license between you and the cloud provider. For example, some IaaS and software providers have created a "bring your own license" (BYOL) plan so you have a way to use your software license in both traditional and cloud environments. Another option is called "pay as you go" (PAYG), which generally integrates the software licenses with the on-demand infrastructure services. For example, say that you're running Microsoft Windows Server and using the PAYG route. If you're paying ten cents an hour for cloud access, a few cents of that fee might be going to Microsoft.

Metering and costs

Clearly, you derive a potential economic benefit by controlling the amount of resources you demand and pay for so that you have just the right match with your requirements. To ensure that users are charged for the resources they request and use, IaaS providers need a consistent and predictable way to measure usage. This process of controlling, measuring, and monitoring the use of compute, network, and storage resources is called *metering*. Ideally, the IaaS provider will have a transparent process for identifying charges incurred by the user. With multiple users accessing resources from the same environment, the IaaS provider needs an accurate method for measuring the physical use of resources to make sure each customer is charged the right amount.

IaaS providers often use the metering process to charge users based on the instance of computing consumed. An *instance* is defined as the CPU power and the memory and storage space consumed in an hour. When an instance is initiated, charges begin to accumulate on an hourly basis until the instance is terminated. Typically, users can make multiple choices during set up, including the amount of compute power, memory, and storage requirements of an instance. Some vendors offer instances that come in various sizes, ranging from small to large. The charge for a very small instance may be as little as two cents an hour; the hourly fee could increase to $2.60 for a large resource-intensive instance running Windows.

Metering to assess the charges for the IaaS services you request begins when the instance is initiated and ends when the instance is terminated. At this point, the virtual machine provisioned for you is removed, and you no longer receive charges. Until this point, the charges apply whether the resources are fully used or are lying idle.

In addition to the basic per-instance charge, your IaaS provider may include charges such as the following (keep in mind that charges can change on a daily basis):

- ✔ **Storage:** A per gigabyte (GB) charge for the persistent storage of data of approximately $0.00015 an hour or $0.10 a month.

- ✔ **Data transfer:** A per GB charge for data transfers of approximately $0.15. This fee may drop to $0.05 per GB if you move large amounts of data during the billing month. Some providers offer free inbound data transfers or free transfers between separate instances on the same provider.

- ✔ **Optional services:** Charges for services such as reserved IP addresses, virtual private network (VPN), advanced monitoring capabilities, or support services.

Because of the variety of costs, many cloud providers offer cost calculators so organizations can estimate their monthly IaaS costs.

Here are the typical billing options:

- ✔ **Pay as you go:** Users are billed for resources used based on instance pricing.
- ✔ **Reserved pricing:** Users are billed an upfront fee, depending on the instance type, and then billed at a discounted hourly usage rate. For some companies this provides the best rates.
- ✔ **Trial use:** Some IaaS providers, such as Amazon, offer free usage tiers that allow users to "try before they buy."

Self-service provisioning

You can't discuss the key characteristics of IaaS without understanding the imperative of self-service. The banking ATM service is a great example of the business value of self-service. Without the availability of the self-service ATM, banks would be required to use costly resources to manage activities of all their customers — even for the most repetitive tasks. With an ATM, repetitive tasks can be handled easily with a self-service interface. The customer makes a direct request to perform routine transactions that conform to predefined business rules.

For example, a customer must have an account to withdraw money. In addition, the customer can't take out more money than is in her account. There may be rules dictating how much money an individual can withdraw from the ATM at one time or in one day. This process is precisely how self-service works in the IaaS public cloud environment. In a private cloud environment, management can enable users to provision resources when they need them based on a set of predefined rules and business priorities. In this way, everyone is satisfied. The business also gets to control expenses and reduce capital expenditures. The business units have the freedom to avoid time-consuming processes that slow down the ability to get the job done.

Many organizations that leverage IaaS opt for a hybrid approach — using private services in combination with public IaaS services. This approach is attractive because a company can leverage its private cloud resources but use trusted public cloud services to manage peak loads. When used in a controlled way, this hybrid approach is effective. Control means that a company establishes rules for when and how business units can use an outside cloud service; thus, the company is better able to control costs. In addition, by implementing distinct usage rules, users can be prevented from storing sensitive data on a public cloud.

A few IaaS vendors are now considering offering private/public cloud environments where appropriate policies may be set to automatically burst from a private to a public cloud. However, this is not yet generally available.

Considering the Role of a Private IaaS

Why would a company choose to implement a private version of IaaS? There are two compelling reasons:

- ✔ The company sees itself as a service provider to its employees and partners.
- ✔ The company needs to control access because of security concerns.

So, a company selecting a private approach creates a pool of resources that can be standardized and easily reused by the IT organization to complete projects. Why standardize? In an IaaS service, IT projects are created in predictable ways. For example, a process might be designed to set up a test environment for code or provision storage to support an application. While certain nuances are different, 80 percent of the time the process within IaaS can be standardized. By standardizing these infrastructure services, the organization gains efficiencies, fewer inadvertent errors, and consistency in managing the development lifecycle. This is the same approach used by a public IaaS vendor to control its costs.

Another benefit of a private cloud service is overall manageability. One of the overarching benefits of IaaS is the ability to gain access to an image or copy of a set of resources via a self-service process.

Although a public cloud vendor uses the self-service portal to ensure that the customer pays for the service, IaaS can be used differently in the private cloud. When a developer provisions a resource from a private cloud, IT management makes sure that when a project is completed, the resource (for example, compute resources or storage) is returned to the pool of resources. This way, IT can better control not only the resources available for projects, but also costs, utilization, and security.

Although a public cloud vendor uses the self-service portal to ensure that the customer pays for the service, IaaS can be used differently in a private cloud. When a developer provisions a resource from a private cloud, IT management can make sure that when a project is completed, the resource (for example, compute resources or storage) is returned to the pool of resources. In this way, IT can better control what resources are available for projects and can control costs, utilization, and security. How IT charges the internal customer is a matter of the business's policy.

Using IaaS

Organizations use IaaS for a variety of needs. Some companies want to leverage IaaS to quickly and economically provision additional compute power, whereas others want to avoid costly and complex maintenance of servers. Some companies find that using IaaS for disaster recovery is highly cost-effective and enables the company to mirror its entire site. In hybrid environments, companies will find a myriad of uses for IaaS. A wise user will evaluate each opportunity to use IaaS against the risk level associated with the IaaS provider and the overall economic risks and benefits.

Using IaaS for discrete projects

Here are some examples where IaaS is used for specific projects:

A team at company X is tasked with creating and testing a new application. The team requires a server for testing and development, but management needs the work done quickly and on the cheap. The team can acquire the resources from IaaS provider.

Company Y hosts a very popular food and cooking website. Normally, company Y's website runs quickly, but before major holidays, the site slows, and last Thanksgiving the site crashed and left cooks wondering what to do with their frozen turkeys. They employ IaaS to deal with any peaks in load.

Both company X and company Y can utilize IaaS to extend their internal IT infrastructure for a short period of time.

These two different companies may each realize similar benefits from using IaaS for discrete projects during a specific period of time. The development and test team will appreciate the high level of control they have for selecting the specific requirements for meeting their needs. The food website company will gain value from the easy and cost-effective way they can extend their IT infrastructure. Here are the key benefits:

- ✔ Creation of virtual machines with almost limitless storage and compute power
- ✔ Flexibility to select the developer tools the team wants to use
- ✔ Flexibility to select the operating system the team requires (Windows, Linux, and so on)
- ✔ Cost savings from eliminating capital expenditures on large systems that will be underutilized much of the year
- ✔ Flexibility to dynamically scale the environment to meet their needs

An organization needs to know its potential risk if its IaaS provider experiences downtime while they are using IaaS. A network outage may be a relatively minor inconvenience or even highly problematic for a specific project, depending on the circumstances.

Amazon EC2 — 2011 service disruption

When IaaS becomes the business, hiccups in service can lead to big headaches. Many customers of companies that live in IaaS don't even know the organization doesn't have traditional data centers until something goes wrong, like the crash of Amazon EC2 in April 2011. This disruption led to some sites becoming completely inoperable.

Amazon EC2 is one of the largest IaaS vendors. Amazon divides its infrastructure into *regions* and then further segments it into smaller areas called *availability zones (AZs)*. A region is analogous to a data center. Amazon has data centers in eight regions throughout the world, including four in the United States, two in Asia, one in Europe, and one in South America. AZs can be thought of as a *cluster* or a group of connected resources. Running an instance in two AZs, even within the same region, in theory insulates problems that occur in an individual AZ. However, AZs can be housed in the same data center and may be logically interconnected, so disruption to one area zone or the entire region could prevent the running of an instance.

April 21, 2011, Amazon's US East (Northern Virginia) data center experienced an outage that brought down sites such as Foursquare, a location-based social networking site; Quora, a question-and-answer service; and, Reddit, a news-sharing site. Problems existed for some Amazon EC2 customers for several days. This disruption exposed the potential risk for companies running all or at least a large portion of their businesses on a public IaaS.

Companies that experienced the biggest problems, such as Quora and Reddit, were likely fully backed up; however, their backup was at the same center that suffered the disruption — companies do so to save money (data transfers within the same data center are free).

Other companies, most notably, Netflix, experienced only minor difficulties during the crash. Although Netflix runs its whole business on Amazon EC2, its site wasn't affected because the company paid a premium to have backups in other Amazon EC2 regions.

When IaaS becomes the business

Increasingly, some companies aren't simply relying on IaaS for bursts of extra compute power, but are running their whole business using IaaS. For example, in 2010 Netflix moved to support the majority of its member traffic using IaaS provided by Amazon's Elastic Compute Cloud (Amazon EC2). Netflix needed to quickly scale its infrastructure to keep pace with the increased demand from a rapidly expanding member base using various new mobile devices. The company used IaaS to run all aspects of its business, ranging from building recommendation systems for members, to storing large amounts of data, to providing backup and redundant environments.

If Netflix had attempted to operate its business using traditional internal data center resources, it's hard to know whether the company would have been able to scale its infrastructure to support increased consumer demand for its services. Regardless, the company would have needed to accurately predict this increased demand several years prior in order to provide enough lead time to build new data centers.

Whereas Netflix is an example of an established company moving to IaaS, many startups never establish data centers and, instead, open shop from the start using IaaS. Zynga, the online social gaming company, which went public in December 2011, was born on IaaS and continues to stay there.

For Netflix, Zynga, and many other companies, IaaS is not simply a fast, cost-effective way of extending their IT needs; it is mission critical. When a company lives on IaaS, it must take extra care when selecting a vendor.

Examining Amazon's Public Elastic Compute Cloud

Currently, the most high-profile IaaS service provider is Amazon Web Services with its Elastic Compute Cloud (Amazon EC2). Amazon didn't start out with a vision to build a big infrastructure services business. Instead, the company built a massive infrastructure to support its own retail business and discovered that its resources were underused. Instead of allowing this asset to sit idle, Amazon decided to leverage this resource while adding to the bottom line. A funny thing happened after this relatively modest plan was put in place: Customers began to find that it could mushroom into something big.

Fast-forward a few years: Today, Amazon has established itself as the gorilla in the market. Amazon's EC2 service was launched in August 2006 and has evolved since with added enhanced features.

Amazon offers the following services to its customers today:

- ✔ **Compute power:** Customers can rent enough compute power to run or develop their own applications.
- ✔ **A web services interface:** Through this interface, customers can create virtual machines that meet their requirements for CPU power, memory, and storage space.
- ✔ **Control over the virtual operating environment:** Customers enjoy the same control they would if they were operating out of their physical data centers.
- ✔ **Elasticity of the service offering:** Users can dynamically add a new instance or terminate an instance as their needs change.

Customers choose from a menu of options to begin to use Amazon's EC2. To use EC2, you must be prepared to answer the following types of questions:

✔ Which instance size do you require for your Virtual servers — micro, small, large, or extra large?

✔ What are your needs in terms of CPU, memory, and storage?

✔ How do you want to back up your virtual machine?

✔ Are you prepared to agree to the rules specified in Amazon's service level agreement?

Amazon EC2 uses Xen virtualization, an open source *hypervisor* — a thin layer of software that allows other operating systems to run on the same system — to create and manage its virtual machines. Instances are based on EC2 Compute Units — defined by Amazon to represent the CPU capacity of physical hardware.

According to Amazon, one EC2 Compute Unit equals a 1.0-1.2 GHz 2007 AMD Opteron or 2007 Intel Xeon processor.

Amazon EC2 offers scalability under the user's control with the user paying for resources by the hour. The use of the term *elastic* in the naming of Amazon's EC2 is significant. Here, elasticity refers to the ability that EC2 users have to easily increase or decrease the infrastructure resources assigned to meet their needs. Users must initiate a request, so the service provided isn't dynamically scalable. Although Amazon itself supports a limited number of operating systems — Linux, Solaris, and Windows — users of EC2 can request the use of any operating system as long as the developer does all the work.

Emerging Players in the IaaS Market

Amazon has been the top dog in IaaS for a number of years, but the market is changing fast. It's inevitable that emerging organizations and companies want a piece of the action. Open source options are emerging as very important in this market.

In this section, we provide an overview of the emerging players in both public and private cloud IaaS, including Eucalyptus, OpenStack, and Red Hat's CloudForms.

Eucalyptus

Eucalyptus Systems is a software company intended to help customers accelerate their movement into a hybrid cloud environment. Therefore, it offers services to create a private cloud. To support public cloud services,

Eucalyptus leverages Amazon's Web Services APIs. The initial software behind the Eucalyptus solution was developed as open source at the University of California, Santa Barbara. Eucalyptus continues to support an open source community while at the same time offering an enterprise version of its software.

Through a partnership with Amazon Web Services (AWS), Eucalyptus has made itself particularly interesting for companies wanting to implement a hybrid cloud. Amazon partnered with Eucalyptus by providing the company with access to its AWS APIs. This means that an organization that develops a private cloud using Eucalyptus has built-in compatibility with AWS offerings. This allows companies to more easily create and move workloads between their private cloud and the public cloud. Eucalyptus faces stiff competition from other open source private cloud platform OpenStack, which is backed by a number of industry leaders.

OpenStack

OpenStack is implementing an open cloud platform aimed at either public or private clouds. The project was initiated jointly by Rackspace and NASA. While the organization is tightly managed by Rackspace, it moved to a separate OpenStack foundation. Although companies can leverage OpenStack to create proprietary implementations, to you, the OpenStack designation requires conformance to a standard implementation of services.

The initiative has begun gaining considerable support from customers and vendors. At this time, there are more than 150 vendors, including Dell, HP, Intel, AMD, and Cisco, who are using OpenStack as the foundation for their cloud offerings. In essence, OpenStack is an open source IaaS initiative built on Ubuntu, an operating system based on the Debian Linux distribution. It can also run on Red Hat's version of the Linux operating system.

OpenStack's goal is to provide a massively-scaled, multi-tenant cloud specification that can run on any hardware. OpenStack is building a large ecosystem of partners interested in adopting its cloud platform. One of the main goals of OpenStack is to provide an independent orchestration layer that supports all of the major hypervisors including VMware's ESX and KVM, and Microsoft's Hyper-V.

OpenStack's services include

- ✔ **Nova:** A compute service, this is the primary IaaS service. It's written in the Python language.
- ✔ **Swift:** This is an object storage service.
- ✔ **Glance:** This image service provides a catalog and repository for virtual disk images. These disk images are mostly used in OpenStack Compute. Although this service is technically optional, any large cloud implementation will need this service.

✔ **Horizon:** A dashboard service, this includes a web-based interface to support the OpenStack services.

✔ **Keystone:** This is an identity service that provides authentication and authorization for OpenStack services including a service catalog.

✔ **Quantum:** This networking service provides an abstracting of networking connectivity through interfaces.

Red Hat's CloudForms

Red Hat, one of the most important open source Linux and infrastructure companies is expanding into cloud services. It created an open source IaaS to allow companies to build private or hybrid clouds with an open source initiative called CloudForms. The CloudForms environment uses Red Hat's JBoss Enterprise Middleware as a set of foundational services for its IaaS. CloudForms includes IaaS tools such as self-service provisioning, application management, configuration management, and deployment and management that allow services to move across environments. CloudForms also offers services to manage virtualization.

What Infrastructure as a Service Means to You

Even if you aren't using IaaS now, it's very likely that your future hybrid environment will incorporate this practical, flexible, and cost-effective cloud service. What does this mean to you?

✔ Think about how you're getting your services.

✔ Understand which services include a set of well-defined interfaces and which ones will lock you into a complex set of services that will be difficult to move away from.

✔ Know why you're using a cloud service. For example, if you need some temporary capacity to test a new application, your requirements will be very different than if you're creating an application that will operate in a cloud.

In addition to understanding potential cloud gains, become familiar with how your infrastructure service provider handles the following capabilities:

✔ Explicit definitions of service level agreements for availability, support, and performance (of provisioning more resource)

✔ A utility computing billing arrangement, relating cost to actual resource use in a measured way

✔ A virtualization environment that enables the configuration of systems (for compute power, bandwidth, and storage) as well as the creation of individual virtual machines (all to be available on an ad hoc basis)

✔ A flexible, extensible, resource-rich environment that's engineered for secure *multi-tenancy* (multiple users or tenants running the software in a shared environment on its servers)

✔ Internet connectivity, including a web services interface to the customer's management environment or its own management environment.

Chapter 6

Exploring Software as a Service

• •

• •

*A*lthough most developers are familiar with using Infrastructure as a Service (IasS), most end users are much more familiar with Software as a Service (SaaS). Software as a Service is the way many business users are first introduced to the cloud, because SaaS applications are designed to implement a specific business process — ranging from accounting to customer relationship management (CRM), collaboration, and human resource management. These business users have increasingly found that SaaS applications represent a more cost-effective, flexible, and secure alternative to traditional on-premises applications.

SaaS is not a stand-alone environment. Instead, these applications and services are frequently used in combination with lots of other cloud and on-premises models. Companies need their SaaS applications to couple with other applications and platforms on their own data center and with other cloud platforms. In this chapter, we take a look at the value of SaaS and how it works in a hybrid world.

Seeing the Characteristics of SaaS

Many companies have discovered that there are great organizational and economic benefits that can be realized by using SaaS applications. They provide the opportunity to have a third-party organization handle all the details that go into keeping complex applications running. As companies become dependent on these applications, they begin to see a pattern of characteristics among the more successful solutions:

✔ Generalized applications that incorporate the right mix of common services so the applications meet the needs of different companies across multiple industries.

✔ True multi-tenancy means that all the users are using the same codebase. However, their configurations and data are stored in separate containers. The next section dives deeper into the benefits of multi-tenant solutions.

✔ Highly elastic SaaS applications can easily scale up or down to support changing needs of a business. If a company increases its sales force, for example, it needs to be able to quickly add more licenses (seats) to its SaaS.

✔ Self-service puts the power to acquire more resources and generally manage an application's deployment directly in the hands of users. Customers can go to their portal and add more licenses, renew their contract, or reduce their number of licenses in a matter of minutes. You no longer need to contact vendors and then wait for them to make the changes. Self-service includes built-in billing, monitoring, and usage information that gives customers a unified view of what they're paying and what they're receiving.

✔ SaaS applications are modular and service-oriented. Without this modular approach, it will be hard to change and difficult to have third-party companies join the ecosystem.

✔ SaaS applications provide sophisticated business process configurators for customers. Each customer can change the process within the standardized SaaS application. For example, a company may want to add a process so a manager has to approve the price being offered to a new customer. A built-in configuration tool enables this to be done on an ad hoc basis without programming.

✔ SaaS applications need to constantly provide fast releases of new features and new capabilities. This must be done without affecting the customer's ability to continue business as usual.

The SaaS vendor must be able to ensure customers that their data and configurations are separate and secure from other customers' data and configurations. Imagine the possible consequences if your competitors use the same SaaS offering that you use and they're able to access your customer lists or intellectual property. Vendors are aware of customer concerns and implement extensive security, both technologically and physically. Ideally, applications should also be able to migrate data in a hybrid environment, which means allowing information to move to a customer's private cloud or a different public cloud.

Multi-Tenancy and Its Benefits

Multi-tenancy means that the SaaS vendor provides a single version of its software for all its customers. This differs from a single-tenant *hosted* solution where the application is housed on a vendor's server but the codebase is unique for each customer.

So, how does multi-tenancy work? Although all users of the software access the same foundational components, the data and configurations that are specific to a customer are stored in a separate and secure container. Users can access all the capabilities of the software, but what isn't shared is their data. The advantages of a multi-tenancy SaaS over a third-party-hosted, single-tenancy application include these:

- ✔ **Lower costs through economies of scale:** With a single-tenancy-hosted solution, SaaS vendors must build out their data center to accommodate new customers. In contrast, in a multi-tenant environment, new users get access to the same basic software, so scaling has far fewer infrastructure implications for vendors (depending on the size of the application and the amount of infrastructure required).

- ✔ **Shared infrastructure leads to lower costs:** SaaS allows companies of all sizes to share infrastructure and data center operational costs. Users don't need to add applications and more hardware to their data centers, and some small- to medium-sized businesses don't even need data centers if they utilize SaaS.

- ✔ **Ongoing maintenance and updates:** End users don't need to pay costly maintenance fees in order to keep their software up to date. New features and updates are included with a SaaS subscription and are rolled out by the vendor.

- ✔ **Configuration can be done while leaving the underlying codebase unchanged:** Although on-premises applications and single-tenant-hosted solutions are often customized, this endeavor is costly and requires changes to an application's code. Additionally, this customization can make upgrades time-consuming, because an upgrade might not be compatible with your customization. Most multi-tenant SaaS solutions are designed to be highly configurable so that businesses can make the application perform the way they want, without changing the underlying code or data structure. Because the code is unchanged, upgrades can be performed easily.

- ✔ **Vendors have a vested interest in making sure everything runs smoothly:** Multi-tenant SaaS providers have, in a sense, all their eggs in one basket. Although this sounds dangerous, it's a benefit to end users. In a single-tenant environment, if there is a service disruption, it may affect only one customer, meaning that the vendor might be slow to respond and fail to take the necessary steps to ensure the problem doesn't reoccur. In contrast, with a multi-tenant solution, a slight glitch could affect all a vendor's customers. It is, therefore, imperative that SaaS vendors invest significant amounts of money and effort into ensuring uptime, continuity, and performance.

The story of a SaaS pioneer: Salesforce.com

Although companies have offered software products as a service for many years, the current generation of highly sophisticated SaaS offerings can be traced back to Salesforce.com. The story of how this SaaS pioneer grew to become a market leader and a look at its current offerings provide insight into the market.

Marc Benioff, the founder of Salesforce.com, had been a marketing executive for Oracle for many years. After leaving and going off on his own, he started Salesforce.com. Being a marketing executive, Marc had a bold marketing moniker for his fledgling company: "No software." The plan was quite simple: Create a way to allow customers to use a popular application — customer relationship management (CRM) — over the Internet. Customers could purchase a seat and use the application over the web. The customer never had to update the software, didn't have to store data on a server, and never had to worry about maintenance fees. If that customer was traveling to a remote location, he could access his sales leads from any PC. There were no capital expenses, with the exception of a PC or some endpoint, such as a tablet.

Initial Salesforce.com customers were small businesses that were willing to take a risk in exchange for not having to buy hardware or hire staff. Also, because there was only a one-month commitment, they knew they could simply take their customer data and go home if it didn't work out for them. Salesforce.com had a more difficult time separating large companies from their data-center focus. Sales and marketing departments at large enterprises began to

implement Salesforce.com by placing the fees to run Salesforce.com on their expense reports. Slowly but surely, Salesforce.com made inroads into large companies that appreciated the ability to avoid buying equipment.

Salesforce.com opened its platform so that independent software vendors (ISVs) could build software that sits on top of the CRM application. Essentially, Salesforce.com built a Platform as a Service, which it named Force.com. ISVs could create SaaS applications on the platform, and Salesforce.com was able to offer additional functionality, such as billing and monitoring, to its customers.

System integrators found that customers who were using Salesforce.com more and more wanted to extend the environment. The application could not simply be "the CRM program" but was part of a greater IT landscape. Companies needed to connect Salesforce.com to other systems, create processes, link to commerce networks, and so on. The system integrators turned Salesforce.com into a hybrid environment that now interacts with data centers behind customers' firewalls, public clouds, and third-party applications built on its Platform as a Service — the secret sauce is the service orientation of the underlying platform. When integrators or other software vendors partner with a company like Salesforce.com, they create a dependency on the Salesforce.com development and deployment model. This dependency allows them to develop more quickly and efficiently, but it also locks them into a single platform.

SaaS Economics

The proliferation of SaaS has changed the way companies pay for and maintain software. The following are some of the most important things to think about when you consider budgeting and SaaS:

✔ **Entry costs are lower with SaaS.** When implementing a SaaS application, customers are often able to get a free trial period to assess the software. Additionally, companies can slowly ramp up the number of *seats* (users) who have access to the application. With traditional on-premises implementations, a company must make a large capital expenditure upfront to acquire the application. It then must install the software and possibly purchase additional hardware to support the implementation.

✔ **Maintenance and support fees are a thing of the past with SaaS.** With on-premises applications, there's a perpetual license software model. Companies need to enter into a contract with a software vendor or services provider to keep software up to date and free from glitches and security vulnerabilities. These contracts are expensive — typically, ranging from 10 to 25 percent of the original purchase price. SaaS sheds these contracts, and instead includes such support in the access fees.

✔ **Upgrades are no longer costly, prolonged procedures with SaaS.** Upgrading a traditional, on-premises application often requires months of testing, the allocation of large budgets, and teams of consultants to ensure that the implementation runs smoothly. Companies often skip upgrades in order to reduce the headaches involved. In a SaaS model, upgrades are performed behind the scenes by the SaaS vendor. All the customers receive the new, updated software at the same time without having to manage a frustrating upgrade process. This ensures that SaaS users are always running the most up-to-date version of the software.

Occasionally, SaaS updates cause problems. For example, if you're running a third-party application that gathers data from the SaaS, the application may fail because the SaaS is no longer working as expected. These problems are typically kept to a minimum because they have to architect their solutions to support a wide variety of partners and their platforms.

How SaaS Fits into the Hybrid Cloud World

SaaS applications rarely sit alone. The reality is companies have an IT landscape that might look something like this: SaaS for CRM, a second SaaS for human resources, in-house analytics hardware behind a firewall, and IA as for testing. Much of this information is fed into their enterprise resource planning (ERP) system that might be housed on their data center. It's critical that processes are enabled that allow information to securely flow among these systems. This hybrid SaaS environment is illustrated in Figure 6-1.

The environment described here truly is a hybrid cloud. Why? Because multiple resources use various delivery options that touch each other and aren't all controlled by the enterprise. These applications somehow ultimately need to work together to provide business value. Of course, a hybrid environment can be simpler or more complex than the one illustrated in Figure 6-1.

What's behind your SaaS application? A vendor might run its software from data centers it operates. Salesforce.com did this out of necessity, because it was an early innovator without other options. Other vendors — for example, SugarCRM — run its offerings on public clouds, such as Amazon EC2. A SaaS running in a vendor's data center isn't necessarily more stable, but great software on an unreliable third party is useless. So, it's important to understand service level agreements (SLAs) (for more on SLAs see Chapter 17).

If you think about the SaaS environment, it too runs on various cloud deployment models (such as private or public) that has various cloud delivery models (such as IaaS or PaaS) supporting it. SaaS on its own is a truly integrated environment that needs to be able to live cooperatively within its own computing environment as well as with other elements in a company's cloud ecosystem. That's what makes a hybrid cloud so complex.

So when a business in your company wants access to all the data so it can run analytics, you can't just say, "Sorry, that's all in the SaaS application." Instead, you can replicate the data onto your private cloud. From there, the analytics team can make a copy of the *golden master* (a single version of the truth for the data — the reference model) to run its fancy number crunching, and other groups, such as developers, can make a copy and use it for testing on a public cloud.

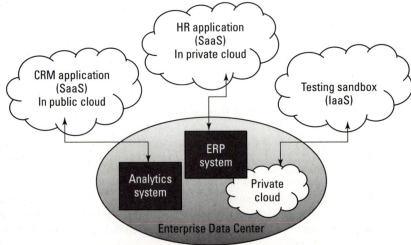

Figure 6-1:
An enterprise hybrid SaaS environment.

Understanding the Hybrid SaaS Ecosystem

In order to create a more feature-rich application, some SaaS vendors have created an *ecosystem*. This is a set of partners that works directly with the vendor, both in technical and go-to-market terms.

How the ecosystem works

This is how it works: A SaaS vendor with thousands of paying customers opens its programming interfaces to other ISVs. These ISVs can then build on top of the SaaS vendor's infrastructure. They, therefore, don't need to write and deploy an entire application, but can focus on their industry-specific code. Messaging middleware, business process services, and other complex programming have already been taken care of by the SaaS vendor that created the ecosystem.

Perhaps the most significant advantage to working in the ecosystem is that the SaaS vendor already has thousands of happy and paying customers. After a partner creates an application, it can market its software through the SaaS vendor's portal in addition to using its own traditional sales force. This has become a standard model used by SaaS vendors to build their brand and power in the market.

Finding out who builds in SaaS vendor ecosystems

ISV partners can be broken into two general categories: small startups and larger, established companies. It might be clear why a small company with limited resources might want to build on top of the Salesforce.com platform, but if you're a large player with your own customer base, why use Salesforce.com or SugarCRM?

Established software vendors with successful applications are receiving pressure to offer a cloud version of their software. The challenge that these larger ISVs face is that in order to have a successful, enterprise-class application, they must write the code from scratch internally. Developing such an environment is costly and can take years to have the reliability and usability that businesses demand.

Smaller ISVs are attracted to SaaS vendor ecosystems because doing so allows them to quickly deploy new software. These companies don't get bogged down by writing the basic code, which is provided to them as a PaaS.

Take a look at Veeva Systems, a software vendor that has developed a cloud-based CRM solution for the pharmaceutical, animal health, and biotechnology industries. Veeva built its software in the Salesforce.com ecosystem. Without Salesforce.com, Veeva would have had to create a completely new platform from scratch — a monumental and expensive endeavor for a small company. Salesforce.com cannot meet the unique needs of every industry, so where Salesforce.com falls short, partners like Veeva step in.

For example, pharmaceutical companies must comply with specific regulations. Veeva has built-in functionality to track and report the required information. Because updates are done by Veeva, when reporting requirements change, it updates the application so all its users have access to the most up-to-date offering and are in compliance with industry practices and government regulations.

The ecosystem relies on the hybrid cloud for success. All the applications in an ecosystem were developed on a PaaS. The vendors creating these programs often run them on IaaS. Additionally, companies often want to back up all the data on their data center. End users simply access the SaaS, and don't realize that behind the scenes multiple public and private cloud environments are being utilized.

Developing in a SaaS vendor's ecosystem

Clearly, there are great benefits for ISVs that build applications in an established environment, but these independent development companies may be at the mercy of the SaaS vendor. If the SaaS vendor does an update, the ISV might find that its application no longer functions in the correct way.

Independent vendors need to make sure they can thoroughly test their software before upgrades. Also, the SaaS vendor may come out with a new feature that renders your application useless to most customers. For example, a company selling a Microsoft Outlook integration tool for Salesforce.com would quickly lose customers if Salesforce.com added built-in integration. Although these issues require ISVs to research a SaaS vendor before developing on its platform, in practice the relationship between the SaaS vendors and their ISV partners is symbiotic — each needs the other for success and growth.

Examining Examples of SaaS Platforms

You may be overwhelmed when you look at how many companies have created SaaS offerings — even companies whose primary focus is the on-premises model feel compelled to offer a SaaS version of their offerings (or are forced to by customer demands).

The reality is that SaaS comes in all shapes and sizes. Applications run the gamut from accounting to customer relationship management, supply chain management, financial management, and human resources. These integrated offers focus on a specific process, such as managing employees' benefits, salaries, and annual performance reviews. These products tend to have several characteristics in common: They're designed with specific business processes built in that customers can modify. They have moved in great numbers to the cloud because customers were finding the platforms too hard to manage and users needed access to the application while on the go.

SaaS is also popular for collaborative applications. This area is dominated by software that focuses on all sorts of collaborative efforts, including web conferencing, document collaboration, project planning, instant messaging, and even e-mail. In a sense, it was inevitable that these platforms would move to the cloud: These tasks occur throughout the organization and need to be easily accessed from many locations.

In the next section, we give you a taste for some of the vendors in the SaaS space, what they offer customers, and the issues to consider. We can't possibly do this topic justice, but we give you a road map for how to understand the offerings and issues.

Packaged SaaS

We've written a lot about how Salesforce.com created CRM as a service and how it also created a rich ecosystem. It took a few years, but the company invested in its infrastructure, built a flexible and modular application, and made the navigation easier. But as with any successful venture, Salesforce.com competitors soon began entering the market in droves.

Knowing which companies to look at in today's market isn't as straightforward as you might think. This market is dynamic, so a company that looks promising today could be gone tomorrow. On the other hand, the small, emerging company that looks too new to consider could land a number of impressive customers and quickly become a major force. Likewise, companies that have been successful as on-premises software providers are streaming into the SaaS market. Some of these companies have come out with clumsy, difficult-to-use offerings, and others have polished cloud versions of their traditional on-premises software.

Companies in the packaged software market include the following:

✔ **NetSuite:** Like Salesforce.com, NetSuite started as a CRM solution in 1998. It added financial accounting, distribution or supply chain management, manufacturing, and human resources and payroll services, and now has a full ERP offering for the small- and medium-sized business market.

www.netsuite.com

✔ **Workday:** Started by David Duffield, the founder of PeopleSoft, Workday, Inc., is a human resources and financial management vendor. The company provides an easy, cost-effective way to run payroll and other processes in different legislative landscapes throughout the world. Although Workday started with a focus on mid-market customers, it now has a number of large enterprises as customers, as well.

www.workday.com

✔ **Intuit:** Provides a financial services suite of products that support accounting services for small- and medium-sized businesses. Some of Intuit's largest brands include QuickBooks, TurboTax, and Quicken, which all have SaaS offerings. The company provides a rich set of interfaces that enables partners to connect their services and applications into its environment.

www.intuit.com

✔ **RightNow:** Acquired by Oracle in October 2011, RightNow provides a CRM suite of products that includes marketing, sales, and various industry solutions.

www.rightnow.com

✔ **Concur:** Focuses on employee spend management. Concur automates cost control via automated processes. Recall the discussion, earlier in this chapter, about SaaS vendor ecosystems — Concur is an example of a company that has not only built its own ecosystem, but has also partnered with Google Apps in order to extend its market reach to new businesses.

www.concur.com

✔ **Oracle CRM On Demand:** Focuses on a broad range of industry targeted solutions.

www.oracle.com

✔ **SugarCRM:** Is a CRM platform built on an open source platform. The company offers support for a fee.

www.sugarcrm.com

✔ **Constant Contact:** A marketing automation platform that partners directly with Salesforce.com and other CRM platforms, Constant Contact automates the process of sending e-mails and other marketing efforts.

www.constantcontact.com

Some of the traditional on-premises software companies have also moved into the packaged SaaS market, including these:

✔ Microsoft with its Dynamics package

http://crm.dynamics.com/online

✔ SAP with its By Design offering for the small- to medium-sized business market

```
www.sap.com/solutions/products/sap-bydesign/index.epx
```

✔ Oracle with its On Demand offering based on its acquisition of Siebel Software

```
www.oracle.com/us/products/ondemand/index.html
```

Collaboration as a service

Collaboration is one of the natural markets for SaaS. There's enough bandwidth, and all companies are connecting to the Internet. In addition, more companies than ever have remote offices and workers across the globe. A team may be easily spread across 100 locations in 40 different countries!

The following list includes some of the companies that are focusing on collaboration as a service today:

✔ **SharePoint Online:** Microsoft's cloud collaboration as a service offering. Office 365 provides users with many of the traditional Microsoft products, such as Microsoft Office, which can now be delivered as a SaaS with collaboration tools built in. Also, Microsoft offers the ability to run its e-mail server (Exchange Online). Customers now have the flexibility of choosing whether to implement Microsoft's collaborative tools either on-premises or as a service.

```
www.cloudshare.com/sharepoint-cloud
```

✔ **IBM SmartCloud for Social Business:** Formerly LotusLive, this collaborative environment includes a set of tools that covers social networking, instant messaging, and the ability to share files and conduct online meetings. IBM is publishing interfaces to allow other collaborative tools to be integrated into the platform.

```
www.ibm.com/cloud-computing/social/us/en/
```

✔ **Google Apps for Business:** As many as 4 million businesses use Google's various collaborative applications, including e-mail, document management, and instant messaging. It publishes APIs so third-party software developers can integrate with the platform. The Google Apps environment has a large Apps Marketplace where ISVs offer a variety of additional functionality.

```
www.google.com/apps/business
```

✔ **Cisco WebEx:** Cisco, which purchased WebEx in 2007, offers WebEx along with other offerings that allow companies to collaborate both internally and with their customers.

```
www.webex.com
```

✔ **Zoho:** An open source collaboration platform, Zoho includes e-mail, document management, project management, and invoice management. It offers APIs to its environment and has begun to integrate its collaboration tools with other companies, such as Microsoft. Zoho offers support for a fee.

`www.zoho.com`

✔ **Citrix GotoMeeting:** Offers an online meeting service as part of its larger suite of virtualization products.

`www.gotomeeting.com`

There are many other players in the field, including Jive Software, DropBox, Yammer, LinkedIn — and even the ubiquitous Facebook is making a play in the business collaboration field.

Other as-a-Service Options in the Cloud

In case all the hundreds (if not thousands) of SaaS options aren't enough, a plethora of as-a-Service models are springing up around the cloud. There are service providers to help you manage your cloud and secure your cloud environment. There are providers to help you deploy desktops in the cloud. The list goes on. This section provides some examples.

Monitoring and management as a service

Is what you see what you get? Maybe. That's why companies using SaaS need to do some of their own monitoring to determine whether their service levels have been met by their SaaS providers. Even more complicated is when companies are using more than one SaaS application in a hybrid model (refer to Figure 6-1 earlier in this chapter). To complicate things even further, you must monitor not just a single application, but also the *combination* of applications.

Companies in the systems management space are positioning themselves for this world. Vendors come at this market from two different perspectives:

✔ From the top down, large telecommunications companies are packaging their capabilities so they can help provide cloud management and monitoring.

✔ You also see traditional companies that provide web-services monitoring now offering services that will tell you whether your website has added new services to support the cloud.

For example, Cloudkick offers monitoring tools as a service for multiple cloud server providers, as well as server management tools. The company was founded in January 2009 and was quickly acquired by

Rackspace, a cloud computing leader, in December 2010, in part because Cloudkick empowers customers to monitor an entire cloud strategy — both public and private.

Security as a service

Almost without exception, vendors providing antivirus software are offering their products as a service. These vendors include all the large IT security players: Symantec, McAfee, CA, and Kaspersky Labs. In addition, companies, such as Hewlett-Packard and IBM, have tools that scan environments for vulnerability scanning and testing.

Identity management — ensuring that people accessing a system are who they say they are and determining what access, if any, should be granted — is an important aspect of a company's security strategy for both on-premises and cloud computing. A growing number of players deliver identity management solutions as SaaS. Symantec, IBM, CA, and Oracle, along with small vendors such as Okta, Ping, and Symplified all either have or are rolling out identity management as a service.

For more on security, see Chapter 15.

Compliance and governance as a service

Compliance and governance tasks are time-consuming and complicated tasks that large companies are required to do. Therefore, offering these capabilities as a service is critical.

Not surprisingly, hundreds of companies have moved into this area. Today a company's full governance, risk, and compliance (GRC) solution can be delivered as a service. Some additional services that have become SaaS include the following:

- ✔ **Patch management:** For security packs and service patches for your applications
- ✔ **Business continuity planning:** To ensure that your software continues to run in the face of a disaster
- ✔ **Discovery of records and messages:** Records management of inactive and semi-active records has become a big SaaS storage type service
- ✔ **Various governance reporting:** Such as SOX (Sarbanes-Oxley), SAS 70 (Statement on Auditing Standard) controls for data, HIPAA (Health Insurance Portability and Accountability Act) healthcare requirements, and GLBA (Gramm-Leach-Bliley Act) requirements

For more on governance, see Chapter 15.

Hybrid Cloud Changes the Nature of SaaS

SaaS provides incredible value to customers, but in practice, SaaS is another element in a hybrid cloud world. Even if you plan to simply use a SaaS service to fill one business need, we expect that you will have more and more of a need to connect systems. The SaaS application your marketing department needs now feeds into your on-premises ERP, and the data is used in your private cloud for analytics, while a development team needs the data on Amazon's EC2 for testing and so on.

We think you see where this is going. As we mention earlier, SaaS can be a complex element in a hybrid cloud. As the market evolves, more SaaS providers will want their applications to work together. Companies will need their SaaS applications to be able to communicate with the applications they have on-premises. All this will have to be secured and monitored. Standards will become ever more important in order for this ecosystem to expand, grow, and succeed. The hybrid cloud is a brave new world. We talk much more about all these factors in Chapters 11, 12, 15, and 18.

Chapter 7

Standing on Platform as a Service

Software development and deployment have always been complex and ever-changing processes. Over time, continual demands have been placed on developers to change software to keep up with new technology trends and changing customer demands. The very definition of what qualifies as a customer is changing dramatically. Today, a customer may be a division within your own company, a business partner, or a buyer of services. At the same time, more companies are creating and deploying software that requires them to work closely with partners to create innovative software-based products, which means the development and deployment processes are much more complicated than ever before.

Development projects may involve many more developers in several locations. In addition, these developers must contend with a variety of configurations, multiple versions of operating systems and middleware, and complex integration with data and processes. The need to abstract complexity away from the teams charged with managing these processes has never been greater.

To help manage this growing level of complexity, many companies are looking at cloud computing as a more streamlined application development and deployment platform. *Platform as a Service* (PaaS) is an environment that abstracts the details and complexity of the development process. As a result, PaaS offers the potential for much more flexibility that enables developers to more quickly and efficiently meet customer demands.

To help you better understand what PaaS is and the business problems it solves, we cover its characteristics in this chapter. We also provide a perspective on how PaaS fits with other important cloud services and how it operates in a hybrid environment.

Understanding Platform as a Service

PaaS is an abstracted and integrated cloud-based environment that supports the development, running, and management of applications. Application components may exist in a cloud environment or may integrate with applications managed in private clouds or in data centers. A primary value of a PaaS environment is that developers don't have to be concerned with some of the lower-level details of the environment. We expect that most organizations will use a combination of some PaaS with traditional on-premises development environments.

If you look at a software stack as a pyramid, as shown in Figure 7-1, Infrastructure as a Service (IaaS) is at the foundational level and includes capabilities such as operating systems, networks, virtual machines, and storage. In the middle is the PaaS environment that includes services for developing and deploying applications. Software as a Service (SaaS) is at the top of the pyramid representing the actual applications offered to end users.

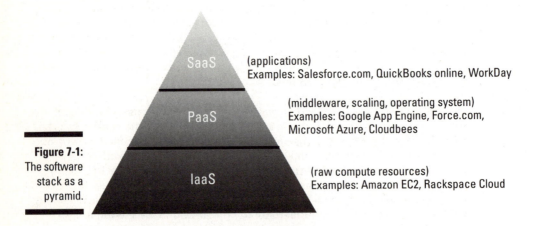

Figure 7-1:
The software stack as a pyramid.

SaaS — (applications)
Examples: Salesforce.com, QuickBooks online, WorkDay

PaaS — (middleware, scaling, operating system)
Examples: Google App Engine, Force.com, Microsoft Azure, Cloudbees

IaaS — (raw compute resources)
Examples: Amazon EC2, Rackspace Cloud

PaaS vendors create a managed environment that brings together a combination of components that would have been managed separately in a traditional development environment. Services integrated in PaaS include middleware, operating systems, and development and deployment services to support software development and delivery organizations. There are also some large enterprises that become, in effect, a PaaS provider to their own internal developers. These organizations follow a similar process of applying best practices to standardize the services developers require to develop and deploy applications. In all situations, the goal of the PaaS provider is to create an abstracted environment that supports an efficient, cost-effective, and repeatable process for the creation and deployment of high-quality applications. These applications are designed to be implemented in public or private cloud environments.

PaaS enables an organization to do the following:

✔ Leverage key middleware services without having to deal with the complexities of managing individual hardware and software elements.

✔ Access a complete stack of development and deployment tools via a web browser, a middleware environment where APIs can be used to plug into selected development and deployment tools. A developer might also leverage a full desktop development environment.

✔ Overcome the challenges of managing lots of individual development and deployment tools by providing a suite of integrated and standardized tools — operating systems, security products, and the like — that meet company requirements.

Platform as a Service (PaaS) can be viewed as having two fundamental parts: the platform and the service. In this chapter, we focus primarily on the platform — the actual software that's delivered to your organization. The service, however, is what really sets PaaS apart. The PaaS vendor doesn't just deliver the software making up the platform; it also continuously services the software. As new updates and new configurations become available, the PaaS vendor can immediately push them to its customers.

One of the decisions you need to make when beginning to use a PaaS is whether you want to maintain the software or if you want the vendor to be the administrator. If you choose to maintain the software yourself, you must set up, configure, maintain, and administer the PaaS yourself (either on a public or private cloud). Alternatively, you can allow the vendor to provide services that handle these tasks. The result is reduced friction between the development and deployment teams. There will, of course, be situations when it's critical for the internal team to control and manage complex software environment.

NIST defines PaaS

The National Institute of Standards and Technology (NIST), a U.S. federal government agency established to design technology standards, has come up with a definition for PaaS. The agency notes that PaaS gives users the ability to create and deploy applications using "programming languages, libraries, services, and tools" supported and provided by the vendor. Additionally, a user "does not manage or control the underlying cloud infrastructure…but has control over the deployed applications and possibly configuration settings for the application-hosting environment." You can find NIST's full definition here, at `http://csrc.nist.gov/publications/nistpubs/800-145/SP800-145.pdf`.

Managing the development lifecycle

It's always been challenging to coordinate processes between those developing applications and those deploying them. Each of these groups has different objectives and often uses different platforms to achieve its individual goals. The process of collaboration becomes even more complicated when teams are spread across multiple time zones. For example, the team in one country may be working on interface design while the team in another country is working on developing one set of business services. A third team in a different location may be working on a completely different set of components.

Although each part of the application might work as intended, when it's time to integrate, build and test problems can arise, often because developers are working on different platforms with a different configuration than operations is working on. Or the latest version of the code isn't all in one place. In some cases, each team is using a different set of tools. Making matters worse, it's difficult for management to get a concrete idea about the state of development across the organization or even across a single complex project.

Managing a fast-paced development environment

In order to respond more rapidly to changing business application needs, companies are moving to an agile development and deployment process. Companies have begun implementing processes that strive to continuously deliver new features and functionality. In the traditional development and deployment model, each new application build contains numerous code changes. These large builds are time-consuming, prone to errors, and may require significant time and money to implement. What makes these problems so troubling is the expectation that software development and deployment must be dynamic to support constantly changing business requirements. This demand to ensure that software models are "always working" is coming from customers who expect their partners to add new capabilities and features in near real time. Competitive pressures are mounting for companies to make their software an important part of their persona in the market.

Not all PaaS delivery models are the same

A number of vendors provide various types of PaaS delivery models. These PaaS services may be tied to a SaaS solution as in the Salesforce.com platform called Force.com, included with a public cloud such as the IBM SmartCloud Enterprise, or provided by a dedicated PaaS vendor such as CloudBees. (See the section, "Exploring Types of PaaS," later in this chapter, for more information on the many variations of PaaS offered by different vendors.) In addition to these vendor-supported public PaaS offerings, enterprises may decide to follow the PaaS model when providing services to their internal users. Companies that follow this approach typically manage very large distributed data centers, and IT actually takes on the role of the service provider.

If you're using a public cloud-based PaaS, the vendor shoulders the responsibility of managing the middleware software resources and the overall development and deployment environment. If you decide to create your own PaaS environment, then, of course, the service management responsibilities fall to you as well.

A public PaaS environment will look and act very different than your traditional development and deployment platform. You'll see some key differences between PaaS and traditional middleware:

✔ Resources aren't delivered as software in PaaS. Instead, the PaaS environment is hosted so that a third-party company is responsible for uptime performance and software updates.

✔ The scope of where development and delivery can take place in a PaaS lives in the cloud rather than a single system.

✔ Because the PaaS is tightly integrated with IaaS services, it offers a consistent way to manage applications. A well-designed PaaS environment includes the programming tools that support middleware tasks outside the PaaS world. Therefore, the PaaS environment can seamlessly link to resources in SaaS applications and data center–based applications.

✔ Middleware and services have no installation and configuration because they're an integral part of the PaaS platform.

A private PaaS environment will also look and act differently than your traditional development and deployment platform. Large enterprises may implement a best-practices approach similar to the PaaS vendors to achieve productivity gains and reduce software development and deployment costs.

✔ Application developers will no longer operate as disconnected units making individualized selections for hardware and software development tools to fit each new project.

✔ Enterprise IT will standardize on a framework for all developers to use to write their code.

Managing middleware complexity

Middleware is the software that allows independent software components to communicate with each other. Middleware enables application services to exchange data, implement business rules and processes, and manage transactions in an orderly and secure manner. Without middleware, each program would sit in isolation and not be able to share data or other messages.

Supporting a variety of middleware platforms

In a perfect world, there would be a single middleware stack to support the development environment for an entire company. But in the real world, an organization's IT infrastructure is typically made up of dozens of different middleware components and development tools purchased over a long period of time. As a result, skilled individuals are required to maintain and manage a complex stack of software and platforms. Companies often find themselves relying on developers who have deep knowledge of a tool or script. Development can move only as fast as those developers.

In a hybrid cloud environment, applications often need to interoperate with other software running on-premises, in a private cloud, or in a public cloud. Without the right middleware, this can get complicated pretty quickly.

Supporting the hybrid of middleware platforms

When you begin to implement a PaaS environment, you will most likely have to deal with a combination of some public cloud-based PaaS and some private PaaS services, as well as traditional application development models. In reality, most organizations will have to combine various platforms and development and deployment services to create the type of business services that customers demand.

Obtaining compute resources

As projects grow in size and complexity, development teams often push the limits of their organizations' compute or storage resources. It is often hard and slow to get machines and configurations to support (often cross-platform) development and testing. Teams sometimes lose weeks while waiting for a centralized procurement organization to allocate the systems they need to complete a project. Because of this procurement bottleneck, developers often hold on to their resources so that they always have the resources they need. This situation ties up unused resources that could be supporting other projects.

Discovering What Changes with PaaS

As complexity increases and as applications are becoming increasingly dynamic, PaaS offers the potential to simplify the world of software development and deployment. PaaS helps reduce the complexity of the development process by

- ✔ Delivering and managing a set of abstracted middleware services that are either hosted in a public PaaS environment or managed in a private cloud environment
- ✔ Ensuring that one standardized set of services is used by those developing and deploying the applications
- ✔ Eliminating the installation and operational burden from an organization

One important benefit of PaaS is that it enables individuals developing applications and individuals deploying those applications to use the same services on the same platform. This approach takes away much of the misunderstanding that happens when two teams with different responsibilities aren't in sync.

By encompassing both development and runtime services, PaaS can streamline the application lifecycle. In this section, we describe just how PaaS can help achieve this streamlining, including standardizing middleware, easing provisioning, working across an organization, and improving control.

Standardizing middleware infrastructure services

In traditional development and deployment environments, individual project teams are likely to select their own preferred development and testing tools, infrastructure, application servers, and the like. The problem with this approach is that it's hard to maintain standards and mistakes are likely to creep in. In contrast, if the organization standardizes on a consistent set of middleware resources, many common errors can be avoided and when problems do occur, they're more easily located and resolved. These development and deployment services can be optimized for the environment, pretested and monitored so that there are no surprises. One benefit of a standardized approach is that all developers in the organization are trained on the same environment, which improves productivity and decreases cost.

Easing service provisioning

A PaaS platform provides a simpler way to provision development services, including build, test, and repository services to help eliminate bottlenecks associated with nonstandard environments. These development services improve efficiency, reduce errors, and ensure consistency in the management of the development lifecycle. Additionally, PaaS makes provisioning of run-time services including application runtime, containers for staging, running, and scaling applications.

Minimizing friction with IT

Traditionally, when a new application server or other middleware is introduced into an organization, IT must make sure that the middleware can access other services that are required to run that application. This requirement can create friction between the software development and operations teams.

Although each team is focused on its own tasks, their managers are focused on solving business problems. Management must ensure that a critical codified business process is able to access the right services and processes to support customers' needs and expectations. The development organization is focused on building the code to support those business customers. On the other hand, the operations team cares that the code is deployed correctly. Although everyone should have the same objectives in mind, each group typically focuses narrowly on its part of the process.

Things usually work when an application is first designed. However, as soon as the application requirements change, the underlying infrastructure must also change and scale to meet the new demands. IT is often unable to simply provision required services and must resort to manual intervention to prepare the infrastructure for what could be dramatically different requirements. This can often create a conflict between IT and a business unit that must tell customers to be patient while the software infrastructure is rebuilt.

With PaaS, these conflicts are minimized. Because the PaaS environment is designed in a modular, service-oriented manner, components can be easily and automatically updated. When PaaS services are provided by a third-party organization, those changes are automatically handled without the user having to deal with the details. When PaaS is implemented in a private cloud, the IT organization has the responsibility of using a self-service interface to provision the new services to the IT organization.

Improving the development lifecycle

PaaS changes the way that development and operations interact with resources. Although development and deployment personnel in a traditional development environment work in isolation from each other, the PaaS environment creates a single unified environment. This unification promotes visibility and accountability across the whole IT organization. For instance, a developer may have tested a recently built application or an application component and assumed that everything is working fine. However, in reality, the application was tested on only one browser. In addition, the developer didn't attempt to test the performance of the application on tablet computers.

With a PaaS platform, the team gets visibility into the *entire* development and deployment lifecycle. The team can see whether software is working, broken, or ready to be released to manufacturing, staged, and so on across the entire application lifecycle.

These functional capabilities are available in a traditional development and deployment environment, but they don't function seamlessly. Often the IT organization has purchased a group of separate tools to support a variety of functions. In a PaaS environment, these capabilities are built in and abstracted as part of the platform.

Streamlining development and deployment: Changing the application lifecycle

In PaaS, support for the application lifecycle, from development through testing, staging, and deployment, is integrated into the platform. The development and the runtime platform are provided as services, so the formal lifecycle of an application is more directly supported. For example, developers and test teams interact with the same hosted application and runtime as the operations people use.

One benefit of an abstracted platform is that it supports development to deployment to operation procedures, thus simplifying the overall development process. Traditionally, much of the integration between development and operations is handled manually. Removing manual processes enables faster development-release cycles, which in turn can support more rigorous methods around quality and continuous integration. See Chapter 14 for more details on the development and deployment environment for PaaS.

How PaaS Abstracts Connectivity and Integration

No application or business service lives in isolation — whether you're talking about a cloud or an on-premises data center. In reality, applications have to communicate and exchange data. The data must be secured throughout all lifecycle stages and accurately mapped between services as needed. To ensure consistent and accurate data across the hybrid cloud, these applications and related services must perform and act as a single integrated environment.

Connecting these applications can be particularly challenging when you consider the various integration scenarios that may occur in cloud environments. First, the PaaS platform residing in a hybrid world has to contend with a variety of applications with complex interfaces that the IT organization has no control over and little visibility into. In addition, even SaaS applications with well-defined interfaces may reside on a variety of different cloud environments. For example, many CRM systems have their own dedicated PaaS environment. Other cloud applications are built as ad hoc projects and aren't designed to work well with other environments. From a process and data integration standpoint, all these various environments need to interact with key systems of record such as general ledger or human resources systems.

PaaS must be architected so that it can handle many unanticipated or complicated business situations.

PaaS integration services generally include connectors, adaptors, and templates for integrating applications in cloud environments. These integration services need to cover various integration scenarios, including the following:

✔ **Connectivity to clouds:** An enterprise ERP system managed in the internal data center needs to integrate with a SaaS customer-relationship management system to ensure that customer sales data is synchronized across these environments.

✔ **Connectivity between clouds:** An application running in an enterprise private cloud environment needs to integrate with a public cloud to increase the compute power available to the application.

✔ **Connectivity in clouds:** Multiple SaaS applications need to integrate to ensure data consistency and reliability.

The value of PaaS services for integration is that it's possible to have a secure, consistent, and standardized way to manage the interaction and delivery of a variety of software components needed for cloud integration. The concept behind a PaaS platform is that the complexity of these integration services is hidden from the team that is developing and deploying the applications.

Exploring Types of PaaS

All PaaS environments aren't the same. Vendors approach PaaS in a number of ways. Some platforms are intrinsically tied to an environment, whereas others are linked to a specific operating system. Other PaaS platforms aren't linked to one cloud environment or one operating system. So, it's important to understand the different approaches, which we discuss in this section.

PaaS anchored to a SaaS environment

Some SaaS offerings have become core business services for their customers. Offerings such as Workday, Salesforce.com, and SugarCRM are replacing traditional on-premises systems of record. To expand their capabilities and their brand, some of these SaaS vendors have created ecosystems that allow independent software vendors (ISVs) to develop applications on top of the vendor's software. PaaS is what enables the ISVs to develop programs in the vendor's ecosystem.

In the following list, each PaaS is anchored to a SaaS environment:

✔ **Force.com:** A PaaS designed by Salesforce.com. As discussed in Chapter 6, this PaaS allows customers to enhance their implementations by inviting ISVs into the Salesforce.com ecosystem. ISVs can sell their software directly to customers using their own channels or can rely on AppExchange, the Salesforce.com application marketplace. Of course Salesforce.com retains a portion of the sale as a commission for promoting the application in its AppExchange market. This operates in much the same way as the Apple App Store. End users receive out-of-the-box interoperability as well as assurances from Salesforce.com that the software has been tested and that it's secure. All applications must meet stringent security testing performed by Salesforce.com to ensure that they're up to the task of handling sensitive data.

✔ **Workday:** Offers a PaaS specifically designed to help customers integrate applications with the Workday financial management and human resource SaaS solutions. Business users and IT developers can leverage services for building, configuring, testing, and deploying integrations.

✔ **Google App Engine:** Allows ISVs to develop applications to work alongside Google Apps. The Google App Engine automatically scales — allocating additional compute power as more and more people implement an application. The Google Apps Marketplace allows users to search all the software that has been developed to work in the Google Apps environment. The applications range from small, free add-ons such as expense-tracking tools to sophisticated accounting solutions.

- **AppScale:** Offers an open-source cloud platform for Google App Engine and is maintained by the RACELab at the University of California, Santa Barbara. It can be deployed on both public clouds and private clouds. This allows organizations to run Google App Engine applications on their own clusters — utilizing unused on-premises compute resources.

- **Intuit Developer Network:** A PaaS that allows ISVs to develop applications that integrate directly with QuickBooks, an on-premises and cloud accounting software aimed at small- to medium-sized businesses. Vendors can market their customized software through the Intuit Marketplace. The Marketplace gives end users access to software that enhances their QuickBooks implementation to fill niche areas for specific industries and circumstances.

PaaS tied to an operating environment

Tying a PaaS to an operating environment makes it easier to perform certain actions within that environment. IaaS providers have begun expanding their offerings up the software stack. Some no longer just provide the nuts and bolts (the operating systems, networking, and so on) but also give you the tools to create your application. For example, Amazon began simply by offering compute power (Amazon EC2) and storage (Amazon S3), but they now have an entire PaaS offering (AWS Elastic Beanstalk, which we discuss further in a moment).

This approach makes sense if the customer is certain to use only a specific IaaS provider to run its applications and doesn't require the depth of a dedicated PaaS provider. Companies like Microsoft with its Azure platform and Amazon with Beanstalk are offering their APIs and abstractions so that developers can build or deploy applications with this support.

Here are examples of PaaS tied to an operating environment:

- **AWS Elastic Beanstalk:** A PaaS that Amazon offers for deploying applications on Amazon Web Services (AWS). Amazon doesn't charge extra for use of its PaaS, but you must, of course, pay for the AWS resources needed to store and run your applications. By utilizing Elastic Beanstalk, organizations are able to auto-scale as demands shift. Elastic Beanstalk enables organizations to add a great deal of automation, while at the same time having overall control of the underlying IaaS resources.

- **Windows Azure:** Based on Windows and SQL abstractions. Microsoft has abstracted a set of development tools, management, and services. For customers with deep expertise with .Net, the movement to the Azure–based PaaS is straightforward. The developer, in essence, ties the development and deployment to the Microsoft infrastructure.

✔ **AT&T Platform as a Service:** Designed to easily deploy applications on the AT&T Synaptic Compute as a Service. Applications can be built from scratch on this platform or developed from already defined application templates.

✔ **IBM SmartCloud Application Services:** An offering through IBM that allows organizations to run Java, web, and enterprise applications on their private cloud or on the IBM public cloud, IBM SmartCloud Enterprise. This offering is well suited for a hybrid environment because it easily allows deployment on a private cloud with the ability to transfer workloads to a public cloud as demand increases.

Open platform PaaS

Open platform-based PaaS is intended to promote an open process and environment that isn't tied to a single cloud implementation. These PaaS vendors allow developers to bring their own platform to the cloud, which offers flexibility — but it can also add complexity and cost.

These platforms are well suited for a hybrid cloud environment because they allow deployment on both public and private clouds. Migration between clouds is eased by an open platform PaaS. For example, testing and early use of an application can take place on a private cloud, but when demand increases, the application can be moved to a public cloud. These open platform PaaS offerings may support only one language or many — if you're a "Microsoft shop," for example, you'll want to make sure the platform works well with .NET.

Here are several examples of open platform PaaS:

✔ **Cloud Foundry:** A VMware-led project that's a PaaS environment for building, deploying, and operating cloud applications. Cloud Foundry supports a number of development languages, including Java, Scala, Ruby, Scala, and .NET. Being an open platform, Cloud Foundry allows for development and deployment on a multitude of public clouds, not just the VMware public clouds — vSphere and vCloud. Cloud Foundry has seen adoption from public cloud providers like Hewlett Packard (HP), which is relying heavily on Cloud Foundry.

✔ **OpenShift:** An open-platform initiative by Red Hat. It supports Java, Perl, PHP, Python, and Ruby applications. OpenShift fully integrates the JBoss Application Server (AS) middleware layer into its offering.

✔ **Engine Yard:** Gives developers writing Ruby on Rails and PHP applications a fully managed PaaS. Engine Yard can be used in conjunction with a number of public cloud providers, such as AWS and private clouds.

- ✔ **CloudBees:** A Java PaaS platform that's independent of the underlying platform and that's intended to allow developers to cover the full application "build, test, run, manage" lifecycle, either on a public or hybrid cloud.

- ✔ **OrangeScape:** A cross-cloud PaaS that's targeted at nonprogrammers who want to create process-oriented business applications. Development is done through the OrangeScape Studio. Final applications can be launched in either a private or public cloud and can be easily migrated between clouds.

- ✔ **Apprenda:** Gives organizations using .NET more flexibility. Instead of relying on Azure, developers can use the Apprenda PaaS to deploy .NET applications on any number of public clouds or on-premises.

- ✔ **DotCloud:** Offers a multi-stack solution that allows developers to build applications in multiple languages. This gives developers greater flexibility by allowing them to choose different languages, databases, and caching and messaging components. Major scripts such as Java, Perl, Ruby, and PHP are supported.

- ✔ **CumuLogic:** A Java PaaS vendor. The company offers a platform for both public and private cloud environments. CumuLogic includes cloud services automation, autoscaling, monitoring, resource management, and user management.

Business Benefits of PaaS

The potential cost savings of IaaS are clear — you can rent compute resources only when you need them. So, you pay only for what you use. PaaS can operate in a similar fashion to IaaS by allowing companies to use a PaaS service during development and deployment, instead of having to purchase many different independent tools.

In a hybrid environment, when the same PaaS environment can support both public and private services, organizations can benefit by this level of flexibility and agility. By providing a homogenous platform, workloads can easily be moved from a private cloud to a public cloud for deployment and efficient scaling. This allows organizations to have a high degree of control on where a particular application is running. Some of the business benefits of PaaS include reduced costs and increased speed of development and deployment.

Reducing costs

By providing the underlying software infrastructure, PaaS can reduce organizational costs. PaaS reduces many of the costs involved with the traditional application development and deployment model, including the ones we discuss here.

Server and storage overhead

Writing and testing new programs are compute-intensive and require large amounts of server and storage space. Typically, once the development and deployment stages are complete, a company's server and storage space lie largely dormant. This underutilized computing capacity requires power, cooling, and maintenance to run, as well as floor space. As a result, organizations often devote considerable amounts of money to unused capacity.

When utilizing a PaaS, companies don't have excess resources in reserve. The development tools are provided by the PaaS, and not all of the iterations of the code need to be stored in the data center. These savings on server and storage overhead are realized whether developing on-premises or in the cloud. When developing in the cloud, although you don't need additional physical servers and storage, you do need to deploy and pay for a larger virtual machine (VM) and more storage.

Network bandwidth

The development and deployment process can put a strain on network bandwidth within a data center. Development teams must perform workload testing to see how the application will perform under different circumstances. This requirement to allocate network resources may slow down the operation of other applications or may require the acquisition of more bandwidth capacity. PaaS enables testing to be done in the cloud, rather than in the data center.

Software maintenance

The cost of managing software updates and changes is often a burden to development and operational organizations and a huge expense in terms of time and money. Although the cost structure of a PaaS requires a per-user, per-month charge, the cost is typically offset by reducing or eliminating software license costs and yearly maintenance fees. The platform vendor manages all patches and updates for the hardware and software and also provides physical and software security for the automation of day-to-day tasks.

Support personnel

To keep software and systems up to date and running smoothly and to fix problems when they occur, organizations must have IT staff at the ready — for everything from storage and archiving to patch management, networks, security, and the help desk. By adopting a standardized platform across an organization, hardware and software conflicts are greatly reduced, resulting in simplified service and support. This level of standardization and automation allows organizations to reduce or refocus its teams away from routine tasks.

A startup finds success with PaaS

Imagine a small services company wanting to roll out a mobile application for airline tracking. To create the application, the development team must bring together large amounts of data from a variety of sources, including airlines, weather forecast modeling, the Federal Aviation Authority (FAA), and local airport alerts. Being part of an emerging company, the team doesn't have an abundance of capital to spend on infrastructure, yet they will be dealing with a massive amount of data. They choose to leverage cloud-based services.

The team is highly technical, so they decide that it makes sense to use an IaaS platform and bring in the set of tools they're already familiar with. So, they have to bring their own operating system, compilers, development tools, and middleware. The process is taking too long and is too cumbersome. To get to market quickly, the team hires developers in five different countries. But the administration and processes to make sure that all the developers are working in synch prove to be complicated and time-consuming.

To speed applications delivery, avoid time-consuming coding, and to save money on hiring a system administrator, the company decides to use a PaaS. To save even more money, the company decides to use a PaaS platform that can be used internally and as a public cloud service.

Now, armed with an abstracted and well-integrated environment, the team finds that it's easier to keep all the developers working together without misunderstandings. Constant interactions of the platform are easier to manage. The company is able to hit the market at the right time with a solution that customers are looking for. The management team finds that it quickly has to support a variety of different platforms and partners' ecosystems. The flexibility of the PaaS environment enables a relatively small development team to accomplish a growing demand from partners and customers. The company is on its way to what looks like a bright future!

Of course, PaaS isn't just for startups and boot-strapped companies. Larger companies are beginning to use PaaS as a way to streamline their development processes.

Careless mistakes

During application development and deployment, there's also a great deal of pressure on teams to get work done quickly. This pressure often results in careless mistakes. Take, for instance, the case of somebody forgetting to load a configuration file. It could take a week before the problem is identified and fixed. Such mistakes add up to time and money and cause deployment delays. With PaaS, such mistakes are reduced or entirely eliminated because the platform has been fully tested and is known to work. Developers don't get tied down with the middleware and tedious tasks that are prone to hasty mistakes.

Lower-skill requirements

Development tools and middleware are complex and aren't standardized. Successfully deploying an application takes a high degree of skill and experience. The learning curve on these skills is steep, and there's also an ongoing need to manage these components. Perhaps only one or two people in an organization have the skills necessary to work with a certain kind of middleware. By providing the development tools and middleware, a PaaS lowers the skill level required to deploy applications and removes the bottleneck that can form while waiting for one specific person's assistance.

Improving speed, flexibility, and agility

In terms of getting products to market fast and aligning agile development practices, continuous delivery is the ultimate goal. PaaS can provide greater speed, flexibility, and agility to the development process. By providing a predictable, heterogeneous application infrastructure, organizations don't get bogged down with enabling applications and can quickly meet the needs of customers. PaaS helps to do the following:

- ✔ Enable faster time to market by allowing development teams to focus on the application

- ✔ Enhance ability to react to changes and opportunities because the organization doesn't have large up-front costs associated with typical application development and deployment

- ✔ Spread capital investments further, which allows a company to be more competitive

Chapter 8

Managing Business Process as a Service

*W*e're all told to think about the three models of cloud computing as Infrastructure as a Service (IaaS), Platform as a Service (PaaS), and Software as a Service (SaaS).

However, before you get too comfortable, think about another cloud computing model that touches the three primary models that we've been discussing: Business Process as a Service (BPaaS).

BPaaS isn't listed along with the big three because it's a wrapper that brings all the other cloud models together. Briefly, it's the way you tell services how to interact with each other based on business rules and business requirements. In this chapter, we focus on how BPaaS works with other models (IaaS, SaaS, PaaS) and the hybrid cloud.

Understanding the Importance of Business Process as a Service

Companies have been automating business processes for decades. Originally, they were forced to do so either manually or programmatically. For example, if a company wanted to make sure that a management system for orders looked up a credit check before issuing a transaction, the company built that request into a program. In some cases, entire business process outsourcing companies might implement processes either manually or through automation.

With the advent of cloud computing, this approach is starting to change. Increasingly, companies are starting to look at a more service-oriented approach to leverage services. Rather than assume you need a packaged application that includes both business logic, data, and processes, it's possible to select a process application that's not tied into a single application. There is a practical reason to select a business process service. First, an organization can select a process that matches business policy. It can then be used in many different application environments. This ensures that a well-defined and, more importantly, a consistent process exists across the organization. For example, a company may have a complex process for processing payroll or managing shipping. This service can be linked to other services in the cloud such as SaaS, as well as to applications in the data center.

Business Process as a Service is any type of horizontal or vertical business process that's delivered based on the cloud services model. These cloud services — which include SaaS, PaaS, and IaaS — are therefore dependent on related services.

Like SaaS cloud services, business processes are beginning to be designed as a packaged offering that can be used in a hybrid manner. After all, business processes are the steps you take or the activities you perform to facilitate the delivery of products or services to your customers or stakeholders. These business processes can really be any service that can be automated, including managing e-mail, shipping a package, or managing customer credit.

The difference between traditional packaged applications and BPaaS is that BPaaS is designed in a service-oriented manner. So, BPaaS is likely to have well-defined interfaces. In addition, a BPaaS is a standardized service for use by many different organizations. Because these services are much more optimized to deliver a service consistently, they can leverage automation, standardization, and repeatability in the way the services are used and delivered. Five characteristics define BPaaS:

- ✔ The BPaaS sits on top of the other three foundational Cloud services: SaaS, PaaS, and IaaS.

- ✔ A BPaaS service is configurable based on the process being designed.

- ✔ A BPaaS service must have well-defined APIs so it can be easily connected to related services.

- ✔ A BPaaS must be able to support multiple languages and multiple deployment environments because a business cannot predict how a business process will be leveraged in the future.

- ✔ A BPaaS environment must be able to handle massive scaling. This means that the service must be able to go from managing a few processes for a couple of customers to being able to support hundreds if not thousands of customers and processes. The service accomplishes that objective by optimizing the underlying cloud services to support this type of elasticity and scaling.

Exploring How BPaaS Works in the Real World

If you've decided to use a hybrid cloud model as a delivery platform for services, you need to understand how to mesh services together based on the processes you want to execute. For example, say that your company decides to use some well-defined cloud-based capabilities to make it more productive.

Following tradition, your larger competitors probably have spent huge amounts of money buying the latest and greatest applications to help streamline operations. Likewise, they've probably hired the biggest consulting firms to help them be more innovative in the market. They've often created systems that enable them to automate complex processes in order to be as efficient as possible.

As a smaller company, you might be at a disadvantage without BPaaS services. You've already discovered the benefit of leveraging various cloud models including sophisticated SaaS and PaaS environments that sit on top of cloud-based infrastructure services. You may, for example, have decided to leverage SaaS-based sales automation, human resources, and accounting services. You've also leveraged the PaaS environment to construct application services that allow you to differentiate yourself from your competitors. You have several different databases of customers, prospects, and partners.

Now here is where PBaaS comes in. You want to be able to use BPaaS workflow tools to link together elements of your cloud services with new processes that might give you a competitive advantage. Also, you know that packaged BPaaS services are readily available that can help you scale this process. Shown in Figure 8-1, a business process service can be linked to a variety of services ranging from SaaS applications, PaaS environments, and IaaS. For example, there may be an analytic process service designed to analyze information coming from a variety of CRM and social media applications.

BPaaS services allow you to experiment with new business process ideas because they're not based on programming each individual business initiative. For example, a packaged BPaaS offering that handles business travel processing or order-to-cash processes may be available, as well as other services that will handle load processing or payroll services, and predesigned services useful for everything from processing claims to managing clinical data for drug trials.

The benefits of cloud-based BPaaS

Like other cloud-based services, BPaaS frees the business and the IT department from having to worry about the underlying services that support the various processes. You don't have to manage or even know about the underlying middleware, networking, or database. Offerings are created so that security is an element of the solution, not an afterthought.

The process services offered by ADP are probably the best-known BPaaS services. ADP helps companies manage their payroll and the accounting and legal aspects related to that process. A company using ADP doesn't have to be concerned that its payment information will be intermixed with information from other companies. ADP can implement payroll services based on its customer's specific business process. For example, some companies pay certain employees every week, while others may be paid monthly. Likewise, a customer might have employees in 20 different states with processes based on rules and governance that ADP implements for its customers. ADP's customers use a subscription model to acquire services and only access the details of their services through an Internet portal. This portal provides all the information the client needs, including costs, reporting, compliance, and data quality.

What BPaaS companies look like

It's worth describing some of the businesses that deliver massively scaled cloud applications and business processes. You may not be aware that these companies provide a business process as a service.

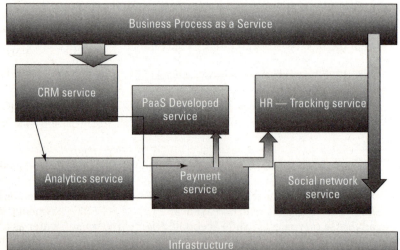

Figure 8-1:
Linking
services
together
based on
process.

Most of the businesses listed here had to cover uncharted business territory when they developed their service. For this reason, the services they offer may not traditionally be thought of as business services — but that's really what they are.

Here's a list of companies in this field and the business processes they deliver:

- **eBay:** Provides an electronic auction service (www.ebay.com)

- **PayPal:** Provides an Internet payment capability as a service (www.paypal.com)

- **Skype:** Owned by Microsoft, Skype provides Voice over IP (VoIP) telephone calls as a service, most of which are free (www.skype.com)

- **Google:** Provides an Internet search capability as a service (www.google.com)

  This service is free when you have access to the Internet. Google also provides an Internet e-mail service, Gmail. Google has quite a few other services, including maps, news aggregation, Google Apps, and so on.

- **YouTube:** Provides video self-publishing as a service and was acquired by Google (www.youtube.com)

- **Yahoo!:** Like Google, Yahoo! (www.yahoo.com) provides an Internet search service and e-mail service

- **Mailchimp and Constant Contact:** Provide services for sending out online newsletters and marketing campaigns (www.mailchimp.com and www.constantcontact.com, respectively)

- **Craigslist:** Offers small ads as a service (www.craigslist.org)

- **WordPress:** Hosts blogs as a service (www.wordpress.org)

- **LinkedIn:** Offers business contacts and networking as a service (www.linkedin.com)

- **Facebook and Twitter:** Provide social networking services that have a huge reach across the globe (www.facebook.com and www.twitter.com, respectively)

This is by no means an exhaustive list, and these services are useful to businesses as well as consumers. Many businesses use eBay, and eBay supports a group of companies that use it as the foundation of their business model. Many businesses depend on PayPal as a way of collecting payments. Businesses advertise on Craigslist and Facebook. A fair number use Twitter as a marketing and public relations outlet. Also, all these businesses have tens of millions of customers. Nearly all of them require very large data centers to cater to their millions of customers.

These companies are able to support these types of business processes because of the massive data centers they've designed to support a specific type of workload. Because their data centers are optimized to support these specialized workloads, they are able to easily support millions of users so efficiently that it's very hard to compete with them.

Looking at web-based business services

You might be inclined to think that web-based businesses are somehow different than the companies to which you outsource your energy generation or the companies that provide your communications, but they're very similar.

Be aware that many of these web-based companies started out without a well-defined revenue stream, and some of them have yet to demonstrate a viable business model for their activities.

This is currently the case, for example, with Twitter, Facebook, and YouTube, all of which exist just because their investors (or Google in the case of YouTube) believe that they will eventually find a profitable way of operating.

Most of the businesses we mention are dominant in their field because they have established strong barriers to entry and because of their scalable infrastructure and their ability to deliver services at a very low cost. Quite a few Internet auction houses existed before eBay began to dominate the field, and there have been several attempts by would-be competitors to penetrate eBay's market, but none have made much of an impact.

Delivering Business Processes from the Cloud

We're at the beginning of this world of hybrid clouds where companies large and small are able to leverage the different cloud models to knit together services with both routine and innovative process environments. The future evolution of many interesting business process services can be characterized as belonging to three different areas:

✔ **Commodity business process services:** These services are common to most businesses and are technically mature. They include services such as e-mail, accounting, and payment services. Although critical to the operations of most businesses, they're not a differentiator. They simply are business requirements. Some commodity services can be quite complex, such as sophisticated accounting process systems.

✔ **Specialized business process services:** These services make a huge difference in the way a company competes. They could be specialized services, such as one used for molecular modeling or predictive analytics. These tend to be highly complex services to build and manage. Also, most companies won't necessarily need them or have the infrastructure to support them on an ongoing basis.

✔ **Foundational building process services:** In some situations, organizations need to customize business processes in unique ways. This is where products to create business process workflows come in. With this type of capability, companies can use templates and best practices from a cloud-based provider to create sophisticated linkages between business partners. This capability requires sophisticated underlying middleware that can broker between services and manage the data between services.

Business processes destined for the cloud

Some applications that embody business processes are inevitably destined for the cloud because of their high number of users and their ease of use in a cloud context.

These applications form two groups:

✔ Existing applications that are migrating to the cloud. The cloud makes the most sense for these established applications (for example, e-mail).

✔ New applications that are taking off in the cloud faster than they are through the use of software installed in data centers, or where use of a data center isn't available. For example, a service that analyzes data from MRI scans in remote applications can provide incredible value in remote locations. Sophisticated collaboration applications can provide a complex process management environment that would be too expensive for a small- or medium-sized business.

Hidden in the cloud

If you haven't had much contact with web businesses, you may not know that nearly all their important business processes are run from the cloud, often at low cost. For example, unless you run a very large website, the web statistics software you use is most likely provided by Google. Your e-mail system likely runs on your web server, which itself is probably hosted by an Internet service provider (ISP). If you carry ads on your website, you're probably using an ad server of some kind, which, again, doesn't run out of your offices. Selling ads to fill the available space on your site is probably outsourced to an advertising broker.

Your website is probably running on software built by someone else with various software modules provided by yet another company. The photographs displayed on your website may well be sourced from another website, and even some of the content may be sourced from content syndication operations.

It's easy to come up with a list of the business processes and applications that will, as a general rule, be run from the cloud in the future. A few organizations will run such applications themselves, for reasons of security or possibly technology integration, but most will not because of the cost.

Business processes already flying high

Many processes sold as on-premises productivity applications will become standard cloud environments. However, this transition will not happen overnight. Companies that make a living selling office software may be reluctant to move to a cloud model. In addition, an important market will remain for sophisticated consumers who deal with very sophisticated processes and will need the process on-premises. So, for now, hybrid business process environments will be the norm. Here is a list of business processes that are already available from the cloud:

- ✔ **Clerical activity:** Office software such as word processing, spreadsheets, and so on

- ✔ **Communications:** Unified communications, e-mail, Instant Messaging (IM), voice, conferencing

- ✔ **Collaboration:** Desktop-to-desktop capabilities, from webinars to collaborative work and file sharing

- ✔ **Data backup and disaster recovery:** The ability to store information in a cloud service for both immediate retrieval and to protect against the loss of a system

- ✔ **Payment technology:** PayPal, credit cards, voucher schemes, and so on

- ✔ **Research:** Including marketing research, technical research, patent research, and almost all other areas of research

- ✔ **Website work:** Design, content, advertising, and SEO

You could add many others to this list — for example, the businesses of insurance, banking, package delivery, and travel and hotel booking. You might not think of these businesses as cloud services, but by any reasonable definition, they are.

TIP

Mashups, service orientation, and other process enablers

The more things change, the more they stay the same. Mashups are the result of combining two related services presented as a single process to a consumer. It's interesting to note how mashups, as a way to link various web-based services together, have morphed into new business models. The ability to create business services with well-defined APIs has become a necessity in the world of hybrid cloud computing. Born in the cloud, companies like Facebook, Twitter, Google, and Amazon are changing the nature of computing for businesses across the globe. All of these types of services and thousands of new services that are invented every day are all foundational business services based on combining processes together. The combination of processes is dramatically affecting the way we create, manage, and collaborate with each other and among businesses.

Predicting the future

BPaaS is one of the fundamental services that's not only changing cloud computing, but also the way some innovative businesses operate today and the way most companies will operate in the future. The value of BPaaS becomes a foundational element of the hybrid cloud model where companies will be expected to link services from their own operations with services from partners, customers, and suppliers.

The foundation of this future state means that these service components must be based on well-designed and model business processes. They must be logical constructs based on how business is conducted, and they must follow business guidelines. Therefore, BPaaS will have to include concrete governance and policy requirements within the structure of that service that is configurable by business management.

One of the best ways to understand what's coming in the future is to look at how some successful born-on-the-web companies operate. Many of these companies have the persona of very large companies with complex and well-designed processes that can be scaled according to demand. These companies assume from their inception that they will build complex customer-facing process management environments using cloud-based models.

Even when web-based businesses are large, many of their business processes are assembled by linking software together, often in a way that's no more sophisticated than simply linking to it from a Web page. Imagine a company that sells a sophisticated pedometer, such as Fitbit, which offers a device that tracks a person's everyday steps, stairs climbed, and calories burned, and automatically syncs that data with a data measurement dashboard. The company has developed sophisticated analytical tools that measure both the steps people take and how their activity compares to others in their age range and at a specific activity level.

The company has a sophisticated distribution model that includes an online sales model and direct sales through retail (say, Best Buy) and online stores like Amazon.com. It, therefore, has to create a sophisticated business process model to link its various distribution partners and keep track of business partners that link to its Application Programming Interfaces.

To attract new customers and ensure that its customer base continues to grow, it must leverage social media and search engine optimization.

Now, try to envisage other businesses running in this way. It's not that hard to do, because the vast majority of small to medium businesses do only one or two unique things — and that means most of their business processes are common, mundane, and a good fit for cloud computing.

Part III

Evaluating the Business Value of the Hybrid Cloud

Model	Open Community	Controlled Open Mode	Contractual Open	Public/Private Hybrid	Private Closed
	Facebook Twitter LinkedIn MyFitnessPal Google Groups	Amazon Web Services Rackspace OpSour	Salesforce.com Workday MailChimp QuickBooks Online	IBM SmartCloud HP Cloud Service Microsoft Azure	Internal but can be implemented by a third-party vendor
Examples					
	No SLA	Simple SLA	SLA with no indemnification	SLA guaranteeing uptime	Explicit SLA Capital expense with ongoing maintenance
	No Contract	Transactional pricing	Contract	Contract	
Characteristics					
	Simple Password Protection	More security	High security provided	Highest level of security	Secure platform
	No governance model	No explicit governance	Governance in place	Explicit governance	Explicit governance

In this part . . .

Why should you think about the hybrid cloud from a business perspective? In this part, we answer that question and discuss how businesses are rethinking IT and reimagining how the hybrid cloud will help to provide innovation and cost-effective delivery of computing resources.

Chapter 9

Embracing the Business Imperative

....

In This Chapter

▶ Understanding the challenges of transforming IT

▶ Exploring the business benefits of the new IT

▶ Getting started in this new world

▶ Discovering the role of the hybrid cloud

▶ Managing workloads in a cost-effective way

....

Most of the discussions surrounding cloud computing tend to focus on the technology and product and services offerings. However, the real value of cloud computing is the way it repositions the information technology (IT) organization to partner with the business in driving innovation and transformation. The ability to bring together a well-constructed data center with private cloud services and a variety of public clouds is the best way to create and drive innovation in business computing. Computing, indeed, has evolved from its original intent of storing and reporting on data. Today, hybrid computing environments are intended to help a company experiment with new business models without having to spend money on speculative endeavors. When business leaders have a variety of resources to experiment with different and unanticipated ways of doing business, they have a better opportunity to succeed. The hybrid cloud environment offers a streamlined and innovative foundation for creativity. This chapter explains how cloud computing and specifically the hybrid cloud environment can help transform business.

Understanding the Challenges of Transforming IT

Increasingly, companies are beginning to understand that their competitive value in the markets they serve is directly related to the way they empower their ecosystem of customers, partners, and suppliers to be a strategic advantage. It's simply not enough to resort to the traditional techniques of managing these relationships. At the same time, companies are recognizing that their longevity depends on their ability to innovate and offer new products and services that leverage their intellectual property.

Without thinking about the use of IT in a new way, this transition cannot happen. Organizations that are transforming themselves are moving away from thinking about IT as a backroom activity. These companies are putting IT in the forefront of empowering innovation and transformation. What does this mean? In brief, it means leveraging all the IT resources across the organization to create a flexible and scalable platform for innovation and change. This level of change requires a dramatic reinvention of IT. A hybrid cloud strategy that leverages the assets and computing models that exist with a continuum of emerging cloud models is at the heart of this transformation.

Setting the stage for action

To change the concept of computing to a hybrid cloud model, management's first step is to understand that the value of information technology is based on the ability to integrate and connect with resources both internally and externally. This method is significantly different than the traditional method of segregating elements of IT within different business units. By focusing on linking resources together rather than isolating them, IT can become the engine of business change. To accomplish this goal requires that management focus on three key elements:

- ✔ Initiating a cloud strategy to change the dynamics of IT. Because of its flexibility, the cloud can become a point of collaboration between business and IT to promote change.

- ✔ Focusing on the right options based on the task at hand. There isn't a single approach that will work to support all situations. A hybrid approach will be pragmatic.

- ✔ Making manageability of resources based on the customer experience a key driver for your strategy.

What the hybrid cloud means to the changing dynamics of IT

Moving IT from operating under an internal business operations model to become an enabler of innovative business models requires that IT be executed without boundaries. Innovative companies can no longer live with strict boundaries among business units, subsidiaries, partners, suppliers, and even customers. For decades, organizations have been looking for ways to leverage their existing assets so that they can expand their business reach. Doing so has been incredibly hard because of the seemingly arbitrary boundaries implemented on account of the inefficiency of IT. With changes in emerging technology enablers, companies are finding new ways to break down these artificial barriers.

The impact is that companies now want to be able to leverage their business rules and processes buried inside their existing business applications. They want to be able to manage the myriad data sources as though they were a single pool of information. This goal can be achieved only if the workloads that control all of these IT sources can be managed effectively. It's a complex task that requires careful business and architectural planning. When these application, process, and data services are freed from their traditional constraints, the business benefits can be compelling.

The Business Benefits of the New IT

Businesses can benefit if IT services can be easily reused and applied to any business problem, opportunity, or innovative idea. For example, imagine that a large retail corporation is looking for new ways to create innovative partnerships that will allow the company to leapfrog competition. Retail is a highly competitive market with low margins. It's difficult to differentiate one company from another. Simply being the low-cost provider will not support growth. The company decides that as a differentiator, it must introduce innovation on various levels:

1. **The company decided that it would enhance its e-commerce site by providing customers with the ability to customize each outfit based on their different needs.**

   It, therefore, leveraged imaging systems so that customers could order outfits based on their exact measurements. To accomplish this, the company had to do the following:

   a. *Partner with an imaging technology company*

   b. *Modify its supply chain to create a system that could synchronize how much merchandise is ordered through a new on-demand consumer model*

2. **To be successful, the company needed to implement new business rules that governed how and when it purchased merchandise based on the level of orders and customer preferences.**

   This business model hadn't been tested before, and thus was risky.

3. **The company decided that it needed to experiment with many different go-to market strategies that would require a highly tuned collaboration with its business partners.**

4. **The company also had to make sure that it was analyzing the results of these experiments to determine which business models were most effective.**

   Looking in the rearview mirror would not be enough; the company needed to be able to look at data across its entire supply chain in order to anticipate the best future business mix of product offerings.

5. **The company needed to create an IT model that would allow maximum flexibility and that would allow customers to basically create their own outfits in real time, online.**

6. **The company needed a way for its business partners to participate in the business model.**

   If one of the experimental models was successful, the company wanted to be able to expand it quickly without time-consuming implementation cycles.

This way of architecting IT as a set of services that are implemented in a flexible cloud-based model is the way companies will compete in the future. Companies that remain tied to ineffective computing models will be unable to compete with competitors that adopt this more dynamic computing model.

Getting Started in This New World

This emerging model that tears down boundaries between traditionally stove-piped systems is the future, but for execution, it requires a set of steps — not a single action. Just as company goals and priorities vary, no two companies will follow the exact same roadmap to transform IT. Therefore, this section is comprised of two parts:

- ✔ A description of the six tasks companies must accomplish to leverage their IT assets in a flexible manner.
- ✔ A real-world example of how one company implemented a hybrid cloud environment to change the dynamics of IT.

Six steps to increase IT flexibility

To leverage IT assets in a flexible manner, companies must accomplish the following tasks:

- ✔ **Seamlessly integrate existing IT with new cloud-based delivery models.** Breaking down the stove pipes among existing applications in the data center and cloud-based services requires a sophisticated approach to integration. Moving data across environments requires metadata mapping that ensures that the integration is accomplished in a meaningful manner.

✔ **Migrate to flexible IT and business processes.** Processes are designed within and across applications throughout the company and across a supply chain. By separating processes from the underlying implementation, companies can gain better leverage of intellectual property. In addition, codifying processes can help management gain better control over how business policy is implemented within systems.

✔ **Create a new model that is holistic so that the underlying services are accurate when used in a new context.** This model must be well-controlled, secured, and predictable. One of the biggest problems with traditional IT is that is has been defined based on solving one specific problem rather than on the overall needs of the organization. So, each time a new problem needs to be solved, a new application is written. The new emerging model is to create a set of services that can work together to solve many problems. These services are architected based on the common services — underlying middleware, business process, and data consistent across the company. These services set the pattern for reuse. Organizations are leveraging the models created with a service oriented architecture (SOA) to achieve these goals. SOA patterns provide the best practices that are at the heart of well-defined cloud environments.

✔ **Create a lifecycle approach where there is a predictable method of changing elements of business services to support business change.** Establishing a more flexible method of managing workloads in different cloud models and on-premises or data center–based delivery models requires that organizations look at the lifecycle of the elements within each environment.

✔ **Ensure manageability across the hybrid environment.** New delivery models don't stop at the data center; they incorporate cloud models and delivery models from partners and suppliers. All these services are now the new definition of what we think the role of the IT organization is becoming. Therefore, all these services must be managed as though the composite were a single integrated environment, rather than a highly distributed one.

✔ **Provide a predictable level of service across all traditional and emerging cloud models.** After an organization takes a hybrid approach based on a combination of different delivery models, creating a consistent level of service is much easier. The new architected environment can now be combined with a service management approach that can be tuned to deliver the level of services customers expect. Not all services will require the same service level. However, in this new service level approach, management can determine which aspects of the environment need more sophisticated levels of predictability, security, and reliability.

Changing the dynamics of IT: One company's experience

The IT organization of a large multi-national company recognized that inefficiencies in its IT processes were inhibiting its ability to support the business. New and innovative business opportunities were slow to get off the ground because of complicated and lengthy IT approval processes. In addition, the process to requisition new infrastructure would often take so long that teams would purchase more than the project required. As demand for new product offerings grew, the supporting applications were moved from smaller machines to larger ones. Likewise, applications which didn't take off as anticipated, sat on underutilized large machines. Given the size of the organization this process was repeated again and again, leaving a proliferation of underutilized and ultimately wasted resources throughout the company. Additionally, the company was not able to effectively manage these distributed systems.

The company had two top priorities:

✔ Providing development teams with fast and efficient access to compute resources

✔ Decreasing the cost of maintaining and delivering infrastructure

At the same time, the organization needed to maintain tight control over customer data to comply with industry regulations. The implementation of a hybrid cloud environment allowed the company to achieve its goals and increase speed to market. Therefore, a private cloud was created to manage applications that touched customer data, and SaaS applications were adopted for human resources, marketing, and customer relations. The data center was streamlined by eliminating unnecessary and redundant applications and now houses the organization's ERP and back-office applications.

The company's private cloud implementation helps to increase standardization and automation while reducing costs. Their implementation strategy includes these four key best practice components:

✔ **Implement a self-provisioning portal:** Users at the company no longer need to wait weeks or months to requisition compute power, but can instead be up and running in minutes. Teams are able to do this through a self-provisioning portal that gives employees with the correct credentials access to pre-approved virtual machines.

What advantage does this give to the organization? Ultimately, the ability to pilot new ideas without the need to make large infrastructure investments. Previously, if teams had a good idea, it could take months just to get to a testing phase. Business teams can now offer new products and services to the market sooner and with more effective market response.

✔ **Establish a code library:** The company created large code libraries including core functionality, common user interfaces, and web services. Without regular attention, registries treated as standalone code repositories can quickly become out of sync. As a result, people stop believing in them and therefore stop using them. To avoid this, a service registry can be built in so that it is automatically in sync.

The code library greatly reduces the time that an architect must spend on coding an application because most of the basic coding has already been completed. Additionally, testing and error-checking efficiency is increased because the majority of the code is standardized and has already been checked. The standardization of application architecture has not only increased speed, but has also driven down the costs of production and increased employee productivity. Overall, the code library provides the organization with greater overall quality by allowing architects to reuse trusted and reliable code.

✔ **Increase use of open source software:** Open source software allowed the company to realize significant cost savings. They were able to slash many of the service fees that they were previously paying for applications.

Caution must be exercised, however, when adding open source software. Once implemented, it becomes an integral part of the hybrid cloud environment.

✔ **Increase commoditization of compute resources:** Creating a hybrid cloud allowed the company to tie together hardware infrastructure that can then function as a single large machine. Large, consistent, highly optimized servers can handle larger workloads and therefore take the place of many smaller machines. They require lower heating, cooling, and power consumption, and they can easily be swapped out as more efficient and faster machines become available.

The Role of the Hybrid Cloud

Cloud computing will play a pivotal role in the emerging model of IT. IT might be tempting to simply assume that the traditional siloed data center can be quickly turned into a private cloud. To create a private cloud requires a modular service architecture that provides for self-service, scalability, and flexible workload management. In fact, many different models of cloud computing can be leveraged in a variety of ways to meet a company's specific requirements, as shown in this list:

✔ **Connect a traditional data center to a cloud environment whether it's public or private.** This will be a requirement for ensuring that the cloud supports important line of business (LOB) applications. Companies can decide based on a new event to move a specific workload from a data center into the cloud, such as when demand for resources suddenly spikes.

✔ **Connect resources between clouds.** In other situations, an IT organization may go this route. Many companies have started their journey to the cloud by signing up for Software as a Service (SaaS), such as customer relationship management (CRM) products like Salesforce.com or SugarCRM. These same companies may use multiple SaaS products and will want to establish connections among these systems. For example, there may be a need to connect CRM with human resource systems and back-office accounting systems.

✔ **Implement a process as a service in order to codify relationships with key business partners.** This is a newer approach that companies are pursuing with partners who are also leveraging cloud-based services.

Putting the Evolution of the Data Center in Perspective

No company can hope to create a streamlined and efficient hybrid cloud environment with a traditional siloed data center structure. Establishing an environment to support these new and emerging business models doesn't happen overnight. It requires a road map and successful planning between IT and business. Each company starts from a different place and has a unique set of business objectives that will impact the route they follow. For example, a mid-size company may move fairly quickly from an internal server environment to implement SaaS and BPaaS in addition to a private cloud. On the other hand, a large enterprise in a highly regulated industry that supports a highly complex traditional data center may need to focus on streamlining its environment prior to implementing cloud technology. This section illustrates what companies with a traditional data center are facing as they begin to rethink the data center.

How siloed IT environments developed

The early data centers had a pretty straightforward role and architecture. These data centers were designed and built to support custom-built enterprise transactional applications. Typically, a single hardware architecture and a single operating system included all the security, systems management, networking, and middleware. The environment was complex and sophisticated, but it was designed to support the intended workloads quite nicely. Then everything changed in the 1980s, when a host of new hardware, operating systems, networks, and middleware became available.

Companies began investing in relatively inexpensive servers and desktops to support a huge revolution in new technologies. Computing became the purview of an increasingly large number of business users. Over time, data centers began to grow out of control. Each time a business discovered a new application, it purchased the application along with a specialized operating system and often specialized hardware. Over time, this environment grew like an untended garden. Data centers became huge, containing thousands of applications — and sometimes hundreds of different versions of those applications. So, what had started out as a well-designed environment with a purpose became a complex environment almost impossible to manage efficiently.

In essence, the data center had become the place where any application and its supporting infrastructure were brought together. The conventional wisdom was that because all computing had been unified into a single physical environment, the economies of scale would add efficiency. The skills of the professionals running the data center would ensure a well-run, efficient computing environment. There would be a single organization with professionals skilled in the field who would manage all the requirements for the IT department. It didn't quite turn out as intended.

Regardless of how sophisticated the professionals running the organization were, gaining economies of scale was impossible because of the disparate nature of the data center. There were simply too many hardware platforms, too much software, and too many silos of disconnected data. The data center was never the unified environment that it was intended to be.

Addressing the challenge of moving from silos to streamlined operations

Recognizing the challenges of the siloed data center, many companies began to look at what could be done to create a more consistent, unified, and well-integrated environment. These companies evaluated which applications were running, what operating systems were supported, and the variety of hardware platforms inside the data centers. Despite efforts to better streamline IT operations, many companies are still struggling to address the complexities inherent in a data center world that must manage hundreds if not thousands of workloads. One measure of data center complexity is the time and expense devoted to managing the tens or even hundreds of different platforms in a large-scale data center. As a result of the large number of different applications and operating systems that IT needs to manage, it is very hard to create a highly automated and standardized data center environment.

Using cloud services to improve IT efficiency and scalability

So how do organizations move from a fragmented data center environment to one that is designed to scale, enable, and encourage change? How do organizations move to a consistent set of underlying infrastructure services that help to increase the quality and stability of the IT environment? Problems with a data center affect all aspects of IT, including software development, deployment, and maintenance. In the complicated world of the traditional data center, meaningful agility cannot be achieved without substantial transformation. The impact is twofold:

- ✔ **The IT organization must be able to gain a full understanding of what is actually running in the data center and why.** There may be applications that are operational but that serve no purpose. For example, an application may have been developed or purchased a decade ago to serve a specific business requirement; over time it hasn't been needed or used, yet it continues to be maintained simply because the IT organization does not have the right level of insight to adequately manage an application over its lifecycle.

- ✔ **Leadership that comes from collaboration between business and IT must take control and turn chaos into a logical data center.** IT and the business need to speak with a unified voice and manage change as a team to drive innovation and growth.

Many companies are finding that the path to a more streamlined data center is one that begins by viewing the data center in a new way. Instead of trying to totally transform complicated and inefficient data center environments, companies are looking at cloud computing as one of the transformative steps to changing perceptions of what data centers are and how they provide value to companies. These companies are beginning to understand that they can achieve their technical and business goals by revolutionizing their data centers through a hybrid computing approach that allows the organization to leverage the right services with the right platform. The idea of a hybrid cloud computing environment is positioned to help with the transition to a more streamlined computing environment.

Case study: From silos to streamlined operations

Here is an example that helps explain how a business begins to streamline its data center. Say that you are the IT director of a major corporation. The business continues to demand that new applications be purchased and built to satisfy new business initiatives. Over time, the pace of business has taken its toll on IT. There's no time to retire old applications or to ensure that there's a single version of an important application. Some of these initiatives are incredibly successful, whereas others simply fade away. In good times, no one really paid attention to how big, complicated, or inefficient the data center became. But the world has changed. Your budget has been cut, but, at the same time, the business expects IT to be front and center in the new business model of the company. You have just finished reading *Hybrid Cloud For Dummies,* and the lessons you learned from the book have given you some good ideas about how to reduce IT costs and improve IT's responsiveness to the business. You make sure to get a number of different perspectives from stakeholders across the organization to ensure that your approach supports business requirements. You take the following steps:

✔ Create a business task force to understand where the business needs were evolving

✔ Implement server virtualization to begin consolidating workloads

✔ Add a public cloud service to quickly allow developers to prototype a new set of application services to demonstrate to the business what is possible and to implement some of these applications

✔ Create a committee to discover what applications are still needed and which ones can be retired

✔ Establish a pool of resources within the data center that can be used as a computing utility

The purpose behind these steps is to create a streamlined environment where consistency and predictability are the rule, not the exception.

An incremental transition

It's becoming clear to both business and IT leaders that business as usual would not support the changing needs for technology that would support business change and the need to innovate with new business models and ideas quickly. However, just as data centers didn't become complicated, hard-to-manage environments overnight, the data center cannot become a highly efficient and streamlined environment instantly. Companies should expect, instead, incremental changes to data centers. What does an incremental transition look like? In essence, company management needs to take a step back and take a hard look at the data center and ask the following questions:

✔ Is the data center streamlined enough to support business change?

✔ Are there too many operating systems and too many types of software in the data center to achieve economies of scale?

✔ Is it possible to separate the kinds of workloads that the data center supports?

These questions may seem straightforward, but the answers may help you begin an incremental tradition to a hybrid cloud environment. Say that you do, indeed, have a well-run and streamlined data center that is very effective in supporting the business. You've probably done a good job at getting rid of applications that aren't used by the business. You've also reduced the number of applications overall and have fewer servers and fewer operating systems. But your work is probably not done.

The process of gaining control over your data center is more complicated than it may seem at the outset. This process could take years. But the task is well worth it. It establishes the foundation for a much more efficient data center. It also sets the stage for a more rational approach to managing computing and workloads. The foundation is set, and the organization is ready to create a hybrid environment designed for a purpose, rather than for whatever comes along.

Managing Workloads in a Cost-Effective Way

When you strip away issues related to specific applications and specific requests, you get to the essence of how computing has begun to evolve. A well-tuned computing environment must be able to manage workloads in an efficient and effective manner. This type of workload management is important in any computing environment; however, it's *mandatory* in a hybrid cloud environment.

Because a hybrid cloud environment is a combination of several different computing models, all the models must be able to come together and act as though they are one cohesive platform. Although enabling different incompatible workloads to work together is possible, deep technical skills are required to mask the differences among implementations.

However, in a hybrid world, an organization wants to be able to have the ability to link workloads together at the time of need without the burden of complex coding. What would this look like in the average environment? Say that you have a sophisticated application, such as a general ledger in the data center. It includes a lot of data about what customers bought and when they bought it and how much they paid. It provides data that can be used to determine the difference in sales over time.

The typical way companies make use of this information is to bring in a reporting tool to determine the right statistics. However, what if the world is more complicated than that? What if not all the data you need is in the data center in the general ledger? Some may be stored in your company's SaaS environment; other data elements may be managed by a partner's public cloud environment. In this scenario, you have less control of the individual workloads, but you don't have less responsibility. It's still imperative that you make sure the data you're using from this hybrid world makes business sense and enables you to make the right decisions.

Chapter 10

Breaking Down the Economics of the Hybrid Cloud

*W*hen company management begins thinking about implementing or utilizing a cloud, one of the first things they think about is the economic impact. Executives who don't fully understand what the cloud is — and certainly don't grasp the concept of hybrid cloud — are saying "we want cloud," because the economics of the cloud can be compelling, and stories often appear in papers and magazines or arise in conversations. Before jumping feet first into the cloud, or implementing a hybrid cloud, it's important to think about what mixture of environments will yield not only the best performance, but also the most savings.

When you begin your thought process around the economic impact of the cloud, you realize that there are no simple answers. You have to consider many different issues. The costs of running an application, such as e-mail or customer relationship management (CRM) is more complicated to calculate than looking at just how much you pay for the software and the expense of employing the required staff to run the application. You must also consider things like cooling, floor space, and capital expenses versus operating expenses — the list goes on. The reality is that organizations — from small and mid-size to the largest global enterprises — are moving toward hybrid cloud environments to increase flexibility and cost efficiencies. Correctly balancing the use of different cloud environments can be challenging for these companies, but correctly achieving the right mixture will optimize their rewards.

In this chapter, you look at the considerations that go into finding the correct balance of cloud, and you also look at a company that shifted their balance with economics in mind. Then, although the economic benefits are discussed throughout this book, we specifically point some of them out. You also look at the economics of traditional on-premises server-based environments compared to cloud-based computing models so you can understand some of the costs involved with each.

Striking the Right Balance of Environments for a Hybrid Cloud

Operational performance, security, economics and flexibility all have a great impact on an organization's cloud strategy. Striking the right balance among public cloud services, private cloud, and the data center can come down to a mix of these factors or can be dominated by just one. Finding the right mixture of environments is critical for your organization to achieve the best value when creating a hybrid cloud strategy. Consider the following:

✔ Public clouds offer amazing capabilities for scalability; however, once you have ongoing knowledge of usage patterns, you may want the greater management and control of a private cloud.

✔ You may want to perform development and testing on one public cloud, because they have great support services, but you may then want to deploy it on a less expensive public cloud when it becomes operational.

✔ Public clouds give customers a great deal of control and flexibility over their costs. Although as time goes on, the costs of renting compute resources add up and it may become more economical to build your own infrastructure and create a private cloud.

✔ Your organization may become too reliant on just a few vendors and decide to build its own cloud to become more self-sufficient. As your private cloud matures, you may even begin having partners use it as a platform. In this case, your company goes from a cloud customer to a provider.

IT — and especially cloud computing — is a dynamic environment that is constantly changing and innovating and will continue to remain so. Vendors are often increasing their offerings and competing with each other for price. It's therefore important that your organization not just adopt a strategy and stick with it; instead you must regularly revisit your approach and consider how the changing landscape affects your economic model.

An online gaming company shifts its mix of environments with economics in mind

Zynga is a good example of a company that has made the economics of the hybrid cloud work to their advantage.

Zynga, the company behind popular online games such as FarmVille, FrontierVille, Mafia Wars, Zynga Poker, and Words with Friends, had to deal with both success and heavy demand on its compute resources as it gained traction in the marketplace. The tipping point for Zynga's move to the cloud was FarmVille, which went from zero users to 10 million in 6 weeks and then to 25 million in five months. Most early Zynga games used Facebook as a platform.

As demand increased, it was clear that Zynga's on-premises infrastructure could not support increasing demand for compute power, storage resources, and bandwidth. Zynga knew that service outages and latency would be received poorly by finicky consumers and would leave the door open for a competitor to quickly come in and capture its market share. As a result, Zynga made the decision to put some of its games on a public cloud server; Farmville alone required over 1,000 public cloud servers! This move allowed them to dynamically requisition additional compute resources as needed. Through automation and management tools, Zynga was able to increase its number of cloud instances as demand required, or when other predefined parameters were met (such as during peak predicted gaming hours). They no longer needed to wring their hands when games grew in popularity, hoping their servers would deliver, but could instead enjoy the success.

Zynga's use of public cloud servers could have continued indefinitely. But as Zynga matured, and received a large capital infusion by going public, it decided to no longer rely totally on other companies' servers, but to instead build a private cloud. The company's private cloud (called zCloud) was created to give Zynga the flexibility and dynamic scaling that it enjoyed with public clouds, while at the same time increasing operational and financial control over its environment. Zynga customized its private cloud to optimize performance for its unique mobile social gaming workloads. One of the financial impacts of investing in a private cloud includes shifting increasing infrastructure expenses from operating expenses (public cloud services) to capital (allowing for the benefits of the depreciation write-offs).

With zCloud, Zynga is able to handle the day-to-day demands of its users, while at the same time leveraging public cloud servers for peak demand periods. Zynga now owns its regular compute requirements and can easily reach into the public cloud during spikes.

Recall that early Zynga games relied on Facebook to provide the platform. With zCloud, Zynga created an optimized social gaming platform open to independent software vendors (ISVs). ISVs are able to partner with Zynga and therefore use the zCloud infrastructure to launch and operate social games.

Zynga's hybrid cloud journey is far from over, but their path is illustrative of how a company can shift its use of various cloud services to best suit its needs. As a young company, Zynga quickly outgrew its physical compute resources and utilized the public cloud to handle dynamic growth and scaling. As Zynga began to better understand its workloads and as it gained capital, zCloud was born. zCloud is highly optimized for social games and allows the company to commoditize its data center. At the same time, Zynga still has the ability to burst into the cloud during peak demand times.

It's likely that Zynga will remain a true hybrid cloud story. Although zCloud is highly customized for gaming, it does not make financial sense for the company to build out the infrastructure to meet demand requirements during just a few peak periods.

Your organization's mixture of different cloud services and use of its data center will change. It's important to have a well thought-out hybrid cloud strategy, but you need to be nimble and willing to change that strategy to better the business.

Economic Benefit of the Cloud

An organization typically has many different types of workloads to manage in its data center, and some of these workloads will be a better fit than others for a cloud environment. Therefore, to optimize your economic benefit from the cloud, you must first have a good understanding of your workload requirements.

Commodity workloads, such as everyday e-mail, collaboration, and messaging applications, are straightforward and well-defined business processes executed over and over again. The economic benefit for workloads with these characteristics comes from leveraging cloud capabilities such as standardization, optimization, and scalability. A commodity workload such as an e-mail application is a good fit for the cloud.

A customer-facing financial application in the heavily regulated financial industry is not likely to be a good fit for the cloud because of security concerns. The reason for this is that any potential economic benefit from the cloud is outweighed by security and compliance issues. An organization may have specialized workloads that are used occasionally by a select group of users. These specialized workloads may have run effectively for many years in the internal data center, so there may be no economic benefit in moving them to the cloud.

After you evaluate your mix of workloads, however, you will find many situations where the standardization, flexibility, and scalability of the cloud can deliver outstanding economic benefit.

A move to the cloud is likely to deliver an economic benefit if you have a need for

✔ **Increased capacity:** Your organization is ramping up for a new but short-term initiative, and you temporarily need some extra CPU capacity and extra storage.

✔ **A Software as a Service (SaaS) solution:** As your company has grown and diversified, everyone on your distributed sales force seems to be running a different version of your internal sales automation tool. You have recently lost out on some big deals based on discrepancies in customer and prospect data across different sales teams. You decide that implementing a SaaS solution to run your sales automation will ensure that all members of the sales team have consistent and accurate information when they need it (see Chapter 6 for more on SaaS).

✔ **Scaled application service:** Running your e-mail system requires more and more servers and lots of system administration time spent on maintenance and upgrades. You decide that a massively scaled application service in the cloud will deliver the performance you require and allow you to move the skilled administration team to focus on other projects.

In the next few sections, you take a look at each of these scenarios from an economic perspective.

Filling the need for capacity

Some pragmatic workloads fit perfectly into the Infrastructure as a Service (IaaS) model. These include basic computing services to support unexpected workloads or test and development requirements.

Considering IaaS for workloads that are outside the normal day-to-day operations makes sense for these reasons:

✔ Building out a full infrastructure for these unpredictable requirements isn't economical. An organization would have to purchase much more capacity than is otherwise required. Given that these resources would be dramatically underutilized, this approach doesn't make fiscal sense.

✔ Being able to procure a resource when it's needed streamlines planning and allows for much faster go-to market models. The IT staff can be more conservative in projecting requirements knowing that if needs expand, it will be able to respond to those changing needs in real time.

So an IaaS model is an economic choice because organizations can access what they need right away, without having to buy new hardware or go through the long process of manual provisioning. In practical terms, this means you must consider the following:

✔ **Software evaluation:** Testing new software is both a cumbersome and a long-lived process. Typically, developers need to acquire servers and specialized development software. Although this is a necessary process, it doesn't add to the bottom line of revenue. It can be time-consuming and expensive to evaluate new software. If that software is available as a service, an organization is more likely to try innovative software because it can quickly evaluate it.

- **System testing:** Similar to software evaluation, resources are required for a relatively short time when testing a system. Despite this, testers typically want to own their own resources, which isn't cost-effective because they will sit idle most of the time. In addition, if someone is testing a fast-growing workload, he has to spend much more money to achieve the same thing than he could via a service for a fraction of the cost. Testing as a service also means that the IT organization can test for situations that cannot be easily replicated within the data center.

- **Seasonal or peak loading:** Some companies are already using IaaS for *cloudbursting* when there are unexpected or planned high-load periods. The flexibility of using IaaS means that the company doesn't have to overinvest in hardware. These companies must be able to adapt to higher loads to protect themselves.

Selecting a SaaS for common applications

Not all SaaS applications are the same in terms of costs to the organization. If the application is fairly independent of the overall applications and information environment of the company, SaaS is a tactical and pragmatic approach. Also, because many SaaS vendors make their application programming interfaces (APIs) available to other vendors and customers, they are able to work in conjunction with third-party SaaS offerings or on-premises offerings. Moreover, SaaS has enormous benefits for organizations that don't want to support their own hardware and support environment.

Reducing your hardware requirements may seem like an obvious benefit, but you may not have considered the additional economic benefit that accrues based on reductions in support and maintenance after you cut back on infrastructure. For example, when you implement a SaaS application, you shift the responsibility of managing new versions and updates to the SaaS provider. You can realize many economic benefits as a result of this shift:

- You can cut back on IT staff or reposition members of the team to other projects.

- End-user productivity improves with a SaaS model that is consistent with more frequent application and seamless upgrades.

- Improved data accuracy based on the consistency and improved automation and availability of the SaaS solution.

However, one of the economic implications of SaaS is that they can create even more silos of applications and data in the IT organization. It is, therefore, important to evaluate the SaaS approach and choices based on how well Software as a Service needs to be integrated with other applications — both in the cloud and in the data center. A SaaS application can easily lead to even more costs if the IT organization has to go back and rearchitect the integration between various on-premises and cloud applications.

OpEx versus CapEx

When the value of cloud solutions are discussed, the conversation often revolves around the ideas of CapEx versus OpEx:

✔ **Capital expenditures (CapEX):** These are investments made by a company to acquire or significantly upgrade assets. These assets could be vehicles, real estate, equipment, software licenses, networking equipment, or servers. Companies either lay out the money up front or pay over time (a capital lease) for the ability to outright own the resource. The company can then depreciate the value of the asset over time.

✔ **Operating expenses (OpEx):** These are funds that must be paid for the ongoing operation of a business. Examples include wages, repairs, utilities, and supplies, as well as cloud services like Infrastructure as a Service, Platform as a Service, and Software as a Service.

OpEx versus CapEx is important because companies are limited in the amount of capital expenses they can make. Organizations often try to avoid sinking capital into resources that do not produce income. This is the reason why many companies choose to lease rather than purchase office space and why many utility companies elect to lease their trucks and other vehicles. They do so primarily for two reasons. First, a company can redirect CapEx to other projects that might be more lucrative; second, companies gain greater agility — a company can easily cut its losses if a project is not successful or can quickly ramp up if it gains traction.

The CapEx versus OpEx discussion often leads to the CapEx person arguing that over a period of three years (the time to depreciate servers) a server costs less than a cloud virtual machine (VM). Of course, you must take into account the fact that you might not be running your VM 24 hours a day, 365 days a year; the physical server has associated costs for maintenance, administrators, power, and so on. The cloud VM has additional costs like storage and bandwidth. However, even if there is a premium for the cloud VM, utilizing cloud services likely still makes business sense because that choice frees up capital for other projects like research and development or marketing and the increase in flexibility and agility.

Selecting a massively scaled application

Some of the earliest cloud adopters are large companies that wanted to take a massively scaled application (such as e-mail) and put it into a cloud. Companies are finding that approach to be a more cost-effective approach. In essence, this is the type of cloud application where the economics can't be matched by the data center. When applications support this type of massively scaled infrastructure, the cloud will often win out. Because massively scaled applications such as e-mail and social media are relatively simple, a vendor can easily standardize and optimize a platform, making it cost-effective to support vast numbers of users at a low cost. By taking advantage of the economies of scale in cloud environments, a massively scaled application is a win-win in the cloud.

When it's not black and white

Not all situations are clear-cut. Accurately forecasting the economics of the cloud can be complicated. The problem for many organizations is that they don't have an accurate picture of data center costs that allows them to consider cloud propositions on an apples-to-apples basis. For example, because companies pay per user per month for a typical SaaS application, the costs over time may appear to be greater than the costs of owning an application outright. The same argument could be made about IaaS services where the customer pays for a unit of work by volume or time. However, it's important to consider the flexibility and agility of the organization to change based on the needs of customers and partners. Some companies are willing to increase their operating costs in exchange for reducing their capital expenses because it gives them long-term flexibility.

The Economics of the Data Center

It's hard for most organizations to accurately predict the actual costs of running any given application in the data center. A particular server may be used to support several different applications. For example, how do you accurately judge how many personnel resources are dedicated to a single application? Although there may be a particular month when your staff is updating one application, those same staff members may be troubleshooting a different application in another month. In some organizations, there may have been attempts to tie computing costs to specific departments, but if so, the model is likely to have been very rough.

Consider, as a simple example, the use of e-mail. Some departments are very heavy users, whereas others barely touch it at all. Pockets *within* a single department may be heavy users. Although technically you can monitor individual use, doing so would require more overhead than it's worth. In addition, overhead costs associated with supporting customers when they forget their password or accidently delete an important message can surpass expectations and add to the overall costs of running an application such as e-mail.

Listing the costs

In order to prepare for your evaluation of on-premises data center costs, you need to look at the costs that are directly and indirectly related to the application or type of workload you want to move to the cloud (public or private). Some of these indirect costs are hard to evaluate, making it difficult to accurately predict the actual costs of running any given application in your company. Here is a fairly comprehensive list of the possible costs, with notes:

✔ **Server costs:** With this and all other hardware components, you're specifically interested in the total annual cost of ownership, which normally consists of the cost of hardware support plus some amortization cost for the purchase of the hardware. Additionally, a particular server may be used to support several different workloads.

✔ **Storage costs:** What are the management and support costs for the storage hardware required for the data associated with this application? Storage costs may be very high for certain types of applications, such as e-mail.

✔ **Network costs:** When a web application you host internally, such as e-mail or collaboration, is moved to the cloud, the strain on your network may be reduced. However, keep in mind that ensuring that users in your company have on-demand access from anywhere to cloud services requires substantial bandwidth.

✔ **Backup and archive costs:** The actual savings on backup costs depend on what the backup strategy will be when the workload moves into the cloud. The same is true of archiving. Say that you're thinking of moving some workloads to the public cloud. Will all backup be done in that cloud? Will your organization still be required to back up a percentage of critical data?

✔ **Business continuity and disaster recovery costs:** In theory, the cloud service will have its own disaster recovery capabilities, so there may be a consequential savings on disaster recovery. However, you need to clearly understand what your cloud provider's disaster recovery capability is. Not all cloud providers have the same definition of disaster recovery. IT management must determine the level of support the cloud provider will offer. This can be an added cost from the provider, or you might seek out a secondary vendor to handle disaster recovery and procedures. Many organizations have redundancy and diversity built into their cloud strategies to mitigate business continuity concerns.

✔ **Data center infrastructure costs:** A whole series of costs — including electricity, floor space, cooling, building maintenance, and so on — go into the data center. Because of the large investment in data centers, moving workloads to a public cloud may not be financially viable if you're only utilizing 40 percent of the data center's compute power. (Of course, you can deploy a private cloud to take advantage of the underutilized space and the advantages of the cloud.)

However, if your data center is 80 percent full and has been expanding at 10 percent a year, you'll soon need a new data center. At that point, you may have to build a data center that could cost as much as $5 million. The cloud will be a much more economical choice in order to divert workloads away from the data center.

✔ **Platform costs:** Some applications run only in specific operating environments — Windows, Linux, HP-UX, IBM z/OS, and so on. The annual maintenance costs for the application operating environment need to be known and calculated as part of the overall costs.

✔ **Software maintenance costs:** What's the annual maintenance cost for the software you may move to a cloud-based service? Although the answer to this question may seem simple, things can easily get complicated if a specific software license is part of a bundled deal or if an application is integrated with other applications in your environment.

✔ **Operational support personnel costs:** A whole set of day-to-day operational costs is associated with running any application. Some costs are general ones that apply to every application, including staff support for everything from storage and archiving, to patch management and networks, to troubleshooting and security. Some support tasks, however, may be particular to a given application, such as database tuning and performance management.

✔ **Infrastructure software costs:** A whole set of infrastructure management software is in use in any installation, and it has an associated cost. For example, management software is typically used for many different applications and can't easily be divided across specific applications.

Increase utilization of resources in hybrid environment

Many organizations have islands of hardware that are underutilized or that lay completely dormant. These islands increase over time. As a new project is started, a team might requisition a two-way box expecting the application to not need many resources. However, as the application demand grows, it outgrows the box and must be migrated to a larger one. Similarly, a team might requisition a larger machine only to find out later that the application is no longer needed. This results in large amounts of white space — where there are resources available, but getting to them proves difficult. By implementing a hybrid cloud strategy, companies are able to utilize these resources and as a result make their data centers more efficient, preventing unnecessary investments in new hardware. Some of the ways a hybrid environment can help save money and increase efficiencies include

✔ **Reducing hardware costs by commoditization:** Organizations that deploy private clouds can greatly reduce server costs by installing larger, more consistent machines. This allows for greater standardization and a smaller data center, which in turn results in lower heating, cooling, and power consumption.

✔ **Decreasing time to market:** Application development can be a slow process. Just gathering the proper compute resources necessary to move forward often takes weeks if not months. With a hybrid cloud, teams can start application development in minutes either on-premises or in a public cloud. This ability to quickly start work can be the difference between introducing an application for a problem that existed six months ago and bringing to market a product that customers need right now.

✔ **Increasing the efficiency of your human talent:** A properly designed hybrid cloud environment has built-in automation and standardization tools. For example, provisioning becomes automated; middleware, operating systems, and the like are standardized; and in some cases, libraries are created to store coding for later reuse. All of this increases an organization's productivity, while at the same time leading to greater quality.

Evaluating Costs in the Hybrid Environment

In order to make a smart economic choice about running workloads in your internal data center versus implementing a public or private cloud, you need to understand some of the subtleties of the cost factors. You also need to consider potential hidden costs associated with the cloud and, in particular, a hybrid cloud. There's always a cost to change, including the following:

- **Management:** Management of a hybrid environment brings additional challenges. You no longer need to simply manage the data center, or even one cloud, but instead multiple environments — on-premises, in your private cloud, and on one, if not multiple, public clouds. People, processes, and software can help with management, but they each have their own costs involved. See Chapter 4 for more details on service management.

- **Data transfer:** When you transfer data, say from your premises to an application in a public cloud, costs are involved. This includes the fee to initially move your data to the cloud. These costs can quickly mount if you have large amounts of data requiring lots of bandwidth. Furthermore, depending on your cloud vendor, you can incur networking fees when moving data between different VMs within the same cloud (for instance, during backup or replication).

- **Customization costs:** If you're migrating an application to the public cloud that was on-premises, there may be costs associated with customizing the application so that it can now work in the hybrid environment. Most likely, some configuration work and testing will be done first. In addition, that application may not be well designed for the highly distributed nature of the cloud environment in its current form, and it may need to be rewritten.

- **Integration costs:** In a hybrid model, you will probably want to integrate various applications. For example, your off-premises CRM application might integrate with your on-premises business intelligence application. Sure, you might have to integrate them if they were both on-premises, but it will probably take you more time to figure it out in a hybrid model.

- **Storage costs:** As you move data and workloads to a hybrid cloud, you will really have to balance and think about your long-term storage costs. In Chapter 16, we talk about how virtual machine image sprawl can take up a lot of space and ultimately use a lot of storage. Likewise, you must plan on how much storage a growing data volume might cost in the cloud.

- **Platform costs:** In some situations, you need to maintain the licenses for technologies such as middleware when you move to the cloud (because most companies end up having a hybrid).

✔ **Software maintenance costs (package software):** This cost may be difficult to calculate if the software license is tied to processor pricing, and the situation could be further complicated if the specific software license is part of a bundled deal or a global usage deal.

✔ **Compliance costs.** Compliance (external or internal) can be an increased cost when using the cloud. It may be necessary to have the cloud service audited to see that it meets the appropriate requirements, which may relate to IT security or recovery procedures or any other such IT activity that must obey compliance standards. This is in addition to your existing on-premises audits. Compliance requirements might come from several sources:

  • _Vendors and partners:_ An example would be credit card companies requiring companies who accept credit cards to comply with the Payment Card Industry Data Security Standard (PCI DSS).

  • _Customers:_ Customers may require that you produce an SSA 16 or similar report to evidence various compliance requirements.

  • _Governmental Bodies:_ Your organization may need to comply with local, national or international compliance standards. These include Health Insurance Portability and Accountability Act (HIPAA), and Sarbanes–Oxley (SOX), along with dozens of others.

  • _Internal compliance:_ You may have compliance requirements that your organization has established. These may be even more specific than externally required compliance.

✔ **Server costs:** If an application is relatively small, running in a virtual server, or perhaps only running occasionally, it's unlikely that moving it to the public cloud will result in any server hardware savings.

✔ **Storage costs:** Similarly, if very little storage is consumed by the application, there may be no reduction in SAN costs.

✔ **Data center infrastructure costs:** The floor space in the data center will not be reduced by the removal of a few servers, and it may make little difference to cooling costs. The change usually needs to be significant in order to bring down these costs.

✔ **Operational support personnel costs:** Savings occur here only if there's a possibility of saving the cost of a staff person or delaying the recruitment of another person.

✔ **Infrastructure software costs:** Infrastructure management software costs may not come down with the movement of a few workloads into the cloud.

Cost calculators

A number of cloud providers and vendors offer calculators for helping you estimate charges for their services or to help you estimate the cost savings of cloud computing.

✔ **Estimating charges:** Some vendors provide monthly calculators for their web services. For example, a calculator might ask you a series of questions about the number of compute instances, storage needs, data transfer, load balancing, and IPs needed, and then provide you with a monthly estimate. Of course, your monthly usage and, therefore, the charges, may vary from the estimates that the calculator provides.

✔ **Calculating total cost of ownership (TCO):** Other vendors offer TCO calculators. These calculators might ask you a series of questions about the type of deployment, the number of servers, storage requirements, and load volatility (for example, the kind of demand you have). Then the calculators will estimate how much you might be able to save versus a data center deployment over five years. These calculators look at such factors as server utilization; facility, power, and hardware costs; the cost of downtime, reduction in deployment, and provisioning time; and cloud administrative costs.

Warning: Of course, you should not base your decision to move to the cloud simply on these calculators. Some of these calculators are marketing tools, at best. However, they can help you wrap your head around some of the costs associated with the factors inherent in the move to the cloud.

From a policy perspective, companies shouldn't simply take an action because it seems cheaper. You need to have a policy on what must stay in the traditional data center or in a private cloud and why (for example, privacy and complexity and singularity of the workload). You should have a policy that states that automation and self-provisioning will support the business and enable it to react quickly to opportunities. There also needs to be a policy that specifies when a workload can safely be moved to a public cloud — and whether the data is safe enough in the private cloud. All these questions are part of the larger economic decision-making process.

Part IV
Creating a Unified Hybrid Environment

The 5th Wave   By Rich Tennant

"I assume everyone on your team is on board with the proposed changes to the system architecture."

In this part . . .

Now, we get into the details of what it actually means to create a hybrid computing environment. In this part, you see the elements required to move to a hybrid cloud environment and what you have to consider from a supporting infrastructure perspective — ranging from cloud management to security and planning.

Chapter 11

Managing and Integrating Data

*T*here's no way around it: The issues surrounding data in the cloud are a big and complicated topic. The reality is that data is the lifeblood of your business. Therefore, the way you manage data, regardless of where it lives, is critical to the health of your company. This data comes in all shapes and sizes. There may be transactional data, customer data, and various kinds of unstructured data, such as documents and images. Your data might be massive in terms of sheer volume. Or it might be coming at you in real time. You may want to use this data for analysis or to provide other business value.

Being able to manage this data and ensure that it's trustworthy is a critical issue in hybrid cloud environments. Depending on the sensitivity of your data and your business requirements, some of this data can be stored on your premises and integrated with a private cloud, whereas other data sources that may not be as sensitive can be stored in a public cloud. Some of it may never leave your premises. There are numerous points to consider, however, and we dive into those in this chapter.

Additionally, in a hybrid world, there can be multiple touchpoints between your data and the cloud. That is why integration is so important in data management. Your data may be on-premises, but integrated with multiple applications in the cloud. Both the integrity of your information and the ability to incorporate cloud-based business services into your company's overall business processes are at great risk unless you can consistently integrate across your hybrid environment. So, in this chapter, we also describe the requirements for integrating across those platforms.

Ensuring Trustworthy Data

In the cloud, company data that was previously secured inside a firewall may now move outside to feed any number of business applications and processes. Although cloud providers must have the proper controls in place to ensure the security and privacy of your data, you are ultimately responsible for your company's data. This means that industry and government regulations created to protect personal and business information still apply even if the data is managed or stored by an outside vendor. For example, the European Union has implemented a complex set of data protection laws for its member states. In addition, industry regulations, such as the Health Insurance Portability and Accountability Act (HIPAA) created to secure the privacy of individual healthcare information, must be followed whether or not your data is in the cloud. Healthcare organizations must require their subcontractors to comply with HIPAA privacy considerations and use reasonable security measures.

Assessing hybrid cloud data risks

You need to be concerned about a number of issues in a hybrid cloud environment. Of course, the level of risk depends on the kind of data that you're trying to secure. This data can range in type from credit card transactions to Social Security data to internal social network site data. You need to decide what kind of data you're willing to either put into the cloud or connect to the cloud based on the risk you're willing to take if that data becomes compromised in some way or if you can't access it. Here are just a few data-related risks to think about:

- **Co-mingling of data:** As we mention in Chapter 15, in a hybrid cloud, there's a good chance that your data will be co-mingled with another company's data on a server. Your neighbors, therefore, matter. For example, if one neighbor is successfully attacked, the attack could affect your data availability or security. Or, if one of your co-tenants engages in malicious activity, you can be affected. Your data might become compromised.

- **Data deletion:** If you end your contract with your service provider and ask it to delete your data, this procedure may not be done in a secure manner. That means some of your data may still be on the provider's disks and that others can access it.

- **Data breaches:** Hackers are very much aware of the new cloud model and the fact that data is moving through the cloud. However, depending on where your data is located, your cloud provider may not have to let you know if its servers are breached. Breach protection laws that protect personal information can vary by country and state.

✔ **Data seizure:** Your data may be co-mingled with other companies' data, which means if one company's data is seized, yours might be, too. For example, in 2009, the FBI raided two Texas data centers and seized a number of servers. Companies that had data on servers that weren't related to the investigation were severely affected. A number went out of business because they couldn't uphold their obligations to their customers.

Hackers and thieves are always one step ahead of the latest security measure, so data protection tools need to be used wisely to provide adequate protection. For example, situations exist where thieves have been able to steal encrypted data. In one recent case, the data was encrypted only up to the point the data was delivered to the applications. At that point, it was decrypted, and that's when the loss occurred. This loss could've been prevented if the receiving application had been allowed to control the decryption process.

Securing data in the cloud

The three key areas of concern related to security and privacy of data are

✔ Location of your data

✔ Control of your data

✔ Secure transport of your data

Cloud providers must ensure the security and privacy of your data, but you are ultimately responsible for your company's data. This means that industry and government regulations created to protect personal and business information still apply even if the data is managed or stored by an outside vendor.

It's important to note that some experts believe that certain kinds of data are just too sensitive for the public/hybrid cloud. This might include highly regulated data, such as medical information. Others believe that if the right level of transparency and controls can be provided, consumers can be protected. In some circles, this is an ongoing debate. Clouds that host regulated data must meet compliance requirements such as Payment Card Industry Data Security Standard (PCI DSS), Sarbanes-Oxley, and HIPAA.

Because security is such a big issue, we've devoted Chapter 15 to it. In addition, if you want to learn more about security in the cloud, we point you to the Cloud Security Alliance (`https://cloudsecurityalliance.org`) for more information.

Beware of attacks by hackers

Attacks that hackers can perpetrate against your systems include man-in-the-middle, sniffing, and side-channel attacks. *Man-in-the-middle* occurs when an attacker intrudes into a communication and is actively monitoring, capturing, and controlling your communication. The attacker can even insert false information into it, by modifying the data. A *sniffer* is an application or device that can read network packets while they're being transferred. The attacker can then read your data as well as figure out your network. A *side-channel* attack uses observations of a system — such as its power consumption or computation time, to crack an encryption system.

The location of data in the cloud

After data goes into the cloud, you may not have control over where it's stored or how it's used. Numerous issues are associated with this situation:

✔ **Specific country laws:** Security and regulatory laws governing data can differ across different geographies. For example, your own country's legal protections may not apply if your data is located outside of it. A foreign government may be able to gain access to your data or keep you from having full control over your data when you need it.

✔ **Transfer of data across country borders:** A global company with subsidiaries or partners (or clients for that matter) in other countries may be concerned about cross-border transfer of data because of local laws. Virtualization makes this an especially tough problem because the cloud provider might not know where the data is at any particular moment, either.

✔ **Secondary use of data:** In public cloud situations, your data or metadata may be vulnerable to alternative or secondary uses by the cloud service provider. Without proper controls or service level agreements in place, your data may be used for marketing purposes. It could be merged with data from other organizations for such alternative uses. Also, the service provider may own any metadata (see the next section for a description of metadata) it has created to help manage your data, thus lessening your ability to maintain control over your data.

The control of data in the cloud

You may or may not have heard the term the *CIA Triad*. No, this isn't about covert operations. CIA stands for *Confidentiality*, *Integrity*, and *Availability*. These three attributes have been around a long time in the world of auditing and management controls; they're critical for data in the cloud environment for the following reasons:

✔ **Confidentiality:** Only authorized parties with the appropriate privileges can access certain data; that is, there's no theft of the data.

✔ **Integrity:** Data is correct and no malicious software (or person) has altered it; that is, there is no tampering with the data.

✔ **Availability:** Network resources are available to authorized users.

These three attributes are directly related to controlling data. *Controls* include the governance policies set in place to make sure that data can be trusted. The integrity, reliability, and confidentiality of your data must be beyond reproach. This holds for cloud providers, too.

You must understand what level of controls will be maintained by your cloud provider and consider how these controls can be audited.

Here's a sampling of different types of controls designed to ensure the confidentiality, integrity, and availability of your data:

✔ **Input validation** controls to ensure that all data input to any system or application are complete, accurate, and reasonable

✔ **Output reconciliation** controls to ensure that data can be reconciled from input to output

✔ **Processing** controls to ensure that data are processed completely and accurately in an application

✔ **Access** controls to ensure that only those who are authorized to access the data can do so. Sensitive data must also be protected in storage and transfer. Encryption can help to do this

✔ **Re-identification** (the process by which anonymized personal data is matched with its true owner) controls to ensure that codes are kept in a separate location to prevent unauthorized access to re-identification information

✔ **Change management** controls to ensure that data can't be changed without proper authorization

✔ **Data destruction** controls to ensure that when data is permanently deleted, it is deleted from everywhere — including all backup and redundant storage sites

The concept of controls in the cloud is so important that the Cloud Security Alliance (`https://cloudsecurityalliance.org`) has put together a list of over 100 controls called the Cloud Controls Matrix (CCM) to guide cloud vendors and assist potential cloud customers in assessing the overall risk of the provider. The matrix outlines the controls, as well as architectural implications and the kinds of cloud delivery models (Infrastructure as a Service [IaaS], Platform as a Service [PaaS], Software as a Service [SaaS]) that the control pertains to.

Controls can be disclosed. When cloud services are certified for ISO 27001 or SSAE 16, the scope of controls should be disclosed. ISO 27001 is an Information Security Management System standard that requires, among other things, that management (of your cloud provider) design a set of risk controls that are deemed unacceptable, which means you should be able to examine this plan. The Statements on Standards for Attestation Engagements No. 16 or SSAE 16, which was developed by the American Institute of Certified Public Accountants (AICPA), has replaced the Statement on Auditing Standards (SAS) 70, which service providers had used in the past. SSAE is now the new standard for reporting controls at service organizations. In SSAE 16, management at the service organization must provide a description of its "system" along with a written statement of assertion rather than a simple description of controls.

Your company needs to develop and publish a consistent set of rules and policies regarding the creation, capture, management, transmission, access, storage, and deletion of confidential and business-critical data. Use techniques, such as encryption and tokenization, to reduce exposure to data theft and misuse. We recommend speaking to your cloud provider regarding what controls it provides for your data.

The secure transport of data in the cloud

Say that you've decided to move some of your data to the cloud. Regarding data transport, keep two things in mind:

✔ Make sure that no one can intercept your data as it moves from point A to point B in the cloud.

✔ Make sure that no data leaks (malicious or otherwise) from any storage in the cloud.

These concepts are not new; the goal of securely transporting data has been around as long as the Internet. The issues you face moving your data from one point to another are really the same kinds of issues you might have faced moving your data from your data center in Pittsburg to the one in Miami.

In the hybrid cloud, the journey from point A to point B might occur any number of ways: within a cloud environment, over the public Internet between an enterprise and cloud provider, or even between clouds.

The security process may include segregating your data from other companies' data, then encrypting it by using an approved method. In addition, you may want to ensure the security of older data that remains with a cloud vendor after you no longer need it.

A *virtual private network* (VPN) is one way to manage the security of data during its transport in a cloud environment. A VPN essentially makes the public network your own private network instead of using a dedicated connection. A well-designed VPN needs to incorporate two things:

> ✔ A *firewall* to act as a barrier between the public Internet and any private network
>
> ✔ *Encryption* to protect your sensitive data from hackers; only the computer you send it to should have the key to decode the data

In addition to transport, in a hybrid world, there will be touchpoints between your data and the cloud. Therefore, it's important to deal with the storage and retrieval of this data. We talk more about storage in Chapter 20. It's important to note, however, that a lot of research has been done over the past decade on storage and retrieval of sensitive information. Some of these techniques use some form of encryption to prevent information leakage. Researchers and experts in the field are now working on other techniques to deal with the challenge of the server performance degradation because of encryption. They're addressing issues related to data partitioning between your on-premises data and a service provider. They're investigating how to deal with distributed query processing over unencrypted and encrypted data.

Integrating Data Across Environments

As soon as you start dealing with the cloud, you must establish a way to deal with the fact that you have data that potentially spans multiple environments. Of course, your data probably does span multiple environments today, but it's under your control. How do you integrate all this data? Most companies very quickly find that they must contend with many different integration scenarios.

Three integration scenarios

The three most common cloud integration scenarios are

> ✔ On-premises data center to cloud
>
> ✔ Connectivity between (or among) clouds
>
> ✔ Connectivity in clouds

We discuss each of these in this section.

On-premises data center to cloud

Connectivity from the data center to the cloud is one of the basic uses of cloud integration. The typical IT organization manages its enterprise resource planning (ERP) system within its data center and uses a SaaS environment to manage sales leads. Sales, order, invoice, and inventory data must be synchronized across these systems for the company to function properly. This can be a major cultural shift for an organization that's used to having full control over its line-of-business applications.

There is little or no control over the architectural structure of the SaaS environment. Consequently, the IT organization needs to establish new processes to institute management between a data center application and a cloud-based application. IT management needs to separate the data elements within the line-of-business applications from unnecessary dependencies. For example, there may be a business process that controls a specific circumstance that interferes with your ability to easily connect between data sources on the cloud.

In addition, specific issues related to using cloud computing environments affect the style of integration. For example, although your company gains huge value from using a SaaS-based customer relationship management (CRM) system, governance requirements demand that customer data be stored behind your firewall. So, when a prospect becomes a customer, the company moves the data into the data center for additional security. This company now has a hybrid environment to manage. The company needs to automate data mobility across clouds in order to transfer and transform customer data to migrate between public and private clouds.

Connectivity among clouds

Companies may need to integrate among a private cloud and public clouds. One common example of this occurs when private cloud resources are insufficient to support peak demand. In this situation, select workloads are allowed to burst into a public cloud environment.

For instance, an entertainment organization is testing the introduction of a new game that supports on-demand group participation. The online gaming community has already shown a great deal of interest surrounding this new capability. The entertainment company wants to test how its web application scales from 20,000 to 1 million concurrent users before going live. They know they need more cycles and more power than they have available on-premises, so they expand their environment by leveraging public cloud resources, such as IBM's Smart Business Development and Test Cloud or Amazon EC2.

Connectivity in clouds

A third type of integration occurs when you need to create bidirectional integration with multiple SaaS applications in order to support a business process. In this case, the connectivity capability itself is in the cloud. For example, a services organization uses sales automation to keep track of its prospects and a different SaaS application to manage commission and salary payments. Many sales situations exist where a cross-brand sales team collaborates in closing a large sales opportunity.

As a result, the sales commission must be split across different sales people. The data in the CRM system needs to be consistent with the data in the payment application, or the people who worked to close the deal won't be paid accurately. Automating this process requires the synchronization of the data between the two SaaS applications.

Because both of these applications are in the cloud, the most efficient approach to synchronizing the data is to use a cloud-based integration capability. Public cloud offerings include connectivity in the cloud for this type of situation.

Choosing an integration method wisely

When considering a hybrid cloud, you need to understand that you lose control over how many things are done. Use an integration method to monitor these connections and make sure standards are met. For example, the SSL/TLS industry standards handshake will help to authenticate using X.509 certificates to ensure that users are legitimate. Part of this handshake process includes creating an encrypted tunnel; some of the security threats this process attempts to protect against are eavesdropping and man-in-the-middle attacks. Secure communication protocols exist that should be followed when communicating with endpoint applications and databases.

Options for cloud data integration

Various options are emerging for cloud data integration. The option that you choose may depend on the business problem you're trying to solve and the kind of cloud deployment you're dealing with:

- ✔ **Software solution:** In this approach, vendors can provide a preconfigured integration pattern or template that jump-starts the effort of integration between applications. One of the benefits of working with a standardized template is that the same template can be reused for other integration projects. The template is typically designed to cover about 60 percent of the requirements for a particular integration. The packages usually also provide a way to visually map the data between source and target systems.

  For example, in your on-premises ERP system, your customer ID might be called ID, and in your cloud application, it's called CUST ID, the visual mapping interface makes this easy to specify that the two fields refer to the same entity. You just draw a line between the two to specify that they're the same. Some packages also allow you to work with more complex mappings as well as provide a way to set up rules for data integration.

- ✔ **Cloud-based tool:** This option is similar in many ways to traditional tools, such as connectors, that can be used to connect specific applications. In this case, end users can buy different components from a provider based on what they need to do. For example, you could buy a component for database connectivity or to transform data going into a database.

✔ **Cloud-based solutions:** In this case, data integration is offered as a service or set of services. For example, a vendor might offer a data replication service to copy data from one source to another and then automatically update it. Or it might offer data quality and assessment services, or services to load data from various format types (such as flat files or databases) into target applications. Or it might offer a packaged web application server and database.

You can find a number of vendors offering solutions in this space, including companies such as Dell Boomi, IBM, Informatica, Pervasive Software, Liaison Technologies, and Talend. Some offer packaged solutions, some offer cloud solutions, and some offer both. The solution you choose will depend on the problem you're trying to solve.

No matter what approach you use, an overriding issue is going to be to make sure that your data maintains its integrity by being complete, accurate, and up to date. You will still have to make sure that you have a master version of your data in place that serves as what is often called a "single version of the truth." In other words, an agreed upon golden master.

Managing Big Data in the Cloud

Perhaps you've heard of the term *big data*? It's getting a lot of attention recently because of the ongoing need to process increasing amounts of data. The key fact about big data is that it exists at the tipping point of the work-arounds that organizations have historically put in place to manage large volumes of complex data. Big data technologies allow people to actually analyze and utilize this data in an effective way.

Master data management (MDM)

MDM is a technique that helps companies establish consistent and accurate definitions of data across their IT assets. It is about breaking down data silos to reach a single version of the truth. For example, you might have multiple systems in your company, each containing customer information. But what is a customer? In the pharmaceutical industry, in one system, a customer might refer to a physician. In another system, it might be a group practice. In yet another system, it might be a hospital that buys drugs in bulk. So, if you're mapping this data together, you need to understand what you're calling a customer or else you'll end up with data that doesn't make any sense when you go to analyze it. That's what master data is all about.

Big data characteristics

Big data generally has three characteristics:

- **Volume:** Big data is big in volume, and although the word big is relative here, currently we're talking on the order of at least terabytes. Many big data implementations are looking to analyze petabytes of information.

Name	Value
Byte	$10^{**}0$
Gigabyte	$10^{**}9$ bytes
Terabyte	$10^{**}12$ bytes
Petabyte	$10^{**}15$ bytes
Exabyte	$10^{**}18$ bytes

- **Variety:** Big data comes in different shapes and sizes. It includes these types of data:

  - *Structured data* is the typical kind of data that analysts are used to dealing with. It includes revenue, number of sales — the type of data you think about including in a database. Structured data is also being produced in new ways in products such as sensors and RFID tags.

  - *Semistructured data* has some structure to it but not in the way you think about tables in a database. It includes EDI formats or XML.

  - *Unstructured data* includes text, image, and audio, including any document, e-mail message, tweet, or blog internal to a company or on the Internet. Unstructured data accounts for about 80 percent of all data.

- **Velocity:** This is the speed at which the data moves. Think about sensors capturing data every millisecond or data streams output from medical equipment. Big data often comes at you in a stream, so it has a real-time nature associated with it.

The cloud is an ideal place for big data because of its scalable storage, compute power, and elastic resources. The cloud model is large-scale; distributed computing and a number of frameworks and technologies have emerged to support this model, including

- **Apache Hadoop:** An open source distributed computing platform written in Java. It is a software library that enables distributed processing across clusters of computers. It's really a distributed file system. It creates a computer pool, each with a Hadoop file system. Hadoop was designed to deal with problems where there's a large amount of complex data. The data can be structured, unstructured, or semistructured. Hadoop can run across a lot of servers that don't share memory or disk. For more information about Hadoop, visit `http://hadoop.apache.org`.

✔ **MapReduce:** A software framework introduced by Google to support distributed computing on large sets of data. It's at the heart of what Hadoop is doing with big data and big data analytics. It's designed to take advantage of cloud resources. This computing is done across numerous computers, called *clusters*. Each cluster is referred to as a *node*. MapReduce can deal with both structured and unstructured data. Users specify a map function that processes a key/value pair to generate a set of intermediate pairs and a reduction function that merges these pairs.

Big data databases

One important appeal of Hadoop is that it can handle different types of data. Parallel database management systems have been on the market for decades. They can support parallel execution because most of the tables are partitioned over the nodes in a cluster, and they can translate SQL commands into a plan that is divided across the nodes in the cluster. However, they mostly deal with structured data because it's hard to fit unstructured, freeform data into the columns and rows in a relational model.

Hadoop has started a movement in what has been called *NoSQL,* meaning not only SQL. The term refers to a set of technologies that is different than relational database systems. One major difference is that they don't use SQL. They are also designed for distributed data stores. There are numerous examples of these kinds of databases, including the following:

✔ **Apache Cassandra:** An open source distributed data management system originally developed by Facebook. It has no stringent structure requirements, so it can handle all different types of data. Experts claim it excels at high-volume, real-time transaction processing. Other open source databases include MongoDB, Apache CouchDB, and Apache HBase.

✔ **Amazon Simple DB:** Amazon likens this database to a spreadsheet in that it has columns and rows with attributes and items stored in each. Unlike a spreadsheet, however, each cell can have multiple values, and each item can have its own set of associated attributes. Amazon then automatically indexes the data. Recently, Amazon announced Amazon Dynamo DB as a way to bring big data NoSQL to the cloud.

✔ **Google Big Table:** This hybrid is sort of like one big table. Because tables can be large, they're split at the row boundaries into tables, which might be hundreds of megabytes or so. MapReduce is often used for generating and modifying data stored in BigTable.

NoSQL doesn't mean that people should not be using SQL. Rather, the idea is that, depending on what your problem is, relational databases and NoSQL databases can coexist in an organization.

Supporting an Analytics Strategy

What good is all that data if you can't do anything active with it? The lure of analytics in the cloud is cloud elasticity. Your data can be processed across clusters of computers. This means that the analysis is occurring across machines. If you need more compute power, you can get it from the cloud.

Big data analytics

Here are some examples of where analytics get big and may require cloud resources:

✔ **Financial services:** Imagine using advanced analytics technologies like predictive analytics to analyze millions of credit card transactions to determine whether they might be fraudulent. Or, on the unstructured side, picture the text in insurance claims being analyzed to determine what might constitute fraud.

For example, take a worker's compensation claim submitted by a worker who may have been reprimanded several times by his boss. This data (or the claim), which came from unstructured sources, can be utilized together with structured data to train an analytical system on what patterns might indicate fraud. As new claims come in, the system can automatically kick out the ones that may need to be investigated.

✔ **Retail:** Just think about the recommendation engines from Amazon and eBay. They're becoming more sophisticated. eBay is utilizing advanced technologies that will look at what you're purchasing, and then, based on models it has of the numerous purchases of other people, make a recommendation.

Another example is the use of advanced analytics over massive amounts of data in real time at big-box stores. Using your loyalty card, based on what you're buying, what you have bought in the past, and what others with similar profiles like you have bought, the store will provide you with coupons for different products you might like.

✔ **Social media analysis:** Imagine all the data being collected across the Internet. This includes blogs, tweets, and newsfeeds. Companies are mining this unstructured data to understand what is being said about them. For example, a consumer packaged goods (CPG) company might mine this data to determine what is being said about them and whether this sentiment is positive or negative. Numerous companies are providing this kind of service in the cloud.

Writing the code to process this data across clusters of machines requires highly trained developers and complex job coordination. With a technology like MapReduce, the same MapReduce job that is developed to run on a single node can distribute this analytic processing power to a group of 1,000 nodes. Say you need immediate analysis of sensor data or social media data that is streaming into your data center or your cloud provider. Parallel processing across multiple computing resources can help to do this, by spreading the analysis across the environment. It gets you to insight faster.

Other cloud analytics

The cloud can be useful in supporting an analytics strategy when your data isn't that big (in contrast to the previous example of big data). Say you work at a company that wants to predict what action your customers will take. You want to use predictive analytics to do this, but you don't have the skills in-house. In this case, you can turn to analytics providers that offer SaaS-based services for help . You provide them your data, and they provide you with the analysis.

A number of cloud-based offerings on the market can either help you analyze your data or provide software in the cloud for you to do the analysis yourself. Maybe you're using a cloud-based CRM and ERP system, and you want to analyze the data that's being generated there. There's a cloud service for that.

If you're thinking about using some of the data services in the cloud, before you sign the contract, remember that data (especially your company's data) is a precious asset, and you need to treat it as such. We recommend discussing certain topics with your potential vendor. We describe those issues in the next section.

Talking to Your Cloud Provider About Data

In addition to issues surrounding security and privacy of your data as covered earlier in the chapter, we recommend talking with your potential vendor about the following issues because when your data leaves your premises in a cloud model, you need to ensure that the proper controls are in place to protect it:

✔ **Data integrity:** What controls does your provider have in place to ensure that the integrity of your data is maintained? For example, are there controls in place to make sure that all data input to any system or application is complete, accurate, and reasonable? What about processing controls to make sure that data processing is accurate? Also, output controls need to be in place. This dovetails into any compliance issues that your particular industry might have.

✔ **Compliance:** You are probably aware of any compliance issues particular to your industry. You need to make sure that your provider can comply with these regulations.

✔ **Loss of data:** Your data is a precious asset. Key to any decision to go with a cloud provider is to find out what provisions are in the contract if the provider does something to your data. If the contract says simply that your monthly fee is waived, you need to ask some more questions.

✔ **Business continuity plans:** What happens if disaster strikes and your cloud vendor's data center goes down? What business continuity plans does your provider have in place — meaning how long is it going to take the provider to get your data back up and running? For example, a SaaS vendor might tell you that they back up data every day, but it might take several days to get the backup onto systems in another facility. You need to determine whether this meets your business imperatives.

✔ **Uptime:** Your provider might tell you that you will be able to access your data 99.999 percent of the time; however, read the contract. Does this uptime include scheduled maintenance?

✔ **Data storage costs:** Pay-as-you-go (you pay for what you use) and no capital purchase is appealing, but you need to read the fine print. For example, how much will it cost you to move your data into the cloud? What about other hidden integration costs? Then how much will it cost to store your data? You should do your own calculations so you're not caught off-guard. You need to find out how the provider is charging for data storage. Some providers offer a tiered pricing structure. Amazon, for example, charges you based on the average storage used throughout the month. This includes all object data and metadata stored in buckets that you created under your account.

✔ **Termination of contract:** How will data be returned if the contract is terminated? If you're using a SaaS provider and it has created data for you, too, will any of that data be returned? You need to ask yourself if this is an issue for you. Some companies just want the data destroyed. So, you need to understand how your provider will destroy your data, in order to make sure it doesn't continue to float around in the cloud.

✔ **Data ownership:** Who owns your data once it goes into the cloud? Some service providers may want to take your data, merge it with other data, and do some analysis.

- **Data access:** What controls are in place to make sure that you and only you (or whoever has access rights) can access your data? In other words, what forms of secure access control are in place? This includes identity management where the primary goal is protecting personal identity information so access to computer resources, applications, data, and services is controlled properly.

- **Threat management:** What software and procedures does your provider have in place to counter a variety of security threats that might affect your data? This includes intrusion protection.

Chapter 12

Managing Hybrid Workloads

. . . .

. . . .

*O*ne of the most important tasks required to manage a hybrid cloud environment is to manage a set of workloads that executes a specific set of commands. This is different than a traditional computing platform where it's assumed that workloads will be executed either on-premises or in a specific remote environment.

In cloud computing environments, workloads are abstracted from their physical implementation. Therefore, managing cloud workloads requires a different approach than companies may be accustomed to in a traditional environment. In this chapter, we discuss the characteristics of workloads in the hybrid cloud world and the ramifications of managing this environment.

What Is a Workload?

At its core, a *workload* is an independent service or collection of code that can be executed. Some industry experts include the application, operating system, and middleware in their definition of a workload. Because a workload is executed across computer assets, another way to look at it is the amount of work that needs to be accomplished by computer resources in a certain period of time.

Of course, different workloads have different characteristics, and the best platform for a particular workload to run on depends on the nature of the specific workload.

All workloads aren't the same

Because computing requirements are varied, so are the workloads. This list explains some of the kinds of workloads you might find in a hybrid cloud environment, and Table 12-1 compares them to each other:

- ✔ **Batch workloads:** These workloads are designed to operate in the background. Typical batch workloads tend to process huge volumes of data. These workloads may include the data produced from a set of cellphone bills or the results of months of online transactions. These workloads require considerable compute and storage resources. Batch workloads are rarely time sensitive and can be scheduled when few real-time tasks are running. Because this data is well documented and predictable, automating this type of workload is relatively easy. Generally, batch workloads are executed on a regular schedule and can take advantage of the economies of scale of public cloud services as a way to process these workloads. Again, as in any cloud environment, the decision of where to execute batch workloads is determined by business rules, governance, and security regulations.

- ✔ **Transactional workloads:** These are the automation of business processes such as billing and order processing. Traditionally, transactional workloads were restricted to a single system. However, with the increasing use of electronic commerce that reaches across partners and suppliers, transactional workloads must be managed across various partners' computing environments. So, there's a need to focus on business processes with these transactional workloads. These workloads are both compute- and storage-intensive. Depending on the cost-benefit analysis, it's likely that complex transactional workloads are best suited to a private cloud.

- ✔ **Analytic workloads:** Organizations may want to use analytic services in a cloud environment to make sense of the vast amounts of data across a complex hybrid environment. This requirement isn't simply a technical one; it's necessary for business partners to benchmark the success of their partnerships and to make adjustments to increase success. In an *analytics workload,* an emphasis is placed on the ability to holistically analyze the data embedded in these workloads across public websites, private clouds, and the data warehouse. These types of analytic workloads tend to require much more real-time computing capability.

- ✔ **High performance workloads:** These have a specialized process with scientific or technical requirements. These workloads are complex and typically require significant compute capabilities. Thus, they're well suited for specialized public clouds optimized for performance.

- ✔ **Database workloads:** These are the most common type of workload, and they affect almost every environment in the data center and the cloud. A database workload must be tuned and managed to support the service that's using that data. A database workload tends to use a lot of I/O (Input/Out) cycles. In some situations, data workloads are small and self-contained; however, in other situations, the data workloads are huge, and the performance requires a sophisticated approach. For example, high-performance database workloads may be implemented on bare metal (directly on the hardware's operating system) to support the business requirement.

Table 12-1	Workloads in the Cloud	
Workload Type	*Focus*	*Is It Time Sensitive?*
Batch workload	Processes large volumes of data in the background	Not time sensitive
Transactional workload	Focuses on large volume of current transactions	Typically requires real time
Analytic workload	Affects large amounts of data for decision making	Depending on the business, could be either batch or real time
High-performance workload	Has scientific or technical focus	Requires huge amounts of compute resources
Database workload	Is highly tuned to application needs	May require specialized hardware integration

Workloads not suited for the cloud

Just as some workloads are suited for the cloud, some are not. A few examples of workloads that you don't want to move to the cloud include:

✔ Workloads that need high-performance network storage. Because these workloads may need to be accessed very quickly, they may not be suited for the cloud where you're dependent on the Internet for network speed.

✔ Legacy application workloads that require very low latency. Often, legacy workloads weren't architected to run in a distributed computing environment. They may serve a particular purpose, and it may not make sense to move them to the cloud.

✔ Database clustering that requires very high throughput (speed) on the network. A large grouping of databases that requires millisecond response time may also not be suited for the cloud.

The massively scaled workload

It is probably clear at this point that all workloads are not the same. For example, a complex line of business application will have hundreds if not thousands of unique workloads that are specific to business processes. When you are dealing with so many unique workloads, it's very difficult to achieve much optimization. However, other workloads are able to be massively scaled. A *massively scaled* workload is able to have millions of users doing the exact same thing. For example, imagine that you have a data center where you are processing one transaction a thousand times a day. You could architect your data center so the hardware, software, storage, and networking are all optimized to be as fast and efficient as possible. If you execute this well, you are able to drive down the cost of processing each transaction to a fraction of the cost of a traditional data center that supports many different workloads.

In the cloud environment, the nature of the workload is critical to both the usability and affordability of a platform. If a workload is very simple, the cost per user is actually very low.

For example, Google's Gmail service is actually a very simple workload that is delivered in a massively scaled data center. Google has been able to optimize the Linux operating system and its software environment to support e-mail in the most efficient manner; therefore, it can easily support hundreds of millions of users. Likewise, Amazon.com with its IaaS supports very simple workloads. Amazon's data centers are optimized to support these workloads so that Amazon can continue to offer new services and support a growing customer base without breaking the bank. In fact, the ability to manage simple workloads in a very efficient manner is the secret behind the success of companies like Facebook and Twitter. These companies can scale their infrastructure rapidly without the scalability problems of traditional complex workload application environments. So, it's not surprising that a company built from the ground up to support these simple workloads can surpass an existing company that has the misfortune of supporting a huge number of complex workloads.

Abstraction and workloads

Workloads can be *abstracted* in cloud environments, meaning that the workload is isolated from the hardware it's running on. In fact, in most situations, the average customer has no idea where the workload runs. Although an individual workload doesn't depend on external elements, it's typically combined with other workloads to execute a business process or task.

The notion of abstraction is critical for how workloads run in the cloud and it's even more important in a hybrid cloud. The only way to create a distributed computing environment consisting of multiple services in multiple locations is to have well-architected, abstracted workloads.

Managing Workloads

Management, in this context, refers to how resources are assigned in order to process workloads. Assignments might be based on resource availability, business priorities, or event scheduling.

The idea of managing workloads has been around for decades. In the unified mainframe computing era, workload management was pretty straightforward. When a task had to be executed, a job was scheduled to run on that system. The instructions for running that task or job were typically written in a complex job-control instruction language. This set of commands helped the IT organization carefully plan the execution of workloads. If a mission-critical workload required a huge amount of time to run, a set of instructions could be established to stop that workload and allow another workload to run. When the second workload finished executing its task, the long-running workload could resume. If there were dependencies that the workload needed to complete a task, a command could be issued to go find that task so it could be executed and then the result added to the workload.

Here are a few principles to consider as you start to think about managing workloads in a cloud model:

✔ **Understand processing requirements.** In other words, you need to understand how your computing resources can execute your workloads on average and at peak demand. In general, IT often engineers its computing resources to meet the peak workload.

✔ **Use modeling resources.** You need to work out what CPU, disk, and memory are needed to execute workloads. Generally, you create some sort of model to do this. Your model might be a simple linear model that calculates the amount of CPU per service, or it might be something more complex.

✔ **Determine the capacity you need.** Optimize your resources based on required response time, number of services, and numerous other variables that need to be considered depending on what you're trying to accomplish with your workload.

The challenge in managing any workload is making sure that it can be executed and delivered at the right performance level. The principle is not that difficult if you're dealing with applications running on one server. However, as IT infrastructures become more complex and heterogeneous (such as in the hybrid cloud), this becomes harder to do.

The load balancer

In distributed computing environments, such as the cloud, a load balancer is often deployed to help ensure that no single machine is overwhelmed. *Load balancing* is the process where IP traffic is distributed across multiple servers. The figure illustrates a simple example of load balancing. Here, the load balancer sits in front of three servers and distributes the load across them. All three servers utilize the same database — the load balancer helps to optimize resource allocation across the servers.

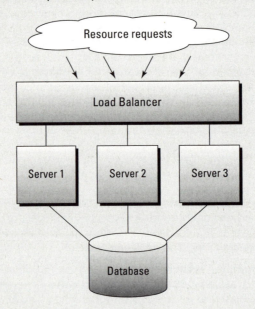

How does it do this? First, it needs to know where the data is coming from. Second, it needs to know which servers it's supposed to distribute the load across. Then it uses an algorithm to determine which machine to give the load to. For example, a popular algorithm is the round-robin algorithm, where a specific region on the distributed platform is used for the first request. Then, the next region is used for the next request, and so on. When the end of the list is reached, the next region used is the first one. And, so on. Of course, there are numerous different algorithms that can be used to balance workloads across servers. The round robin is just one of them.

Workload Complexities in the Hybrid Cloud Environment

The world is a lot more complicated with the hybrid cloud than it was with a single architecture (if only the world were still so simple!). With the advent of a hybrid cloud world, many more applications and services exist across geographies that have to run. Some workloads may be permanent and need to run constantly, such as an online commerce site or a control system that manages a critical environmental process. Virtualized workloads add another level of complexity. Business services and various application models are added into the mix as well.

In a hybrid cloud environment, your workloads may be running on different clouds, running different kinds of infrastructures using different operating systems. You're bringing together workloads from different environments that often have to behave as though they're a unified system.

Operationalizing workloads

What is the connection between workloads and workload management in the cloud? It's actually at the center of determining whether you have a well performing cloud environment or not. This is true whether you are a service provider offering either a public or private cloud to customers, or if you're managing an internal private cloud to benefit internal customers and external customers and partners.

You may think that all you have to do is get some automation software (to automatically schedule resources and to perform some other functions associated with allocating resources) and you're set. When you look at workloads from an operational perspective, it becomes clear that lots of issues need to be taken into account when determining how you create an overall hybrid cloud environment that both performs at a quality level and meets security and governance requirements. This is not a static requirement; from an operational perspective, organizations need to be able to dynamically change workload management based on changing business requirements.

For example, say a workload is now being used within a geography that has different rules for where data must be placed. If the data has to be stored within a country, then that workload has to be managed differently than the same workload running in a country without this type of governance requirement. With fewer restrictions, IT operations is free to move workloads to locations that have the bandwidth or capacity to meet the quality of service required by the business. In fact, the ability to change and move workloads based on business requirements is at the heart of operational issues in the cloud.

APIs: Key to managing cloud workloads

Application programming interfaces (APIs) enable a software product or service to communicate with another product or service. For example, if you're a software developer who has written a spreadsheet program and you want to allow another developer to add some specialized functions to enhance your application, you can provide the developer with an API that enables him to write to your application. The API specifies how the one application can work together with another one. It provides the rules and the interfaces. The developer doesn't need to know the nitty-gritty of your application because the API abstracts the way these programs can work together.

 An API also provides an abstracted way to exchange data and services. Because of this abstraction, the API can hide things from developers. For example, you don't want an outside developer to learn the details of your internal security, so those details of the system are hidden. The API allows the developer to execute only the intended task.

As you've probably surmised by now, APIs are important for managing workloads in a cloud environment. The Amazon Elastic Compute Cloud environment offers a rich set of APIs that allows customers to build their own workloads on top of Amazon's compute and storage services. In fact, every company that offers a foundational cloud service such as IaaS, SaaS, and PaaS develops APIs for its customers.

Everything is great as long as you manage your workload within the environment where you created it or where you will deploy it. However, many organizations are beginning to face the fact that different APIs aren't always compatible. For example, one API may be built to support a 32-bit operating system, and the cloud environment that the developer wants to move the workload to supports a 64-bit implementation. To make the transition from a 32-bit model to a 64-bit model requires extensive programming.

To better understand the complexities of the problem, consider what happens when you create workloads in the Amazon IaaS platform. Here are three common scenarios you might encounter:

✔ Amazon lets you create a set of connections to the network as a security group by assigning a permanent IP (Internet Protocol) address. If you try to connect this public service with a private cloud service, you'll find incompatibilities at the networking level.

✔ You create a workload for storage on Amazon and a second workload for storage in another public cloud for redundancy. You have a third storage workload running in the private cloud. When changes occur, you don't have a standard way to manage these three storage services. This situation can allow errors, thus preventing the three storage workloads from functioning as intended.

✔ Cloud APIs are all different. Although Amazon APIs have become a de facto standard, many more APIs have emerged in the market. For example, there is the Open Cloud initiative, the Open Cloud Stack, the IBM Smart Cloud, and the Microsoft Windows Azure market. None of these cloud APIs are compatible with each other.

The question becomes, how do you manage workloads across incompatible environments?

The necessity of a standard workload layer

As you see from the previous example, no standard API allows the developer to work with different cloud models provided by different cloud vendors. What is actually needed is a standard layer that creates compatibility among cloud workloads. In service orientation, the XML model allows for interoperability among business services. There's no equivalent model for the hybrid cloud.

Of course, you can always find ways to work around complicated problems. For example, in the cellphone market, vendors end up implementing both the U.S. and the European wireless connectivity standard into each phone set. Likewise, in hybrid workload management, companies such as cloud management provider RightScale (`www.rightscale.com`), IBM's Workload Deployer (`www.IBM.com`), and BMC's Control-M (`www.BMC.com`) create customizable templates that allow developers to make allowances for the differences in APIs and thus are able to deploy and migrate workloads.

Portability of workloads

Discussing APIs and standards is essential because workload management is fundamental to the operation of the hybrid cloud. In a hybrid cloud environment, being able to move workloads around and optimize them based on the business problem being addressed is critical. Despite the fact that workloads are abstracted, they are built with middleware and operating systems. In addition, workloads must be tuned to perform well in a specific hardware environment. In today's hybrid computing world, a lot of manual intervention is needed to achieve workload portability. However, we anticipate future standards and well-defined approaches that will make hybrid cloud workload management a reality.

The advent of hybrid computing will lead to the evolution of a new component in cloud computing. The broker of hybrid service workloads will provide a layer that will examine the infrastructure of the underlying cloud-based service and provide a consistent and predictable way to handle different workloads as though they were built the same way. We expect that this hybrid service workload broker will provide the hybrid workload management that the market will demand. When standards evolve, the need for part of this layer will go away, but the broad use of standards takes time.

Managing hybrid workloads

Managing workloads in a hybrid cloud environment requires a set of distinctive steps, including these:

✔ Keeping track of dependencies among specific services, such as Software as a Service, and Business Process as a Services like credit checking services. The management environment needs to manage these relationships.

   • Workloads need to be scheduled based on business policy and required dependencies for third-party processes.

   • The workloads need to be monitored and optimized based on the company's service-level requirements.

✔ Governance of workload management is essential for success. The IT organization needs to guarantee that corporate and governmental regulations are adhered to. For example, in the hybrid world, it may be necessary to execute a workload in a particular country. In other situations, some data must be stored within a special secure environment.

For more information about management in the hybrid environment, see Chapter 4.

Making Workload Management Transparent

In the hybrid cloud environment, providing transparency to a set of workloads is important, no matter where they're physically located and which virtualization technologies are used. So, successful vendors look at workload automation from a holistic perspective. Organizations must also be able to include their on-premises systems as part of the overall workload management environment. As data centers become more streamlined and focused, including those workloads as part of an overall hybrid-distributed computing environment will become easier.

Obviously, there's a huge value to balancing workloads in a hybrid cloud environment. In a traditional data center, workloads tend to be constructed as complete applications rather than independent workloads. Typically, when an application is complex and expensive to operate, costs are simply spread out across the departments that leverage the application. The criteria for success has been accessibility to that application in the data center that needs to connect to resources located in the hybrid cloud. Now, the criteria for success is a model that combines the need for performance, reliability, and security in a constantly changing world. The challenge is to create a customer experience that is flexible, affordable, and predictable.

Balancing the acceptable level of risk and the acceptable level of service is delicate. So, before you make decisions related to workload management in a hybrid cloud, ask yourself the following questions:

- ✔ What is the purpose of your workloads and how do they support the business?
- ✔ What are the legal risks that are unacceptable?
- ✔ What is the reputation of the public cloud providers?
- ✔ How well does your internal organization understand the various internal and external workloads that need to be supported?

You need to be practical in how you address these questions. As we have pointed out in this chapter, there are many different types of workloads. If the workloads require real-time performance, you need to keep those workloads as close to the source of the transactions as possible. However, some workloads can run with less stringent performance and can be placed in a less expensive cloud model. However, you shouldn't compromise the reputation of your company. Therefore, you need to do you homework. You need to work with business leaders in your company that can pinpoint the risks you need to avoid. Part of that risk is selecting a cloud provider that is here today and gone tomorrow. Workload management must be viewed as an overall part of your hybrid cloud management strategy. Therefore, planning for managing workloads goes hand in hand with a strong cloud strategy plan.

Chapter 13

Architectural Considerations for the Hybrid Environment

*U*nderstanding all the different models available for cloud deployments is important, but to be successful in the hybrid cloud world, you need to understand the architectural view. The *architectural view* includes both the underlying processes and computing elements combined with best practices needed to create a model that can stand the test of time. Start by asking these questions:

Who are the constituents that will be served by the cloud?

What functions are needed to meet your company's requirements?

What's the nature of the workloads that you need to support in the cloud?

What are the range of on-premises services that need to interact with your cloud services?

The reality is that cloud computing is part of your overall computing model. As with everything else in the world, nothing is black and white. There are tradeoffs to be made. However, at the end of the day, the way you plan and execute your computing environment will be tied directly to your optimal customer experience. In this chapter, we discuss the open issues and considerations in planning an environment that serve the best interest of your internal and external customers.

What type of constituents does your cloud serve?

Three constituents that are part of the cloud ecosystem determine how you view the cloud architecture:

- **Cloud consumers:** The individuals and groups within an organization that use different types of cloud services to get a task accomplished. A cloud consumer could be a developer using compute services from a public cloud or a partner that uses a private cloud environment to purchase products or services.

- **Cloud service provider:** These can be commercial vendors or companies that create their own capabilities. The commercial vendors sell their services to cloud consumers. In contrast, a company might decide to become an internal cloud service provider to its own employees, partners, and customers — either as an internal service or as a profit center. These providers also create applications or services for these environments.

- **Cloud broker:** A cloud broker brings together services from a variety of suppliers to create an overall hybrid cloud environment. An organization that provides brokering services may be in charge of negotiating the contract between the provider and the consumer of services.

Depending on what your organization does will set the requirements for how you plan your cloud architecture. If you're a cloud consumer, you have the responsibility to select the right set of services based on your business requirements. You don't need to think about how to necessarily architect each element; instead think about how to link elements together that you'll use. A cloud consumer has to be careful not to create a set of disconnected silos that can't be managed.

In contrast, if your organization is a cloud service provider, you'll spend a lot more time architecting the elements. You also need to understand how to build applications and business services that are optimized for this environment. These service creators need to be concerned with consistency of the services that they're building so that they can support their customers — both short-term and for the long run.

A cloud service provider can be a commercial vendor selling services, or it could be an internal resource designed for the use of employees and partners. The cloud service provider has to create an entire environment that can easily connect with an ecosystem of partners.

Putting the Pieces Together

How do all the components of a cloud model fit together from an architectural perspective? Figure 13-1, which is from the National Institute of Standards and Technology (www.nist.gov/index.html), depicts the various cloud services and how they relate to each other based on the three constituents. On the left side of this diagram, the cloud service consumer represents the types of consumers of cloud services. This includes all those consumers, such as the end user of a service, bringing a group of services together for internal and external users; and the business management that needs to have these services available as part of business strategy implementation. Within this category are the applications, middleware, infrastructure, and services that are built based on on-premises computing models. In addition, this model depicts the role of the cloud auditor. This organization provides the oversight either by an internal or an external group that makes sure that the consumer group meets its obligations.

Cloud service providers

Cloud service providers (see the center of Figure 13-1) represent all the models of cloud services that we discuss in Chapters 5–8. A cloud service provider might be a commercial company or a corporation that decides to become its own cloud service operator. Cloud providers may provide the underlying physical and virtualized resources needed to run various cloud services. They also may create the actual applications and business services that operate in these environments.

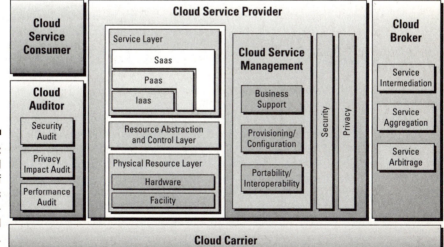

Figure 13-1: The National Institute of Standards and Technology cloud architecture.

These various cloud models don't exist in isolation — they're all related to each other. In addition, there's an entire ecosystem of partners that support various vendors with offerings. The cloud service provider provides a unified architecture to support and manage these services in a consistent manner. Managing these services is a major requirement for any cloud service provider. These management platforms have to provide both support for the operation of the various services as well as managing the way they perform to support business requirements.

The cloud provider has to support all of the important cloud models that we discuss in Chapters 5 through 8. In addition to SaaS, PaaS, and IaaS, we would like to add Business Process as a Service (BPaaS) — which is not included in the NIST diagram — because we think that it's an important fourth cloud delivery model. In addition to supporting the physical and virtual environment, it is important to remember that all of these cloud models and the supporting environment have to be linked together in the form of service orchestration. Without service orchestration, each service would become an independent silo.

Clearly, all the components in the cloud provider model must be managed. There have to be services to support the business, to manage configurations, and to provision the right resources on demand. Management services must also support interoperability and service portability. For more details on cloud management, take a look at Chapter 4.

Planning for Deployment

The hybrid cloud isn't a single architectural model; rather, it's a combination of a lot of different services that are located on different platforms. Therefore, there isn't a simple way to define a hybrid architecture. Instead, from an architecture perspective, it's important to look at the relationship among the services that are used together. Therefore, the usage of cloud management technologies (see Chapter 4 for more details on hybrid cloud management) needs to be considered as part of the architectural framework of the hybrid cloud.

In the hybrid cloud, you will never bring all services and elements together as though they were one system. Instead, you need to have a clear understanding of the distributed services and how they relate to each other. Many of the approaches require the creation of best-practices templates that can be used to create the right linkages between services. One of the best practices needed is to be able to keep track of what task a specific service executes, the rules for how it can be used, as well as definitions and dependencies. But the issues don't stop with dependency. In a world where you're going to leverage services based on different physical and virtual environments, you need to think about how the entire environment behaves under different circumstances. A well-designed hybrid cloud environment has to be built to support change. Change can be the addition of an additional cloud service, such as a SaaS application or a new business partner and their set of services. In essence, hybrid models have five primary architectural considerations:

✔ Latency and performance

✔ Security

✔ Governance

✔ Reliability in the context of change

We discuss each one throughout this section.

Latency: Performance matters

When planning your hybrid model, you need to consider the overall perfor-mance of your platform, which means that you have to monitor and measure your entire environment. For example, say that a critical issue for your business is the speed at which customers' orders are confirmed. If you don't handle this issue efficiently, customers won't be happy and may move to another supplier. So, you may want to keep transaction management running within a private cloud or data center environment. If you were to use a public cloud transaction management service, the latency involved in moving data between networks would cause service delays. In addition, some applications require regular access to and manipulation of complex data. If this were to happen on a regular basis, you might not be able to perform as customers expect. In this situation, stick with either your current on-premises solution or a well-architected private cloud environment. On the other hand, you may discover that for other applications, such as customer management or human resource management workloads, a SaaS application provides acceptable latency to meet the needs of your constituents.

In addition to the performance of a specific cloud service, you need to consider the location of a service. A service in a public cloud may be fine for one type of use but may have unacceptable latency when several services need to exchange data very rapidly. Therefore, part of the hybrid architecture requires that you understand what role each service plays and how those services need to interact with each other.

Determining when to use a public versus private service depends on the context of what service is being delivered to the customer. The choices you make will depend on the task being executed. Therefore, you need to build the need for flexibility into the way you plan for latency in a hybrid cloud environment. For example, if you're setting up a collaborative workspace with three partners, a public cloud environment will be cost-effective, and depending on the type of collaboration, this environment may perform well based on the type of collaboration being conducted.

However, if you have set up a mission-critical, high-volume transaction management platform, performance must be optimized. In contrast, if customers are looking up information occasionally or if data can be easily distributed, latency will not be an overarching problem. Many services have low volumes of data, in which case the system won't constantly reach for massive amounts of data from on-premises data sources. These environments are practical for a public cloud platform environment.

Although people typically think of individual models and services, it's worth looking at the issue of latency differently. Instead of assuming that each service runs as a stand-alone service, imagine that you combine a number of services to create a composite service. For example, say that you have a service where latency must be very low, but you want to take advantage of an inexpensive public commodity service in combination with a secure private cloud and some on-premise services. In this situation, you must determine which components of the environment will benefit from the public cloud services so that they match the overall service level requirement. As the needs of the organization change, it will be important to be able to change the location of a service if a different level of performance is required. There are situations where the volume of data that a customer needs to access has expanded so much that a different configuration will be needed.

Can encapsulation reduce latency?

In a service-oriented approach to computing, you can tightly couple a set of services that must execute with low latency. Pioneers in the services oriented architecture (SOA) market learned the hard way that loosely *coupling* (or connecting) business services doesn't always provide the level of performance an organization needs. After learning this lesson, companies began tightly coupling services that needed faster performance. You can apply these same techniques to a cloud environment.

Creating *encapsulated services* (services where the elements needed to execute a service are combined together and provided with a clearly defined interface) that work as advertised isn't easy. Technologists have struggled with getting this right for years. For example, the best practice of isolating underlying systems and software from the composite service is often ignored. Although this can be a huge problem within a data center, it can be *disastrous* in a hybrid cloud environment. Simply put, if you have a dependency to an outside service running in an encapsulated service that is used within a hybrid cloud environment, this dependency will cause failures. That failure may not happen until the dependent service is suddenly changed. For example, the service might require a certain version of a database. When that database is updated, the service will still look for the old version of the database. So, even when you do tightly couple services to reduce latency, you still need to follow the principle of loose coupling — services should be free of dependencies. At the end of the day, a well-constructed hybrid cloud must follow good engineering principles.

Security: Planning in context

When planning your hybrid environment, at the outset, you need to think about the security requirements for customers. What type of environment are you providing for your customers? Are you creating an informational resource that might be tied to a set of product data sheets? However, if you've created a platform that manages private health data, you must ensure that you've created the level of protection and privacy your customers demand. (Check Chapter 15 for more details about security and governance.) You need to understand these considerations before you begin your design. So, make sure your cloud providers can match your requirements.

Governance: Getting the right balance

Like security, governance requirements will determine how you plan and architect your hybrid cloud environment. Many industries have rules of engagement that are considered best practices. If you're part of an industry that's required to meet sophisticated governance requirements, it's important to select partners that meet your needs. You may discover that you can't use a third party for this part of your environment. Likewise, many countries have strict guidelines and requirements for how private data must be handled. In some countries, for example, an individual's data must be stored physically within that country. These types of governance requirements demand that IT organizations plan their platform with this in mind. This means including process management services that determine where data must be stored. Which means that, in some countries, data is stored in a single physical data center. In other countries, data may be highly distributed across geographies without violating rules. Some cloud providers can implement automated policies that ensure that certain services run based on these rules.

Again, it's critical to validate that your cloud vendors can meet your business requirements. For example, you must make sure that you can deploy your application and data in a specific country or region if necessary. The bottom line is that you have to match your architectural plan with the governance requirements in both your company and the industry.

Managing co-location

In the real world, compromise is a requirement for making computing perform well at an affordable price. In a perfect world, cost would never be an issue, but in complicated environments, compromise is a reality. The trick is to be able to manage across a hybrid environment that creates an architecturally balanced approach. So, when planning your hybrid cloud environment, you need to first select applications that fit well into the benefits and limitations of the cloud. Applications that do not match well for such a public cloud environment may need to stay on-premises, either on a traditional middleware deployment or in a private cloud environment. When companies or cloud creators have carefully architected their applications or services, they will be well-positioned to support a hybrid cloud environment.

Creating flexibility in the model

Companies looking at cloud computing typically assume that it's an all or nothing model. However, cloud computing is simply part of an overall distributed architectural plan. Within an architectural framework, determining business, performance, and customer goals is important, and to do so, you must take into account all aspects of computing.

As we mention earlier in this chapter, you need to consider the issue of latency of overall performance and latency of managing data. If applications and services being offered to customers are based on a tightly coupled set of services with many dependencies, a public cloud service will cause serious problems with performance. However, if the organization is creating and leveraging a platform of well-defined and loosely coupled services that are designed to be easily linked together at runtime, a public cloud service is ideal.

Most organizations have a combination of these two scenarios; thus, architecturally, you need to think of your platform as a combination of data center, private cloud, and public cloud services. When you approach architectural considerations from this holistic perspective, the customer is well served and protected.

Some vendors will actually help you by providing several deployment options (public, private, data center) from the same platform, making it easier for your company to have a unified platform that can adapt to a wide number of use cases and constraints.

Setting the Right Policies and Business Rules

Companies generally think about policy and business rules from an overall governance perspective. On the contrary, making policies and rules operational in a hybrid cloud environment means that these dictates must be integrated from an architectural perspective. Building a policy or rule into the actual application may be straightforward in an on-premises environment. In a hybrid environment, however, you must make sure those policy requirements can be applied across components. For example, if a policy requires that personal data about French customers is stored in a physical server in France, this policy must be designed as a middleware service that controls the movement of data based on rules and conditions. It's not practical to try to implement each rule and policy inside each component of the hybrid environment.

Navigating the Choices in a Hybrid World

The great thing about a hybrid cloud is that the environment allows you to select the right service for the right task. But, you might ask, how do I select the right balance of services from an architectural perspective? Think about the collection of requirements from a business perspective and match that perspective to an architectural approach.

In general, you want the platforms you select to be appropriate for the service level requirements of the business. If a portion of your environment requires real-time performance and guaranteed uptime, you will choose a public service with a sophisticated Quality of Service (QoS) or a completely private service that your company controls. For services such as customer relationship management, where availability and manageability are the most important business concerns, a SaaS environment makes business sense. From both an architectural and a business process perspective, you must decide which services need to interact with each other and which ones are, in essence, stand-alone services. In the end, you want to end up with a highly optimized environment that matches the needs of the customers that you need to support.

Optimizing for Workloads

Being able to optimize workloads across environments is one of the fundamental architectural principles of hybrid cloud computing. (For more on workload management, see Chapter 12.) Unless workload optimization and balancing are one of the starting points, satisfying customer requirements will be difficult. One way to allow interoperability across workloads is through federation. *Federation* is a technique for linking together different environments at the interface level. Common interfaces across different public and private cloud services are needed. Even if various services aren't federated, consumers of cloud services must at least have an uncomplicated way to access data or business services across different environments and networks. Keep in mind, however, that the creation of true portability and interoperability of workloads across hybrid cloud environments is at an early stage.

Supporting a Dynamic Lifecycle

The lifecycle of cloud computing is different in many ways from the lifecycle of a traditional computing environment. The architecture of the cloud environment is predicated on the ability to abstract the details away from users based on a services-oriented architecture. As a result of the cloud, you must think about the term lifecycle in a new way. Now the focus isn't on disconnected tools and capabilities; instead, the cloud begins to enforce a discipline that has been missing in traditional computing environments. One of the benefits of a cloud environment is that it is designed to support change. To support changing numbers of users, applications, and workloads requires an environment that is architected for change. Therefore, the lifecycle of working with the architecture has to expect changes. One day you might be supporting 100 developers who are working on a new experimental application that will be gone in a month. The architecture has to expect shifts in workloads.

Your business will gain real benefits by approaching cloud computing as a dynamic architectural model that speeds the development and deployment of applications and that makes linking services together easier. For example, you might find that by tying together development and deployment in the cloud environment that there are fewer misunderstandings between those developing applications and those deploying those applications. In addition, when a company adds new employees through an acquisition, it will be straightforward to provision additional capacity or to add more users to a SaaS application. Because security becomes a service within the cloud environment, it is much easier to update and change security requirements.

As you start thinking about supporting a dynamic lifecycle to support a hybrid cloud environment, consider the following:

✔ Think about an overall services-based model that breaks down traditional disconnected silos of applications, processes, and services.

✔ Think about creating an environment with fewer dependencies so that when you add new cloud services, you'll have the flexibility to advance as the industry advances.

✔ Think about the performance requirements that will give your customers excellent experiences.

✔ Think about creating a predictable, safe, and well-governed environment that will support business operations in the long run.

Part V
Operationalizing Hybrid Clouds

The 5th Wave   By Rich Tennant

"We take network security here very seriously."

In this part . . .

The hybrid cloud is only as good as the operational support it provides to your internal users, customers, and partners. In this section, we address issues — such as manageability and planning for the future — that make the hybrid cloud work in the real world.

Chapter 14

Development and Deployment in a Hybrid Cloud

*T*he typical enterprise utilizes many applications. Some of these may be large, monolithic legacy applications that are built in-house and customized. There may be smaller homegrown applications, too. You might use packaged enterprise applications for ERP and business intelligence. You may even be using SaaS applications purchased from a service provider. There's also a good chance that, if you've embraced the cloud as an organization, you'll make the decision to actually build some new applications that will run in it.

You may want to work with your partners via a cloud service or even deploy some cloud-based applications specifically for your sales team. In this chapter, we examine how to build, deploy, and manage applications in the cloud and for the cloud.

Examining Changes for Development and Deployment in a Cloud

There are numerous scenarios in which you might want to write an application for the hybrid cloud. Here are a few:

✔ You want to write an application for the cloud that will work with the customized applications you already have in place.

✔ You want to write applications that can work on-premises and reach into the cloud. For example, these applications may burst into the cloud for peak situations.

✔ You may want to write applications for the cloud that can be leveraged across multiple clouds.

Of course, the market is still very nascent when it comes to building and deploying hybrid cloud–based applications. So, what's important? Some parts of the puzzle include

✔ **Service orientation:** In Chapter 3, we discuss service orientation in the cloud. As we mention in that chapter, service orientation is an architectural approach based on implementing business processes as software services. These business services consist of a set of loosely coupled components — designed to minimize dependencies — assembled to support a well-defined business task. Enterprises that have invested in designing infrastructure with a service-oriented approach will be in a better position to integrate internal services with cloud services. Enterprises that have focused on taking existing infrastructure and wrapping key components so they can be exposed as services are ready to begin to integrate service in a hybrid environment.

✔ **Scalability:** Applications will need to be architected to work in a cloud so they can scale out across cloud boundaries. It's not just about writing an application that's going to live on a few servers. It's about building them to utilize potentially many servers. When people familiar with the cloud talk about scalability, they use the terms *scale-up* versus *scale-out*. Scale-up refers to increasing memory/CPU on the server, and scale out refers to scaling resources across many, many nodes. You need to architect an application in a way to work across machines. You also need to predict how an application behaves because it needs to be built in a way that can support this cloud horizontal scalability. In other words, the code needs to potentially work as pieces across multiple machines. This includes the facts that the application will need to support a stateless protocol model (that is, each call on an object can stand alone), that each piece of code is modular with loose coupling (as described in the previous bullet), and that the same code can be run across multiple machines.

✔ **Service synchronization and dependencies:** An application might include databases, message services, and other services. Traditionally, if an application needed a certain service, say a database service, the service was handled by mapping references to physical addresses. Of course, this changes in the cloud because you may not know the IP addresses beforehand, which means that finding resources needs to be part of the application.

✔ **Availability:** Experts also advise that developers need to consider a plan for failure, including considerations around *Mean Time to Failure* (MTTF, the predicted elapsed time between system failures) and *Mean Time to Recovery* (MTTR).

If you look at any one enterprise, there's a good chance you'll find a mix of development environments and processes. Development may be done in silos for siloed applications. Developers may be restricted by the lack of resources. Perhaps the tools they're using were developed to handle the most complex problems. As companies transition to developing in the cloud, it's important for them to begin understanding how to abstract away some of the complexity. Of course, doing so will take time.

Big benefits of developing and deploying applications to the cloud are its elasticity and scalability. The infrastructure you need for development and deployment can be automatically scaled up or down, based on the requirements of the application. This field is evolving, however, and it pays to do the math. Many vendors will charge based on the utilization of underlying resources, which might include usage per hour, processing, bandwidth, and storage.

We've been talking about developers in both medium- and large-sized corporations that are building applications to run complex businesses. There's a whole different class of developers — the Internet-scale developer— who may be interested in different sets of problems than enterprise developers. These Internet developers address problems that, from the get-go, are ready for scale and building for performance and failures of the Internet. One example of an Internet-scale developer is a social media analytics services company that develops analytics that cull through massive amounts of social media data. This developer may be using new suites of tools like those we mention in Chapter 11 for data and big data.

Developing and Delivering Applications with PaaS

One way organizations are looking to develop applications in the cloud and for the cloud is by using a PaaS approach. Developing in a PaaS environment differs from the way development organizations have designed software over the past few decades. In a traditional model, the development team may select a variety of different tools — operating systems, middleware, security products, and the like. If the team is very experienced, this is a fine choice. Many organizations have been very effective with this approach. However, typically, there are problems in managing complexity — especially in an era where more and more aspects of daily life are controlled by software.

We talk about some of these factors in the previous section, but the following list highlights a few factors that make it hard for development teams to synchronize their efforts, whether their work environment is on-premises or in the cloud:

✔ Teams are distributed across business units or different geographic regions of a company.

✔ Software code needs to work across multiple platforms and devices.

✔ The software development process requires individual components that all need to work together in a service-oriented way.

✔ Market dynamics lead to a faster software development lifecycle.

All of these factors lead up to one thing. The software quality and time to develop will suffer unless the team has a way to test for, locate, and fix errors early in the software development process.

In a PaaS model, the development organization uses a platform and its services to help develop and deploy applications to the cloud. The platform consists of a group of services that can help to streamline the process. We now explain these services in more detail.

Developing applications using PaaS

PaaS is a kind of cloud development platform. It provides hosted services used during development, such as middleware and operating systems. Over the past few years, as early adopter companies started to develop for the cloud, often developers cobbled together their own cloud development platform. In a PaaS however, these services are always available for a developer to use without having to install or maintain software.

Application development services are the core of PaaS support for the development process. They're the anchor services that streamline the process of developing applications in the cloud. A PaaS platform

✔ Provides the developer with a complete environment to provision, develop, build, test, and stage applications

✔ Abstracts the details from the developer so that developers can focus on the task of coding and not on supporting the systems needed for development and testing

Integrated development environments (IDEs) are commonly used by developers on their desktop in traditional environments and can also be used with shared cloud services when using PaaS. There are some key advantages for a developer when the IDE is used with the cloud. You can still use your existing IDE on your desktop, but it becomes much easier and faster to share your code with other members of your team. You can push your code into a shared repository in the cloud so everyone has immediate access to the same code and tools.

Also, you can test your code during development against the same systems your end users will access, using services provided by the PaaS. As a result, errors in the code are found earlier, and the resulting applications are delivered faster.

Throughout this section, we list some of the most important software development services that may be offered by your PaaS provider.

It's important to note that a PaaS development environment may require you to limit how you develop in order to be compatible with the underlying services. For example, suppose you want to update your application and choose to go with tools that aren't part of the prescribed environment. You can still do this, but you lose some of the efficiency of working within a more controlled environment. If you break the mold and do the update outside the framework, you need to do it manually. This means that there is the risk of vendor lock-in with a PaaS. Some vendors are entering the market claiming that their software won't lock you in. So, it's important to ask a lot of questions.

Hosted software configuration management services

Developers use software configuration management services to keep track of the different versions and modules of code that are created during the software development process. The code is stored in an online repository. GitHub (https://github.com) is an example of a popular hosted service used for this purpose.

These software configuration management services help a developer manage the sandbox environment used to create and test code. The developer stores software code (sometimes also known as a *forge*) in the sandbox. This environment needs to include the right operating system and tools, such as source code editors, debuggers, compilers, performance profilers, and source code management systems (to know when and how a piece of software has changed).

Build services

The PaaS should be able to support a variety of application build processes that allow developers to combine services into a deployable application. There are several steps in the build process, including writing code, compiling code into an executable file, invoking code, and running and then testing the code. When creating an application, developers generally produce multiple modules of code with dependencies. The build services in the PaaS should help developers keep track of the individual modules of code. An example of a tool for this is Maven (http://maven.apache.org). Maven is used by many Java developers to build and assemble their applications as well as to manage dependencies on other third-party software modules.

Web application server

The PaaS environment can help developers quickly test the applications they're building by allowing developers to deploy using the production run-time system. This type of testing is important because a developer typically creates a web application using his own local environment, and because of the difficulty of getting access to more than a single machine, the developer's environment may be very different from the production environment. To tighten testing cycles, the developer might use an in-process web application server that works perfectly on a local environment, but then behaves differently in production. The PasS makes it easy to access and isolate production systems, so that developers can stop wasting time mocking up simulations and avoid the risk of discovering runtime errors in production or at late stages of delivery.

Frameworks

Developers typically use a development framework to help them create quality software that performs well under varying conditions. Although frameworks are used in traditional software environments, these frameworks can be more consistently shared across large distributed teams when used in a PaaS environment. Some of the key benefits of using frameworks in a PaaS environment include

- ✔ The ability to quickly establish a consistent structure for an application
- ✔ Ready access to secure and tested foundational software modules for coding
- ✔ Easy access to runtime services for testing to make sure that the application will run properly in production

Spring (`www.springsource.org`) is one of the most commonly used application development frameworks for Enterprise Java.

Database services

One of the most important tests for a new application is how it will work with real end-user data. This type of testing often presents a challenge for developers because the application may be intended to work with data stored in a very large and complex database. Developers often install a lightweight database in their development environment in order to test the code with data, but then aren't able to test against a true production database during the development phase.

One of the major advantages of developing in a PaaS environment is that the developer can have immediate access to a database with the same characteristics of the eventual production database. For example, if the application will need to call a MySQL database in production, the developer can leverage PaaS database services to test the code with hosted MySQL database already provided by the PaaS.

Testing tools

Testing services can be built into the PaaS platform or provided by its eco-system of services. These services can include user-interface testing or load testing. Access to these tools is beneficial to companies of all sizes; however, the impact on small to mid-size companies can be huge. Smaller companies may not have the resources to purchase and maintain the state of the art tools designed to improve the quality of the development process. These smaller teams can use PaaS to have access to the same best practice environment that many of the larger competitors have built in-house at a very high price. For example, Jenkins is the most widely used continuous integration server; it initiates build jobs as developers' check-in code.

Performance analysis tools

There are limits to how many different kinds of tests can be applied to the code in a developer's local environment. Performance analysis, including production profiling and load testing, is hard for a developer to do on her own. For example, it's difficult for a developer to replicate the wide range of machines and networks that may be found in end-user environments. Examples of cloud-based tools designed for this purpose include these two:

- **SOASTA:** (www.soasta.com) Leverages cluster of cloud machines to simulate user load on your application based on a number of criteria (number and type of clients, geographical location, load pattern, and so on)

- **New Relic:** (www.newrelic.com) Designed to provide insight to end-user behavior, monitor server behavior, and identify bottlenecks

From development to test to production coordination services

The PaaS provider can provide services that enable updates of cloud applications without interrupting services. For example, in your data center, you most likely roll out the new version of the software to one segment of users at a time. With PaaS, you can make sure that the flow between development, testing, and deployment is more seamless. PaaS can help you to guarantee no loss of uptime.

Although these concerns cross more into deployment, they also affect development. For example, a Java web application might make use of a session store to ensure state is maintained in the event of failure and across updates. The PaaS provider can help by providing a built-in session store capability and by automatically coordinating the update rollout process. So, the developer can make use of the session store directly, and also test to make sure it always works properly during the development lifecycle. As the application is updated, the developer can also ensure that application-level changes work across versions using the same session store.

Deploying applications using PaaS

PaaS automates many aspects of the deployment lifecycle that are typically managed by IT development staff in traditional environments. Some of the deployment functions built into PaaS platforms are

- ✔ Allocation of resources
- ✔ Staging and testing applications
- ✔ Installing, configuring, and securing load balancers and application servers
- ✔ Installing, configuring, and securing databases
- ✔ Monitoring and notification services

The standardization of PaaS deployment lifecycle services means that the services are both easier to deploy and easier to maintain in a consistent manner. In a PaaS environment, all the key deployment functions are abstracted from the developer. As a result, PaaS makes the process of updating applications once they've been deployed faster and more efficient.

You may be wondering what will happen if you try to change those predetermined patterns. As we stated in the previous section, there is a tradeoff you need to make to leverage many of the benefits of PaaS, and that tradeoff is that you may be locked into the PaaS platform tools. It's a decision you need to make.

Staging and testing applications in PaaS

The PaaS environment allows for greater flexibility in the way that deployment teams create *staging areas* for their applications — staging areas are environments used to test changes to a private version of an application before the new or revised application goes live. Setting up the staging area appropriately can take a lot of time and manual effort on the part of the IT team. The staging area needs to completely replicate the databases, web servers, connections, and other dynamic components of the application environment, or you run the risk of allowing errors into your live system. All of this can be quickly and easily handled with PaaS, which allows developers to focus more on meeting customer requirements and less on IT infrastructure issues.

As a user of PaaS deployment services, you expect the following in your staging environment:

- ✔ Full mirror of your live environment for the switch
- ✔ Rollback to environment previous to change if errors are found
- ✔ Partitioning of existing cloud resources for phased deployment and testing within predefined limits

Load balancing and secure connection services

Your PaaS provider needs to ensure that the load balancing service will adequately support your end users regardless of how they access your application (desktop, mobile). You want assurance that your end users will always be routed over a secure channel to a live endpoint.

Data management services

Users of PaaS services need to trust that their provider will maintain all service level agreements related to scalability and isolation of their data. You need to be confident that all requests for more disk space or additional instances as well as any updates to your database will affect only your data.

In Chapter 7, we provide an overview of some vendors that are providing PaaS services. These include heavyweights like Amazon Web Services, Google Apps, and Microsoft Windows Azure. Other providers include Appistry, CloudBees, and OpenShift.

Monitoring and notification services

All aspects of the PaaS environment that may affect end-user performance need to be monitored. It's critical that security issues are given the utmost attention by your PaaS environment.

Your runtime environment needs as much security and protection as your development environment to support customer and suppliers.

To monitor security and prevent intrusion or denial of service attacks, your PaaS provider will need to scan networks, operating systems, and applications. In addition, you will need to have sufficient insight into the monitoring capabilities to satisfy audit requirements.

Questions for your PaaS provider

A well-designed PaaS environment has enough flexibility and modularity to be useful in many different scenarios and to handle a wide range of development objectives. In addition, the PaaS environment must be able to support developers with a wide range of services that encompass the entire software development lifecycle. You can use the following list of questions to ensure that your PaaS provider offers the right set of flexible services so you can make the most of your PaaS development and deployment environment.

- Can you choose from a menu of à la carte services so you can select the services that are right for you?
- Can you start slowly with just a few services and then add on later if needed?

- ✔ Are your choices constrained in any way based on the specifications of your PaaS provider?

- ✔ Will the PaaS provider host the specific services you want to use, so you can use them in the PaaS environment and don't have to host them yourself?

- ✔ Are sophisticated build and testing services made available in such a way as to encourage early identification of software coding errors?

- ✔ How will the provider ensure that your web application can scale? How will the provider guarantee that your web application can take on an unanticipated increased load and still perform?

- ✔ What is the provider's solution for autoscaling and high availability?

- ✔ If one of your machines goes down, how will the provider ensure that end-user experience stays the same?

- ✔ What is the provider's plan for disaster recovery? Does it support running in multiple regions so that your application will automatically be supported in an alternative region if your base region is struck by a disaster?

- ✔ Is the provider's development framework easily accessible and easy to update during runtime? The PaaS needs to make it possible to make the updates. If you update the frameworks in your PaaS, will all your dependent frameworks be updated automatically?

The same set of PaaS services will not be right for everyone. You should demand flexibility and a variety of options from your PaaS vendor.

Internet-scale development using PaaS

When you start with platforms like PaaS that abstracts you from the underlying infrastructure, in some ways you go on faith that they can support you. The key questions are how much of the infrastructure do you need to manage, and can your PaaS provider achieve this scale? Some Internet developers may start in a PaaS, but then outgrow it when they begin developing a really big application. In this case, developers may need to manage their own software in an IaaS, using some services offered by the IaaS provider and customizing their own services. A different mindset may be required for this kind of developer who may be using Hadoop or NoSQL technologies (which we talk about in Chapter 11).

At Internet scale, application workloads may be running across thousands of nodes across the world. You will need an intimate understanding of how your application runs against infrastructure.

Managing Heterogeneous Applications

When your application is on your premises, you control it. This means you control the whole stack — the infrastructure, the operating system, the middleware, the data, the application, and the runtime environment. In a PaaS environment, the PaaS provider manages everything up to the application and possibly the database. The provider is dealing with installs, updates, and patches to the production environment. It's a self-managed environment. The issue becomes this — how can you manage cloud applications together with those developed on-premises? You need to measure the impact of IT performance on the business that, by definition, now includes the performance of the cloud provider.

Here's a simple scenario that drives home this point. Assume you have contracted with a PaaS provider to build and deploy your application. The application starts to have a problem. When something goes wrong, figuring out the source can be tough. The key is to be able to trace the source of the problem quickly. Did the platform provider just upgrade the operating system? Is there a power outage? Was there a security breach on the provider's end? Or is it something on your end?

Gaining visibility

The bottom line is that you must be able to gain visibility into at least three areas:

- ✔ **Security:** To monitor security, you need to scan networks, operating systems, and applications in order to prevent intrusion or denial of service attacks.

- ✔ **Performance:** You need to ensure that the cloud's performance doesn't go below the agreed-upon service level.

- ✔ **Service availability:** You need a tool that can help you determine the availability of your services. You can use this tool to monitor whether your cloud provider is up or down and is meeting its service level agreements.

Negotiating these service levels is often a dance between IT and the provider. You should ask your service provider how it monitors security, performance, and availability. Make sure you're comfortable with the approach. Additionally, your provider should furnish a dashboard to give you visibility into those services that you're using on a regular basis. Ideally, you want a dashboard that gives you uniform visibility across your own resources and those of your PaaS provider.

Tracking service level agreements

A *service level agreement* (SLA) is a contractual obligation between you and your cloud provider. IT and the service provider must work together to establish these SLAs. Typical SLAs include the following:

- ✔ Response times
- ✔ Availability on any given day
- ✔ Overall uptime target
- ✔ Agreed-on response times and procedures in the event a service goes down

The agreement theoretically gives you some assurance that the provider will meet certain service levels. However, you need to determine what levels of downtime and other parameters you're willing to accept. For more about SLAs, see Chapter 17.

Considering access and integration

Another issue to think about is access to your services and integration between the application you want to deploy to the cloud and other services it depends on. For example, you need to determine what kind of *access control services* your provider offers so that only those people who are supposed to access your application during development and deployment can do so.

What about after the application is deployed? This is related to the security question mentioned in the previous section. Does your vendor provide the level of authentication and authorization you feel comfortable with? Additionally, what about the data? Traditional access control usually assumes that the owner of the application and the data are located in the same place (that is, on your premises). This is not the case in the cloud. Say that you've decided to move your application to the cloud, but you don't want to move your database or even replicate your data there. You will need to ensure that the right level of security exists between your on-premises data and your cloud application.

Additionally, there can be many points of integration with an application in the cloud. The application may integrate with a customer relationship management application in your organization. The application may integrate with other services in the cloud. A key criterion for a PaaS provider is to provide well-documented and well-defined interfaces for your use. In other words, at the center of integration capabilities between applications in the cloud or on-premises are Application Programming Interfaces (APIs). These APIs, which are part of the PaaS platform, enable companies to quickly integrate their services into a wide variety of applications on a diverse set of platforms. Before choosing a PaaS vendor, make sure it can support the applications and services you need to integrate together.

Avoiding lock-in

Although the PaaS approach has many benefits, it can have some disadvantages. One drawback of PaaS is that it may lock you in to use a particular development environment and stack of software components. PaaS offerings usually have some proprietary elements (perhaps the component libraries). Consequently, you may be wedded to the vendor's platform and unable to move your application elsewhere without rewriting it to some degree. If you become dissatisfied with your PaaS provider, you may face substantial expense if you suddenly need to rewrite applications to satisfy the requirements of another PaaS vendor.

The fear of vendor lock-in has led to the emergence of a new variety of PaaS: Open Platform as a Service. This service offers the same approach as PaaS, except there's no constraint on choice of development and delivery software. If lock-in is important to you, then ask questions before signing a vendor's contract.

Chapter 15

Promoting Cloud Security and Governance

Security is first, second, and third on the list of any IT manager who's thinking about the cloud. Whether you're looking at creating a private cloud, leveraging a public cloud, or implementing a hybrid environment, you must have a security strategy. Security is something you can never *really* relax about since the state of the art is constantly evolving. Hand-in-hand with this security strategy needs to be a *governance strategy* — a way to ensure accountability by all parties involved in your hybrid cloud deployment.

Managing security in the cloud needs to be viewed as a shared responsibility across the organization. You can implement all the latest technical security controls and still face security risks if your end users don't have a clear understanding of their role in keeping the cloud environment secure. Cloud services provide non-IT professionals with more control over their IT environment than ever before. As a result, the organization benefits from increased efficiency, flexibility, and productivity. However, there is also a much greater likelihood that an end user can impact security if they don't understand the implications of their actions.

In this chapter, we examine the security risks and governance considerations for companies working in hybrid cloud environments. There is a lot to consider, and understanding security is a moving target. Ultimately, education is key to ensuring that everyone in the organization has an understanding of his or her roles and responsibilities with regard to security.

How Using a Cloud Provider Impacts Security Risks

A company planning to secure its IT environment generally focuses on a broad range of vulnerabilities to its data center as well as ways to safeguard sensitive corporate, customer, and partner information wherever it's located. A hybrid cloud environment changes things because, although ultimately it's your company's responsibility to protect and secure your applications and information, many challenges arise when you're working with an external provider. Here are a few of those challenges:

- ✔ **Multi-tenancy:** In a multi-tenant architecture, a software application partitions its data and configuration so that each customer has a customized virtual application instance. However, your applications and data exist on the same servers as other companies using the same service provider, and these users are accessing their resources simultaneously. You may not know the names of the other companies that are sharing these servers. So, if one company's data or application is breached or fails for any number of reasons, your application may be affected.

- ✔ **Attacks that affect you, even though you aren't the target:** If your company makes use of a public cloud, you may be the collateral damage in an attack, even if it wasn't meant for you. Consider a virus attack, for example. Because you're sharing an environment with others, even though you may not be a target, your resources may be affected, resulting in a service interruption, or worse.

- ✔ **Incident response:** In a cloud environment, you may not have control over how quickly incidents are handled. For example, some cloud providers may not tell you about a security incident until they've confirmed that an actual incident occurred. As a result, you won't know something has happened until it affects your business. Additionally, if you become aware of an incident, you may not have access to servers to perform an analysis of what went wrong.

- ✔ **Visibility:** The preceding example illustrates that in many cloud environments, you may not be able to see what your provider is doing. In other words, you may not have control over your visibility into your resources that are running in the cloud. This situation is especially troublesome if you need to ensure that your provider is following compliance regulations or laws.

- ✔ **Non-vetted employees:** Although your company may go through an extensive background check on all of your employees, you're now trusting that no malicious insiders work at your cloud provider. This concern is real because close to 50 percent of security breaches are caused by insiders (or by people getting help from insiders). If your company is going to use a cloud service, you need to have a plan to deal with inside as well as outside threats.

✔ **Data issues:** If you're putting your data in the cloud, you need to be concerned about a number of issues, including the following:

- Making sure no unauthorized person can access this data.

- Understanding how this data will be segregated from other companies' data in a multi-tenant environment.

- Understanding how your data will be destroyed if you terminate your contract.

- Understanding where your data will be physically located.

- Understanding how your data is treated as it moves from your location to your provider's servers. Data issues are so important in a hybrid cloud environment that we've devoted a whole chapter (Chapter 11) to it.

✔ **Multiple cloud vendors:** Some cloud providers may actually be storing your data on a different cloud provider's platform. For example, cloud provider A may need extra capacity and move your account to a separate cloud environment supported by cloud provider B. It is therefore important to understand where your data in the cloud is actually located. Once you gain this information, you must make sure all of the parties are complying with your security requirements. In the earlier example, for instance, you need to make sure that Vendors A and B are both doing a thorough job of vetting employees.

Different applications and resources might demand different levels of security. If you're not providing time-sensitive data to the cloud, for example, you may not be as concerned about incident response time as someone who does. The point is this: You need to ask yourself how much you have invested in what you're putting into your cloud environment. If you're very concerned about what happens if there's a service interruption or what happens to your resources, you need to practice due diligence. What happens in the cloud can affect your cloud resources as well as those on your business's premises. It's best to be prepared.

Even when cloud operators have good security at the physical, network, operating system, and application levels, your company is responsible for protecting and securing its applications and information.

How Internal End Users Impact Security Risks

The cloud has helped to bring IT into the hands of the non-IT professional. It is easy, fast, and cheap for a business user to contract with any number of cloud services. And with the increase in the use of mobile devices, business users can easily access and share company data wherever they are located. The IT team no longer holds all of the control. This democratization of IT brings with it the problem that non-IT professionals are just not aware of the risks that cloud computing can have. This is not their fault; they've never had to think about IT security in the past. Some of the reasons why include:

- ✔ For the most part their interactions with cloud computing is through various SaaS programs ranging from enterprise level applications like Workday and Salesforce.com to consumer applications like Facebook, Flickr, Yelp, LinkedIn, and many others. Users of these SaaS offerings typically take for granted the complex security that is built into each level of the application.

- ✔ Employees are used to acquiring compute resources from the IT team. The IT team is of course well aware of security risks and follows best practices for things like systems configuration, software maintenance, and access control.

- ✔ Compute power that teams were traditionally acquiring from IT were from an internal data center that has strong security measures in place.

The reality is that non-IT teams typically don't know why the data center is secure, nor have they ever cared — all they need to know is that it "works." They don't realize that most of the technologies involved in making the data center secure are not built into basic public cloud virtual machines. In fact, some cloud vendors make it very clear in their SLAs that users are completely responsible for securing their cloud environment — not something somebody pulling out their corporate card to spin up a virtual machine is likely to appreciate.

Security measures taken by the IT department can be easily undermined by well-meaning business users who do not have an understanding of best practices for maintaining security in cloud environments. For example, sharing of passcodes for a SaaS application is a common practice in some companies and can lead to secure information ending up in the wrong hands.

Sharing the Responsibility for Cloud Security with Your Cloud Provider

If you are using the public cloud, your company is sharing common infrastructure with other companies. This concept of sharing is at the heart of the cloud model – you get access to advanced virtual server environments at a lower cost because you share this infrastructure with others. But in addition to these benefits, you are also sharing security risks. Your cloud provider has the responsibility of securing the physical and logical aspects of the infrastructure and operation system in the cloud environment. You can minimize some of your security risks by choosing the right cloud provider. However, in some cloud environments, you need to share security responsibilities with your cloud provider. For example, if you are using IaaS, you are responsible for the security of your virtual resources once they have been provisioned.

As described in the previous section, the cloud provides your business users with a greater level of control over their IT environment. IT users also have much greater control over provisioning IT assets. Without understanding the risk involved, users have the potential to easily provision images without providing the right level of attention to security. You need to manage resources provisioned in the cloud with the same attention to security as used in your internal data center. All users of cloud virtual machines need to understand that all provisioned instances must adhere to your company security standards.

After you have provisioned an image, you need to take responsibility for the patch management of that instance as well as additional images you create from that instance. For example, you need to keep up-to-date with vendor bulletins and apply required security updates, fixes, and patches to your software.

Having an inadequate identity management process opens up vulnerabilities that can impact the security of your environment. You can also put other customers of your cloud provider at risk if you have a weak identity management process and create vulnerabilities and open points of entry for hackers. You will need to have a process for:

✔ User ID request process

✔ User ID approval process

✔ User ID revalidation process

✔ User ID revocation process

✔ Password management guidelines

✔ Password strength guidelines

If you fail to maintain the right level of security, your cloud provider may decide you are a poor risk and can refuse to provide you with services.

Exploring the Risks of Running in the Cloud

We've talked a bit about some of the factors that lead to security risks in the cloud environment. Now, we go into a little more detail about the specific kinds of risks you might face, beginning with the categories of security risks. According to the National Institute of Standards and Technology (NIST), a government standards body, computer systems are subject to many threats ranging from loss of data to loss of a whole computing facility because of fire or natural disaster. These losses can come from trusted employees or from hackers. NIST divides these risks into the following categories:

✔ Errors and omissions including data errors or programming errors

✔ Fraud and theft

✔ Employee sabotage

✔ Loss of physical infrastructure support

✔ Malicious hackers

✔ Malicious code

✔ Threats to individual personal privacy

Many of the same security risks that companies face when dealing with their own computer systems are found in the cloud, but there are some important twists. The Cloud Security Alliance (CSA — `http://cloudsecurity alliance.org`), an organization dedicated to ensuring security best practices in the cloud, noted in its recent publication, "Security Guidance for Critical Areas of Focus in Cloud Computing," that significant areas of operational security risk in the cloud include the following:

✔ **Traditional security:** A hybrid cloud environment changes traditional security because you're no longer totally in control. Some of the computing assets you're using aren't on your premises. Now, you must ensure that strong traditional security measures are being followed by your cloud provider. Traditional security includes

- *Physical security* covers security of IT equipment, network assets, and telecommunications infrastructure. CSA recommends both "active and passive" defenses for physical security (see the section, "Assess your cloud vendor," which also includes equipment protection and location.

- *Human resource security* deals with the people side of the equation — ensuring background checks, confidentiality, and segregation of duties (that is, those who develop applications don't operate them).

- *Business continuity* plans need to be part of any service level agreement (see Chapter 17 for more information on SLAs) to ensure that the provider meets its service level agreement for continuous operation with you.

- *Disaster recovery* plans must ensure that your assets (for example, data and applications) are protected.

✔ **Incident handling:** A hybrid cloud environment changes incident handling in at least two ways. First, whereas you may have control over your own data center, if an incident occurs, you'll need to work with your service provider, because the service provider controls at least part of the infrastructure. Second, the multi-tenant nature of the cloud often makes investigating an incident more complicated. For example, because information may be co-mingled, log analysis may be difficult, since your service provider is trying to maintain privacy. You need to find out how your service provider defines an incident and make sure you can negotiate how you'll work with the provider to ensure that everyone is satisfied.

✔ **Application security:** When an application is in the cloud, it's exposed to every sort of security threat. The CSA divides application security into different areas, including securing the software development lifecycle in the cloud; authentication, authorization, and compliance; identity management, application authorization management (for updating application and the like), application monitoring, application penetration testing, and risk management.

✔ **Encryption and key management:** Data encryption refers to a set of algorithms that can transform text into a form called *cyphertext,* which is an encrypted form of plain text that unauthorized parties can't read. The recipient of an encrypted message uses a key that triggers the algorithm to decrypt the data and provide it in its original state to the authorized user. Therefore, you can encrypt data and ensure that only the intended recipient can decrypt it.

In the public cloud, some organizations may be tempted to encrypt all their information because they're concerned about its movement to the cloud and how safe it is once it's in the cloud. Recently, experts in the field have begun to consider other security measures besides encryption that can be used in the cloud. (We tackle a few of those security measures in the later section that deals with encryption options.)

✔ **Identity and access management:** Identity management is a very broad topic that applies to many areas of the data center. The goal of identity management is to manage identity information so that access to computer resources, applications, data, and services is controlled properly. Identity management changes significantly in the cloud. In a traditional data center, you might use a directory service for authentication and then deploy the application in a firewall safe zone. The cloud often requires multiple forms of identity to ensure that access to resources is secure. (We also cover this topic in a bit more detail in the identity management section, later in this chapter.)

With the increasing use of cloud computing, wireless technology, and mobile devices, you no longer have well-defined boundaries regarding what is internal and what is external to your systems. On an ongoing basis, you must assess whether holes or vulnerabilities exist across servers, network, infrastructure components, and endpoints, and then continuously monitor them. In other words, you need to be able to trust your own infrastructure as well as a cloud provider's.

Digging deeper into identity management

Identity management helps prevent security breaches and plays a significant role in helping a company meet IT security compliance regulations. In a cloud environment, where you don't own the infrastructure and may not control the applications, you may need to think about identity management in a slightly different way. For example, the CSA notes that in the cloud, an identity isn't just a person's identity. Identities also exist for devices, code, and other resources that exist off-premises. The CSA notes, "It becomes necessary to identify all of the entities associated with a transaction." A username and password simply aren't enough. Perimeter security with a firewall isn't enough.

In the cloud, identity and attributes (that is, facets of identity that link to the identity) can come from many systems. These facets may feed into an *entitlement layer* that contains the rules for authorization and access to the different layers at a provider's site. These layers include the network layer, the system layer, the application layer, the data layer, and the process layer.

Think about the cloud. Machines can be decommissioned quickly and then brought up online again. New machines can be provisioned on the fly. Data can be moved to different machines when the need arises. Your company may want to communicate with different partners and cloud providers. All of this can affect security and identity management practices.

The Jericho Forum, part of the Open Group (www.opengroup.org) that addresses the development of open, vendor-neutral IT standards and certifications, has recently published a set of principles called the Identity, Entitlement and Access Management (IdEA) Commandments. These best practices are meant to promote open and interoperable standards that can be used to help build strong identity management processes for systems, services, and data. Although not specifically developed for the cloud, they are meant to deal with systems that have become *de-perimiterized* (that is, where there is no hardened perimeter security because information is flowing between organizations). The cloud certainly falls into this category. There are 14 commandments, which include the following:

- ✔ All core identities must be protected to ensure their secrecy and integrity.

- ✔ Identifiers must be trustworthy.

- ✔ The authoritative source of identity will be the unique identifier or credentials offered by the persona representing that entity.

- ✔ An entity can have multiple separate personas (identities) and related unique identifiers.

- ✔ A persona must, in specific use cases, be able to be seen as the same (that is, to substitute one persona for a currently interacting persona).

- ✔ The attribute owner is responsible for the protection and appropriate disclosure of the attribute.

- ✔ Connecting attributes to a persona must be easy and verifiable.

- ✔ The source of the attribute should be as close to the authoritative source as possible.

- ✔ A resource owner must define entitlement.

- ✔ Access decisions must be relevant, valid, and bidirectional.

- ✔ Users of an entity's attributes are accountable for protecting the attributes.

- ✔ Principals can delegate authority to another persona to act on behalf of a persona.

- ✔ Authorized principals may acquire access to (seize) another entity's persona.

- ✔ A persona may represent, or be represented by, more than one entity.

For full descriptions of these Commandments, go to The Open Group website and enter **Commandments** in the Search box.

Understanding data protection options

Some experts believe that different kinds of data require different forms of protection and that, in some cases in a cloud environment, data encryption might, in fact, be overkill. You could encrypt everything. You could encrypt data, for example, when you write it to your own disk, when you send it to a cloud provider, and when you store it in a cloud provider's database. You could encrypt at every layer.

Encrypting everything in a comprehensive way reduces your exposure; however, encryption poses a performance penalty. For example, many experts advise managing your own keys rather than letting a cloud provider do so, and that can become complicated. Keeping track of too many keys can be a nightmare. Additionally, encrypting everything can create other issues. For example, if you're trying to encrypt data in a database, you will have to examine data as it's moving (point-to-point encryption) and also while it's being stored in the database. This procedure can be costly and complicated. Also, even when you think you've encrypted everything and you're safe, that may not be the case.

One of the long-standing weaknesses with encryption strategies is that your data is at risk before and after it's encrypted. For example, in a major data breach at Hannaford Supermarkets in 2008, the hackers hid in the network for months and were able to steal payment data when customers used their credit card at the point-of-sale. This breach took place *before* the data was encrypted.

Maintaining a large number of keys can be impractical, and managing the storing, archiving, and accessing of the keys is difficult. In order to alleviate this problem, generate and compute encryption keys as needed to reduce complexity and improve security.

Here are some other available data safeguarding techniques:

- **Anonymizing the data:** When data is anonymized, all of the data that describes the data (called *metadata*) is removed. This might include someone's name or Social Security number or address. Although this technique can protect some personal identification, hence privacy, you need to be really careful about the amount of information you strip out. If it's not enough, hackers can still figure out who the data pertains to.

- **Tokenization:** This technique protects sensitive data by replacing it with random tokens or alias values that mean nothing to someone who gains unauthorized access to this data. This technique decreases the chance that thieves could do anything with the data. Tokenization can protect credit card information, passwords, personal information, and the like. Some experts argue that it's more secure than encryption.

- **Cloud database controls:** In this technique, access controls are built into the database in order to protect the whole database so that each piece of data doesn't need to be encrypted.

Developing a Secure Hybrid Environment

A thoughtful approach to security can succeed in mitigating against many security risks. Here are some pointers about how to develop a secure hybrid environment.

Assess your current state

In a hybrid environment, security starts with assessing your current state. We recommend that you begin by answering a set of questions that can help you form your approach to your security strategy. Here are a few important questions to consider:

- Have you evaluated your own traditional security infrastructure recently?

- How do you control access rights to applications and networks — both those within your company and those outside your firewall? Who has the right to access IT resources? How do you ensure that only the right identities gain access to your applications and information?

- Can you identify web application vulnerabilities and risks and then correct any weaknesses?

✔ Do you have a way of tracking your security risk over time so you can easily share updated information with those who need it?

✔ Are your server environments protected at all times from external security threats?

✔ Do you maintain your own keys, if you are using encryption, or do you get them from a trusted, reliable provider? Do you use standard algorithms?

✔ Are you able to monitor and quantify security risks in real time?

✔ Can you implement security policies consistently across all types of on-premises and cloud architectures?

✔ How do you protect all your data no matter where it's stored?

✔ Can you satisfy auditing and reporting requirements for data in the cloud?

✔ Can you meet the compliance requirements of your industry?

✔ What is your application security program?

✔ What are your disaster and recovery plans? How do you ensure service continuity?

Assess your cloud vendor

A hybrid cloud environment poses a special set of challenges when it comes to security and governance. Hybrid clouds utilize your own infrastructure plus that of your service provider. For example, data may be stored on your premises but processed in the cloud. This means that your own on-premises infrastructure may be connected to a more public cloud, which is going to affect the kinds of security controls you need to have in place.

Controls must be in place for perimeter security, access, data integrity, malware, and the like — not only at your location, but also with your cloud provider. Cloud service providers each have their own way of managing security. They may or may not be compatible with the compliance and overall security plan of your organization. It's absolutely critical that your company not bury its head in the sand by assuming that the cloud provider has security covered.

You need to verify that your cloud provider ensures the same level of security that you demand internally (or a superior level, if you're looking to improve your overall security strategy). You must ask a lot of hard questions to guarantee that your company's security and governance strategy can be integrated with your provider's.

Here are some tips that can get you started and that may also be useful in assessing your security strategy:

✔ Ask your cloud provider what kind of companies they service. Also ask questions about system architecture in order to understand more about how multi-tenancy is handled.

✔ Visit the facility unannounced in order to understand what physical security measures are in place. According to the CSA, this means walking through all areas, from the reception area to the generator room and even inspecting the fuel tanks. You also need to check for perimeter security (for example, check how people access the building) and whether the operator is prepared for a crisis (for example, fire extinguishers, alarms, and the like).

✔ Check where the cloud provider is located. For example, is it in a high crime area or an area prone to natural disasters such as earthquakes or flooding?

✔ What sort of up-to-date documentation does the cloud provider have in place? Does it have incident response plans? Emergency response plans? Backup plans? Restoration plans? Background checks of security personnel and other staff members?

✔ What sort of certifications does the provider have in place? Do cloud security personnel have certifications such as CISSP, CISA, and ITIL. Find out which third parties have done a review.

✔ Find out where your data will be stored. If your company has compliance regulations it must meet about data residing in foreign countries, this is important to know. Refer to Chapter 11 for more about data management issues.

✔ Find out who will have access to your data. Also check to see how data will be protected.

✔ Find out more about the provider's data backup and retention plans. You will want to know if your data is co-mingled with other data. If you want your data back when you terminate your contract, these issues may be important.

✔ How will your provider prevent denial-of-service (DoS) attacks?

✔ What sort of maintenance contracts does your provider have in place for its equipment?

✔ Does your cloud provider utilize continuous monitoring of its operations? Can you have visibility into this monitoring capability?

✔ How are incidents detected? How is information logged?

✔ How are incidents handled? What is the definition of an incident? Who is your point of contact at your service provider? What are the roles and responsibilities of team members?

✔ How does your provider handle application security and data security?

✔ What metrics does your cloud provider monitor to ensure that applications remain secure?

This list proposes a lot of questions, and we don't expect you to be able to answer them in a few seconds. We present them because the information you'll gather should be the foundation for assessing your current security environment.

Given the importance of security in the cloud environment, you might assume that a major cloud service provider will have a set of comprehensive service level agreements for its customers. In fact, many of the standard agreements are intended to protect the service provider — not the customer. So, your company really must understand the contract as well as the infrastructure, processes, and certifications your cloud provider holds.

You must clearly articulate your cloud security requirements and governance strategy and determine accountability. If your cloud provider doesn't want to talk about these items, you should probably consider a new cloud provider. On the other hand, your cloud provider may actually have some tricks up its sleeve that can improve your own security! In fact, it probably does.

Completing this assessment will give you a lot to think about. At that point, you'll have an idea about the strengths and weaknesses in your own security environment, as well as any issues you need to discuss with your cloud provider. You'll have a better idea of the tools and techniques you may have to put in place, both on your own premises as well as in the cloud. And, your provider may surprise you. Cloud providers are now making it their business to understand the ins and outs of security. This means that you should not be surprised if they have a much better handle on security than you do! Here are some additional pointers:

✔ If your company is large and you are implementing a complex cloud environment, it makes sense to have security people on staff that can help you do your assessments and assess security products.

✔ In most circumstances, approach cloud security from a risk-management perspective. If your organization has risk-management specialists, involve them in cloud security planning.

✔ Try to create general awareness of security risks by educating and warning staff members about specific dangers. It is easy to become complacent; however, threats come from within and from outside the organization.

✔ Regularly have external IT security consultants check your company's IT security policy and IT network and the policies and practices of all your cloud service providers.

✔ Stay abreast of news about IT security breaches in other companies and the causes of those breaches.

✔ Continue to review backup and disaster-recovery systems in light of your security strategy. Apart from anything else, security breaches can require complete application recovery.

✔ Review your governance strategies on an ongoing basis to make sure that your cloud security strategy is enforced. We discuss governance in the next section.

Discovering Risk and Maintaining Your Cloud Governance Strategy

An effective cloud security strategy requires enforcement and accountability. This is where *governance* comes in. Basically, governance is about applying policies — the organizing principles and rules that determine how an organization should behave — relating to using services. In the cloud world, governance helps to define how multiple organizations behave, because multiple parties across different companies will be part of the governance plan.

IT governance is really a combination of policy, process, and controls. The role of IT governance is to implement, maintain, and continuously improve these controls. IT governance does the following:

- Ensures that IT assets (systems, processes, and so on) are implemented and used according to agreed upon policies and procedures
- Ensures that these assets are properly controlled and maintained
- Ensures that these assets are providing value to the organization

IT governance, therefore, has to include the techniques and policies that measure and control how systems are managed. However, IT doesn't stand alone in the governance process. In order for governance to be effective, it must be holistic. It's as much about organizational issues and how people work together to achieve business goals as it is about technology. A critical part of governance is establishing organizational relationships between business and IT, as well as defining how people will work together across organizational boundaries. So, the best kind of governance occurs when IT and the business are working together.

Implementing a governance strategy

How does governance typically work? IT governance usually involves establishing a board made up of business and IT representatives. The board creates rules and processes that the organization must follow to ensure that policies are being met. These rules and processes might include the following:

- Understanding business issues such as regulatory requirements or funding
- Establishing best practices and monitoring these processes
- Assigning responsibility for things such as programming standards, proper design, review, certifications, and monitoring applications

When you moving into a hybrid cloud environment, you want your governance board to deal with issues related to how your compute resources are handled on your premises, as well as deal with your cloud provider. Cloud governance is a shared responsibility between the user of cloud services and the cloud provider. Understanding the boundaries of responsibility and defining an appropriate governance strategy within your organization require careful balance.

A successful governance strategy in a hybrid environment requires a negotiated agreement between you and your cloud provider(s). Generally, several goals are involved in cloud governance, including risk and monitoring performance.

Your governance strategy needs to be supported in two ways:

- ✔ **Understanding the compliance and risk measures the business must follow:** What does your business require to meet IT, corporate, industry, and government requirements? For example, can your business share data across international borders? These requirements must be supported through technical controls, automation, and strict governance of processes, data, and workflows.

- ✔ **Understanding the performance goals of the business:** Perhaps you measure your business performance in terms of sales revenue, profitability, stock price, quality of product or service provided, and timely delivery. Your cloud provider needs to be able to support these goals and help you optimize your business performance.

Risks worth noting

Each industry has a set of governance principles based on its regulatory and competitive environment and its view of risk. There are different levels of risk. For example, in certain companies, information cannot be shared across international boundaries. In financial services, certain data practices need to be followed. In software development, there are risks associated with getting the product on the market on time. In the healthcare industry, there are patient privacy concerns.

Although a business's CIO may work with the business to put together a certain set of rules to manage risks, everyone in the business must understand the risks. To make our point, suppose you have a corporate policy stating that no data from a credit card system can be used by the company's marketing analysis systems. Now, suppose that the CIO discovers that the marketing analysis system used this information. In this case, the business is put at risk, and IT governance fails. Clearly, not only the CIO needed to know the rules set in place to manage risks.

Here is a list of risks to consider as you move into a hybrid model:

- ✔ **Audit and compliance risks:** Include issues around data jurisdiction, data access control, and maintaining an audit trail.

- ✔ **Security risks:** Include data integrity and data confidentiality and privacy.

- ✔ **Other information risks:** Include protection of intellectual property.

- ✔ **Performance and availability risks:** Include the level of availability and performance your business requires to successfully operate — for example, alerts, notifications, and provider business continuity plans. In addition, does the provider have forensic information, in case something does go wrong?

- ✔ **Interoperability risks:** Associated with developing a service that might be composed of multiple services. Are you assured that the infrastructure will continue to support your service? What if one of the services you're using changes? What policies are in place to ensure that you will be notified of a change?

- ✔ **Contract risks:** Associated with not reading between the lines of your contract. For example, who owns your data in the cloud? If the service goes down, how will you be compensated? What happens if the provider goes out of business?

- ✔ **Billing risks:** Associated with ensuring that you're billed correctly and only for the resources you consume.

Measuring and monitoring performance

You can measure business performance by comparing production, sales, revenue, stock price, and customer satisfaction with your goals. You can measure IT performance by comparing server, application, and network uptime; service resolution time; budgets; and project completion dates with your goals. Businesses use all these measures to rate their performance compared with that of competitors and the expectations of customers, partners, and shareholders. In cloud computing, you need to measure the affect of IT performance on the business, which by definition now includes the performance of the cloud provider.

Of course, your own internal governance committee needs to answer the following types of questions to get started:

- ✔ How can IT performance measures support the business?

- ✔ What should management measure and monitor to ensure successful IT governance?

- ✔ Are customers able to get responses to requests in the expected amount of time?

✔ Is customer transaction data safe from unauthorized access?

✔ Can management get the right information at the right time?

✔ Can you demonstrate to business management that your organization can recover from anticipated outages without damaging customer loyalty?

✔ Are you able to monitor systems proactively so that you can make repairs before faulty services affect rules and regulations?

✔ Can you justify your IT investments to business management?

These questions need to be answered whether or not you're using a cloud provider.

Making governance work

We believe that effective management of the cloud will be part people and processes and part technology. It's really a three-part solution.

✔ Your organization needs to set up a governance body to deal with cloud issues and to put processes in place to work with the business around enforcement (this body can be your existing governance board, if you like). This board will have oversight responsibilities and will collaborate with the business (it should include business members). It can also develop best practices.

✔ Your organization needs to have governance bodies in the cloud that deal with standardization of services and other shared infrastructure issues. You need some sort of interface to this group. Your level of involvement depends on your level of involvement in the cloud.

✔ Your organization also needs to have technology in the mix that helps your organization automatically monitor what happens in the cloud.

Chapter 16

Virtualization and the Hybrid Cloud

Any discussion of cloud computing usually includes virtualization. *Virtualization* is the process of using computer resources to imitate other computer resources or whole computers. Virtualization is really one of the foundational technology for cloud computing and serves as an enabler for many types of cloud implementations.

In this chapter, we present an overview of virtualization. One of the most important uses of virtualization is on the server, so we focus strongly on that. We also examine what virtualization means in a hybrid cloud. Because managing virtualization is so important, and there are a lot of twists in the hybrid world, we end the chapter with these issues.

Defining Virtualization

Virtualization separates resources and services from the underlying physical delivery environment. With its use, you can create many virtual systems within a single physical system. A primary driver for virtualization is consolidating servers, which provides organizations with efficiency and potential cost savings.

Characteristics

Virtualization has three characteristics that make it ideal for cloud computing:

✔ **Partitioning:** In virtualization, many applications and operating systems are supported in a single physical system by portioning (separating) the available resources.

✔ **Isolation:** Each virtual machine is isolated from its host physical system and other virtualized machines. Because of this isolation, if one virtual instance crashes, the other virtual machines aren't affected. In addition, data isn't shared between one virtual container and another.

✔ **Encapsulation:** A virtual machine can be represented (and even stored) as a single file, so you can identify it easily based on the services it provides. For example, the encapsulated process could be a business service. This encapsulated virtual machine could be presented to an application as a complete entity. Thus, encapsulation could protect each application so that it doesn't interfere with another application.

Here's a nontechnical analogy to help you think about virtualization. Some experts have likened virtualization to an apartment building. Individual apartments share a building. They are each isolated, but they share utilities in a more efficient model than a house might.

In *server virtualization,* one physical server is partitioned into multiple virtual servers. For example, the hardware resources of a machine — including the random access memory (RAM), CPU, hard disk, and network controller — can be virtualized into a series of virtual machines that run their own applications and operating system on these machines. A thin layer of software is actually inserted onto the hardware that contains a virtual machine monitor or *hypervisor,* which is described in the next section.

Using a hypervisor in virtualization

System virtualization can be approached through hardware partitioning or hypervisor technology. *Hardware partitioning* subdivides a physical server into fractions, each of which can run an operating system. Although this model supports consolidation of hardware, according to experts, it doesn't have the full benefits of resource sharing and emulation that hypervisors do.

A *hypervisor* allows multiple operating systems to share a single host. It knows how to act as a traffic cop to make things happen in an orderly manner. The hypervisor sits at the lowest levels of the hardware environment and uses a thin layer of code in software to enable dynamic resource sharing. The hypervisor makes it seem like each operating system has the resources all to itself.

A short history of virtualization

IBM introduced virtualization in the early 1960s to enable users to run more than one operating system on a mainframe. Mainframe virtualization became less relevant in the 1980s and 1990s. Indeed, in the 1990s, companies stopped worrying about the efficiency of the computer platform because computers were becoming so powerful.

For more than a decade, IT organizations expanded the capabilities of their data centers by adding servers. Servers had become so cheap that each time a new application was added, it was easier to buy a new server than to share resources with other applications. Eventually, organizations realized that maintaining, upgrading, and managing a large (and growing) number of servers was getting out of hand. The number of support-staff employees required to operate the data center was climbing swiftly, so the manpower cost of maintaining the data center (as a percentage of total cost) was rising. At the same time, other costs were growing in an unpredicted manner, particularly the costs of electricity (to power the computers), air conditioning (to cool them), and floor space (to house them).

One of the main problems was that the servers were horribly inefficient. In the days of the mainframe, great efforts were made to use 100 percent of the computer's CPU and memory resources. Even under normal circumstances, it was possible to achieve a better than 95 percent utilization. On the cheap servers that IT departments had been deploying, however, CPU inefficiency was often 6 percent

or less — sometimes as low as 2 percent. Memory and disk input/output (I/O) usage were similarly low.

This situation seems almost insane until you realize that many applications simply don't require a great deal of resources, and with the servers that were being delivered by the year 2000, you didn't put more than one application on a server. Why? Because the operating systems that almost everyone had — Windows and Linux, typically — couldn't effectively schedule resource use between competing applications. In a competitive hardware market, vendors began increasing the power of the servers, at an affordable price. Most of these servers had more power than a typical application needed. If an organization decided to stay with older but lower-powered hardware, it couldn't find people to maintain those aging platforms.

If you had an application that only ever needed 4 percent of a current CPU, what were you going to do other than provide it with its own server? Some companies actually used old PCs for some applications of this kind, maintaining the PCs for themselves; but there's a limit to the amount of old equipment that you can reuse.

The solution to this squandering of resources was to add scheduling capability to computers, which is precisely what one IT vendor, VMware, introduced. Adding scheduling changed the dynamics of computer optimization and set the stage for the modern virtualization revolution. The mainframe is dead; long live the mainframe!

Because in cloud computing you need to support many different operating environments, the hypervisor becomes an ideal delivery mechanism. The hypervisor lets you show the same application on lots of systems without having to physically copy that application onto each system. One twist: Because of the hypervisor architecture, it can load any (or many) different operating system as though it were just another application. So, the hypervisor is a very practical way of getting things virtualized quickly and efficiently.

You need to understand the nature of the hypervisor. It's designed like a mainframe OS rather than like the Windows OS. The hypervisor, therefore, schedules the access that guest operating systems have, everything from the CPU, to memory, to disk I/O, to other I/O mechanisms. With virtualization technology, you can set up the hypervisor to split the physical computer's resources. Resources can be split 50:50 or 80:20 between two guest operating systems, for example.

The beauty of this arrangement is that the hypervisor does all of the heavy lifting. The guest operating system doesn't care (or have any idea) that it's running in a virtual partition; it thinks it has a computer all to itself.

There are basically two types of hypervisors:

- ✔ **Type 1 hypervisors** run directly on the hardware platform. They achieve higher efficiency because they're running directly on the platform.

- ✔ **Type 2 hypervisors** run on the host operating system. They are often used when there's a need to support a broad range of I/O devices.

Exploring Why Companies Adopt Server Virtualization

Companies adopt virtualization for a number of reasons. As stated previously, virtualization helps to consolidate infrastructure, which can lead to a number of business benefits including decreasing the costs associated with maintaining a lot of servers. Virtualization is appealing to companies for technical reasons, too, including the fact that it might help in business continuity, disaster recovery, and resource availability. We delve into some of these benefits in the following sections.

Why companies adopt server virtualization

Companies find virtualization attractive for a number of reasons:

✔ **Consolidation efficiencies:** Migrating physical servers to virtual machines reduces the number of physical servers and the costs associated with maintaining them. Virtualization improves space utilization in data centers, and on the application side, helps to remove application compatibility issues because applications are isolated on virtual machines. Since there are now more applications on a machine, this virtualization helps to more fully utilize servers.

✔ **Cost reduction:** Combining server virtualization and consolidation boosts resource utilization, and a consolidated data center reduces power requirements. A smaller energy footprint reduces costs.

✔ **Faster server provisioning:** Companies can develop one standard "golden" (the reference standard) virtual server build that can be rolled out across multiple servers as needed.

✔ **Increased availability:** Virtualized servers offer features that often aren't found on physical servers. These features may include distributed resource scheduling, live migration, and fault tolerance, which helps to keep the servers running.

✔ **Business continuity/disaster recovery:** Virtualization abstracts (suppresses the details and provides only the relevant information) away the underlying hardware requirements, which can help with disaster recovery because you don't need to worry about having the exact machine on hand if disaster strikes. The costs savings associated with fewer servers also means that more money is available for disaster recovery plans.

Abstracting hardware assets

Another benefit of virtualization is the way that it abstracts hardware assets, in essence allowing a single piece of hardware to be used for multiple tasks. Here are some of the hardware abstraction types:

✔ **File system virtualization:** Virtual machines can access different file systems and storage resources via a common interface.

✔ **Virtual symmetric multiprocessing:** A single virtual machine can use multiple physical processors simultaneously and thus pretend to be a server cluster. It can emulate a fairly large grid of physical servers.

✔ **Virtual high-availability support:** If a virtual machine fails, that virtual machine needs to automatically restart on another server.

✔ **Distributed resource scheduler:** You could think of the scheduler as being the super-hypervisor that manages all of the other hypervisors. This mechanism assigns and balances computing capability dynamically across a collection of hardware resources that support the virtual machines. Therefore, a process can be moved to a different resource when it becomes available.

✔ **Virtual infrastructure client console:** This console provides an interface that allows administrators to connect remotely to virtual center management servers or to an individual hypervisor so that the server and the hypervisor can be managed manually.

Server Virtualization and the Hybrid Cloud

By now, we think you understand what virtualization is all about. You know that virtualization is so important because it decouples the software from the hardware. *Decoupling* means that software is put in a separate container so that it is isolated from the operating system. Although the cloud infrastructure doesn't require virtualization, virtualization is often a component of a cloud deployment. The point is that virtualization is important in the cloud because it provides a level of abstraction. The abstraction doesn't need to be virtualization, per se; it might be done another way (like a grid), but you need a way to do this abstraction in order to provide functions for end users.

Clouds are often laid on top of this virtual server substrate. It is a foundational technology. When building a cloud infrastructure (whether you're building a private cloud or a public cloud), you generally think about it as a distributed environment that's dynamically allocated or provisioned. Virtualization enables this distributed environment. Virtualization is most concrete on a server level. For example, this is really what IaaS is all about — a distributed resource that can be dynamically allocated.

Whether to virtualize your infrastructure depends on the workload you're dealing with. For example, some experts caution that if your workload is running analytics across thousands of nodes at full capacity on a big data problem, using a virtualized environment might not make sense.

What is abstraction?

The idea behind abstraction is to minimize the complexity of something by hiding the details and providing only the relevant information. For example, if you were going to pick up someone that you've never met before, he might tell you the location to meet him, how tall he is, his hair color, and what he will be wearing. He doesn't need to tell you where he was born, how much money he has in the bank, his birth date, and so on. That's the idea with abstraction — it's about providing a high level specification rather than going into lots and lots of detail about how something works. In the cloud, for instance, in an IaaS delivery model, the infrastructure is abstracted from the user.

As companies build out their virtual data centers, many find that the next logical move is to implement a private cloud. This provides them with more flexibility around provisioning resources. However, in a *hybrid* model, your company may want to bridge your private cloud to a public cloud. Here are some examples:

- ✔ **Application bursting:** When spikes in resources for a particular application are required that overwhelm your private data center, you may want to borrow resources from the public cloud.

- ✔ **Moving virtual machines:** It's exciting to think that you might be able to balance loads between private and public clouds at the virtual machine level. In this way, you could run them where they're the most effective.

Ideally, in a hybrid cloud there needs to be a shared, standardized environment or at least some kind of consistent virtualization infrastructure between your on-premises private cloud and what exists in the public cloud. Several approaches have emerged:

- ✔ **Compatibility:** Large vendors such as VMware, IBM, Microsoft, and HP are putting offerings on the market that enable enterprises (and service providers) to move virtual machines between on- and off-premises infra-structures. Often, these infrastructures use the same technology platforms as you have on-premises. This makes it easier to be consistent. VMware is even certifying cloud providers that offer a globally consistent IaaS service that can be provisioned via a GUI interface.

- ✔ **Virtual Private Cloud (VPC) services:** Cloud vendors like Amazon are offering a VPC service. The Amazon VPC, for example, lets you provision a private, isolated section of the Amazon Web Services (AWS) cloud where you can launch AWS resources in a virtual network that you define.

- ✔ **Open source software:** These open source projects are looking to bring together public and private cloud infrastructures. One example of this is Eucalyptus (www.eucalyptus.com). Eucalyptus utilizes virtualiza-tion software to create resource pools that can be scaled up or down. A Eucalyptus private cloud is fully compatible with Amazon APIs, which makes it easier for organizations to migrate virtual servers between a private cloud and a public cloud environment.

- ✔ **Cloud management services:** Other third-party providers, such as RightScale (www.rightscale.com), are providing cloud management services. For example, RightScale provides a cloud configuration framework that are templates to configure and operate servers. It also provides an automation engine to help provision and monitor server deployments.

Desktop virtualization

Just as virtualization refers to separating resources and services from the underlying physical delivery environment, conceptually, desktop virtualization refers to separating the desktop environment from the physical machine. This kind of virtualization has gotten a lot of attention over the past few years.

The term desktop virtualization can be somewhat misleading, given that organizations are making use of all kinds of devices — smartphones, tablets, notebooks, and PCs. In fact, desktop virtualization is sometimes called *client* virtualization or even *endpoint* virtualization. Also, the desktop virtualization model is changing. Whereas several years ago, people talked about virtualizing a desktop to a server, and this is still a primary desktop virtualization model, newer models are emerging.

Virtualizing the desktop can happen in a number of ways. On the server side this can include

✔ **Terminal server:** In this approach, a desktop is provided to a user from a remote server. The operating system is not stored on the device. Only the screen image is actually transmitted to the user, who may have a thin client (it has no hard disk) or possibly an old PC.

✔ **Operating system streaming:** In this approach, the OS software is passed to the client device — but only as much of the software as needed at any point in time. Technically, this process is called *streaming.* Some of the processing occurs on the disk and some in local memory. The Windows OS, for example, and its applications are split between the client and the server. Streaming applications run at about the same speed as does reading the

application from the disk. You can use this approach by utilizing PCs on a desktop or by using thin clients. The model requires a constant connection, which is why it's typically used with desktops.

✔ **Server-hosted virtual desktop:** Here virtual PCs (complete emulations of a PC) are created on a server. The user has what *appears* on the server to be a complete PC. In actuality, the server-hosted virtual desktop is remotely executing the operating system on the server, and the graphics are being sent to a desktop over a network. Sometimes people refer to this kind of client virtualization as a *virtual desktop infrastructure* (VDI). This is one of the most popular forms of desktop virtualization. VDI provides the capability to have shared client sessions on the server rather than on the client. The software you need to use sits on the server, and an image can be viewed on your device.

For example, in healthcare, clinicians are using VDI desktops to gain access to information in patient rooms and offices. In science labs, where space is at a premium and contaminant-free work areas are a priority, virtualized desktops eliminate the server and other hardware from the room. Other examples include using virtualized desktops for temporary workers or remote workers who need access to applications, and even for traders who need to move around the trading floor but need access to information on demand. Moving the desktop to the data center (whether a public or private one) covers every possible means of replacing physical PCs with graphics terminals (also called thin clients).

Managing Virtualization

A management infrastructure is going to be key in a hybrid cloud world. In fact, when virtualization is used in cloud computing, it's quite possible that the management software you use in your data center will fall short. You need to consider how you want to handle management, which includes provisioning resources as well as dealing with security and capacity planning. Face it: This is new territory. Although it's still early, different models are emerging. For example, some of the virtualization vendors are offering management solutions. Service management vendors are also looking to provide tools to manage hybrid virtualization.

When managing virtualization, the service provider (whether it's your IT organization or a cloud provider) must be able to do the following:

✔ Know and understand the relationships among all elements of the network.

✔ Be able to change things dynamically when elements within this universe change.

✔ Keep placement of virtual resources in step with all the other information held in the *configuration management database* (CMDB). A CMDB stores configuration items that detail the attributes of individual entities in an IT environment. Given that few organizations have anything approaching a comprehensive CMDB, that's asking a lot. In fact, ideally the CMDB should capture how all service management capabilities are integrated.

You're going to have to decide who your hybrid cloud administrator will be and the skills she will need to do the job. Following are some of the issues associated with managing a virtualized hybrid cloud.

Handling foundational issues

Managing a virtual environment involves foundational issues that determine how well the components function as a system. The foundations have to be in sync between the public and private worlds. This means that management needs to understand how the following issues will be treated:

✔ **Licenses management:** Many license agreements tie the license fee to physical servers rather than virtual servers. Resolve these licenses before using the associated software in a virtual environment. The constraints of such licenses may become an obstacle to efficiency.

✔ **Service levels:** Measuring, managing, and maintaining service levels can become more complicated simply because the environment itself is more complicated. When a public cloud is added to the mix, the cloud consumer is responsible for establishing service levels for both internally virtualized environments and those living in the cloud.

✔ **Network management:** The real target of network management becomes the virtual network, which may be harder to manage than the physical network.

✔ **Capacity planning:** Although it's convenient to think that all servers deliver roughly the same capacity, they don't. With virtualization, you have more control of hardware purchases and can plan network resources accordingly.

Managing virtualization in hybrid environments

In a virtualized hybrid environment, you'll have lots of images of the environment across multiple environments. However, you'll need to treat all resources together as though they were a single system, as opposed to an image here or there. If you don't, you'll end up having resources that are there but not being used in an effective manner. The issue is how you manage these images in a virtualized hybrid environment. Figure 16-1 illustrates just how complicated this management can be. You can see that you have multiple virtual machines, across multiple environments.

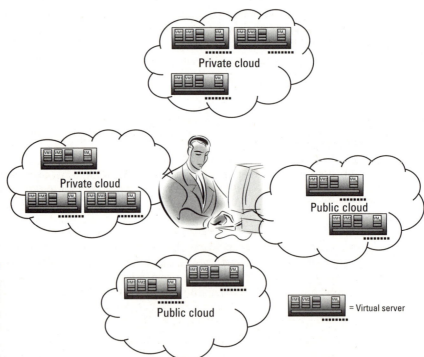

Figure 16-1:
Virtual
machines
in a hybrid
cloud.

A strong management platform needs to deal with the issues that we describe in this section.

Provisioning software

Provisioning software lets you manually adjust the virtualized environment. Using provisioning software, you can create new virtual machines and modify existing ones to add or reduce resources. This type of provisioning is essential to managing workloads and to moving applications and services from one physical environment to another. Provisioning software enables the following:

✔ Migration of running virtual machines from one physical server to another

✔ Automatic restart of failed virtual machines on a separate physical server

✔ Clustering, or grouping, of virtual machines across different physical servers

In a hybrid environment, you'll have to make sure that cloud providers offer provisioning software in a consistent manner and can work with your internal resources.

Hardware provisioning

Before virtualization, hardware provisioning was simply a matter of commissioning new hardware and configuring it to run new applications (or possibly repurposing it to run some new application).

Virtualization makes this process a little simpler in one way: You don't have to link the setup of new hardware to the instantiation of a new application. Now, you can add a server to the pool and enable it to run virtual machines. Thereafter, those virtual machines are ready when they're needed. When you add a new application, your cloud data center administrator or your service provider (via a self-service interface) will enable you to configure it to run on a virtual machine.

One of the key benefits that companies have found with cloud computing is the ability to quickly and effectively provide additional hardware resources from IaaS providers.

Provisioning is now the act of allocating a virtual machine to a specific server from a central console. Be aware of a catch, however. You can run into trouble if you go too far. You may decide to virtualize entire sets of applications and virtualize the servers that those applications are running on, for example. Although you may get some optimization, you also create too many silos that are too hard to manage. You may have optimized your environment so much that you have no room to accommodate peak loads.

The hypervisor, referenced earlier in this chapter, lets a physical server run many virtual machines at the same time. In a sense, one server does the work of maybe ten. That arrangement is a neat one, but you may not be able to shift those kinds of workloads without consequences. A server running 20 virtual machines, for example, may still have the same network connection with the same traffic limitation, which could act as a bottleneck. Alternatively, if all those applications use local disks, many of them may need to use a SAN or NAS (described in Chapter 20) — and that requirement may have implications in terms of performance.

Security issues

Using virtual machines complicates IT security in a big way for companies running hybrid cloud environments. Virtualization changes the definition of what a server is, so security is no longer trying to protect a physical server or a collection of servers that an application runs on. Instead, it's protecting collections of virtual machines running across multiple environments. Here, as a result, are some security issues that arise:

- ✔ **Perimeter security:** In a hybrid cloud, the data center is no longer a single entity that you can protect. You now have to ask yourself what your perimeter security looks like.

- ✔ **Hypervisor security:** Just as an OS attack is possible, a hacker can also take control of a hypervisor. If the hacker gains control of the hypervisor, he gains control of everything that it controls; therefore, he could do a lot of damage. The hypervisor should have no externally accessible ports that can be accessed by a hacker, and it should be as invisible as possible to a network. It should not have to be patched often.

- ✔ **Storage security:** If data is written to a local storage machine and then not cleaned when reallocated to another virtual machine, data leakage can occur.

- ✔ **Configuration and change management:** The simple act of changing configurations or patching the software on virtual machines becomes much more complex if the software is locked away in virtual images. In the virtual world, you no longer have a fixed static address to update the configuration.

- ✔ **Network monitoring:** Current network defenses are based on physical networks. In the virtualized environment, the network is no longer physical; its configuration can actually change dynamically, which makes network monitoring difficult. To fix this problem, you must have software products (available from companies such as VMware, IBM, CA, and HP) that can monitor virtual networks.

We won't use the acronym SaaS for security as a service, because that would be confusing, and security as a service is really a subset of SaaS. However, note that a class of vendors does provide security as a service — in other words, to help monitor and control certain kinds of hybrid deployments.

Capacity planning

Capacity planning refers to the estimation of how much computer hardware, software, connection infrastructure, and space will be needed over a certain period of time. Although capacity planning in a data center means a lot of forecasting, capacity planning in the cloud model is theoretically easier because of the elastic nature of the cloud. However, that doesn't mean you shouldn't do it. You still need to have some idea of what work loads will go where and what the performance will be. Otherwise, although you think you might have infinite resources, you may find that you don't, or that your costs become uncontrollable.

For example, virtualized servers can get 95 percent utilization, and virtualization makes creating images easy. You may wonder what's wrong with that. The problem is that people create images and then don't get rid of them. These images can be haphazard. You can end up with blobs where you don't know what's inside. Besides being a security issue, this situation can lead to a proliferation of images. IBM notes that a typical virtual image can range in size from 5GB to 20GB. So, even though virtualization was created to control server sprawl, it's also created *image sprawl,* where images are left after a virtual machine is taken offline. This situation can lead to high storage costs, especially because often virtual machines automatically ask for storage.

Chapter 17

Employing Service Level Agreements

*T*he problem of coming up with the right level of service for the right task at the right time is an age-old problem in the computing world. It's no wonder. If you ask the typical computer user if he wants the systems and applications to have incredibly rapid performance with no downtime, the answer will always be, "Of course." However, in the real world, there's always a balance among performance, uptime, and costs.

This tension is the same in a cloud environment, with this difference: In a cloud, you're not dealing with a single system that you control; you're typically dealing with a hybrid environment that includes public and private computing services. This chapter explains what it means to manage the level of service in a hybrid world.

Defining Service Level Agreements

A *service level agreement* (SLA) is a document that captures the understanding between a service user and a service provider that defines uptime, availability, and performance. The SLA is also the contractual agreement between the participants in a service delivery contract. In the world of computing, an SLA is typically written based on the expectation that a system could be operational 99.99 percent of the month. It may also specify that the service provider's help desk will respond to an outage in a set amount of time. Also, there's an expectation that the service provider will not share a company's information with anyone and that data will be preserved for a set period of time and backed up on a regular basis.

SLAs inside the firewall

Typically, two types of SLAs are in a traditional on-premises computing environment:

- ✔ An SLA between the business and IT
- ✔ An SLA between the business and an outside services provider

In both situations, a contract specifies both expectations and penalties. Clearly, an SLA with an outside service provider is more explicit because it's a legally binding contract.

Between the business and IT, the SLA takes on a different flavor. For example, members of the accounting department may need the assurance that they will have the highest level of service when accountants are finalizing their end-of-the-month reporting. On the other hand, in the middle of the month, a lower level of service is acceptable. The manager of the accounting department understands that he will pay a higher fee at the end of the month and a smaller amount in the middle of the month. When accounting is based on an on-premises model, the fee may be in the form of a charge back based on usage of IT resources. On the other hand, if that same accounting department is using a SaaS accounting service, the company may have to purchase a more robust service package from the vendor.

Other issues important to the accounting department include things such as a high level of security for financial data and a secure connection between the office and the suppliers that are paid via an online service.

The cloud SLA

In a hybrid cloud environment, the SLA becomes more complicated than in an SLA for a private cloud service, which is very similar if not identical to the SLA between a business unit and the IT organization. (After all, the private cloud is a service within the data center that is optimized for self-service provisioning for internal customers and business partners.) Each cloud public service provider — whether it is a provider of IaaS, SaaS, BPaaS, or PaaS — will provide SLAs to cover the types of guarantees they are willing to provide to customers. But the problem for a business that might use a combination of public and private cloud services would ideally like to have a single SLA for the hybrid environment.

The bottom line is that it is hard to manage individual cloud services as though it were a single cloud environment; in reality, a hybrid cloud is a combination of many different services from many different vendors. The consumer sees the IT organization as responsible for providing them the type of service they expect. Therefore, the IT organization has to manage the SLA provided by each public cloud vendor, the SLA it has for the services it provides, and rationalize the combination.

When a company uses public cloud services, there are different expectations for an acceptable service level between the consumer and the provider. The consumer of the services expects on-demand access to services like e-mail or customer relationship management that they depend on. The service provider, on the other hand, wants to limit its liability in case of a service interruption. For example, a developer might go to Amazon.com to experiment with developing an application. That developer uses a credit card to pay for the service and builds the prototype application. Because that application is an experiment, the developer may be less concerned if the service is down for an hour. In fact, the developer might not even think about the service level at all. However, if that same developer is building an important application using Amazon.com, the expectation of uptime performance will change.

However, this starts to change if your organization uses public cloud services in combination with private cloud services as part of an overall computing environment. In this case, there may be an expectation that the public cloud service provider follows the same rules as the internal IT organization. Yet, this is not always the case, unless the public cloud service is designed and marketed with a higher level of service.

To get an idea about what you'll be dealing with, check out the SLA on Amazon.com's website. In case you don't feel like reading this fine print, it basically means that if the service doesn't achieve 99.95 percent uptime and your service is down for more than five minutes, you're eligible for a 10 percent credit. However, if the outage is related to your service provider, your software, your systems, weather, and so on, the outage is not Amazon's responsibility.

Although you might be pleased to know that a public cloud service provider will give you some money back, the issue is actually more complicated than it might appear at first glance. Say that you spent $5,000 to buy some compute capability from a public cloud provider. There's an outage that the company took responsibility for. You are sent a check for $50. But this money does not reflect the lost opportunities that may result from an outage. For example, imagine that during an outage, several important customers who were about to place significant orders were unable to execute their orders. One customer simply delayed the purchase until the following month. However, another customer actually went to a competitor. That sale was lost, which quite likely led to lost customer confidence. The bottom line is that an SLA has to take into account the impact of the service on the customer experience and revenue.

An SLA is a piece of paper, isn't it?

As much as we would like to promise you that if you simply create a hybrid cloud SLA, life will be perfect — we can't. The SLA is no better than the thinking and planning that goes on behind it. Although we think you need to think about an SLA for your hybrid environment, don't get lulled into thinking that's enough. Instead, you need to spend your time planning and coordinating.

The hybrid cloud offers a lot of flexibility that can be an economic and business benefit. However, the service level has to be understood from a holistic perspective. So, as a starting point, remember these three rules:

✔ **Read the fine print.** Remember that your cloud providers' agreements are there to protect them, not you.

✔ **Coordinate.** Look at your cloud services as an overall computing environment. You need to understand which services work together and which ones are stand-alone. For example, the public cloud service that's used to try to create new applications probably won't be part of the coordinated plan. However, the three SaaS applications that are part of a single business process need to have a coordinated SLA.

✔ **Think cloud management.** It's easy to be lulled into thinking that service levels are the responsibility of the cloud vendors you're working with. The truth is that the customer experience is still your responsibility.

Keeping Track of the Pieces

If your company is using a private cloud in combination with a public cloud service, what do you do to ensure that you are satisfying the needs of your consumers? This is a difficult question to answer. In fact, today there really isn't a great solution to this problem, but there are a number of factors to think about:

✔ Many business units will use public cloud services to create projects outside the control of IT. When these services become critical to the business, IT is often brought in after the fact.

✔ Any number of SaaS applications may become mission-critical within the company. Although the advantages of avoiding the day-to-day management and maintenance of these applications are huge, they often aren't viewed as part of the overall computing environment of the company. In addition, different SaaS applications become interconnected so that they can complete a business process. So, there are huge dependencies between these services that have to be taken into account.

✔ In addition to full SaaS applications, often key business services, such as commerce networks, payment services, and so on, are now essential services within businesses. Various on-premises applications as well as other SaaS applications depend on these services.

All of the pieces have an SLA associated with them. Each one of these environments provides a contract about the level of uptime, performance, and security. However, few vendors would be able to have the technology infrastructure or the cash to be able to guarantee the service of one of its business partners or of a third-party cloud service that its customer uses. Therefore, a hybrid SLA is something that the business itself will have to control by managing relationships with its service providers.

Creating a Hybrid SLA

Given the current state of the world, what should a business do about managing service levels across cloud models? We recommend starting at "home" and thinking about what's most important to the business. Thus, the SLA process begins by setting up a set of principles and requirements that are important to your organization's success in the market. Each company will have different requirements and priorities, but the following questions and comments can help get you started on your hybrid SLA journey:

✔ **What is the overall level of service that your business units require for applications, infrastructure, and processes?** When you understand your limitations, you will be in a better position to decide which cloud services to select based not just on price but also on the SLA the company offers. For example, perhaps a public cloud service proposes a comprehensive uptime SLA based on offering redundancy of all their services. Or a service provider might provide a virtual private network that gives you extra security you need. Another company might indemnify your company against any legal action based on their failure to live up to an SLA. When you understand the needs of each business unit, you can decide where you can afford a quick-and-dirty public service and where you need the high-priced option. You will also know when, in fact, you need to keep a service behind your firewall in the private cloud or the data center.

✔ **What type of penalties can you negotiate with cloud service providers?** When you understand the areas where you need a higher level of service, you can potentially negotiate contract terms that meet business requirements. Remember that an SLA is a contract for service that has to match your business requirements.

✔ **Managing the integrity and security of data must be a priority.** You need to understand the value of all the data managed in your hybrid cloud environment. All data is not the same. Some data (for example, company financial results and pending deals) needs a high level of protection. Other data (for example, background information and industry statistics) is important, but its loss will not affect the health of the company. Likewise, some countries restrict where and how personal information is stored. An SLA must cover all these issues.

✔ **What happens if, suddenly, key components of your hybrid environment become unavailable?** Part of your overall hybrid SLA has to include a way to handle disasters. Do the cloud providers and your private cloud have a coordinated plan to get things working again? Can you find a way to create a coordinated SLA between the important parties? This will be a new idea to many public cloud providers and the IT organization, so expect to have an important education process. Start sooner rather than later.

✔ **Understanding where the buck stops in terms of monitoring activity is a priority.** The responsibility for monitoring what's happening in the hybrid cloud is with the organization itself. Therefore, you need to think about the type of tools and techniques that will allow you to have access to performance monitoring for each service you use. At the same time, you need to have a service management strategy that will allow you to look at the entire picture of your hybrid environment.

Creating a Hybrid Management SLA Dashboard

Regarding management of the SLA of a hybrid cloud environment, think in terms of a dashboard that allows you to have visibility into the combination of services and then the ability to detect which part of your hybrid environment is causing the problems.

Here is an example that might help you think about this issue: Imagine that you are in charge of managing a sales force. You have a direct sales force, a group of contract sales people, and a distributor that sell your products. You look at the overall performance of the entire hybrid sales organization, and you notice that sales are off by 25 percent from the prior month. What does this mean? Is everyone having problems? Instead of panicking, you take a look at each group. It turns out that the distributor was acquired by another company and the team that had been selling a lot of your products was reassigned to different accounts. In fact, when you take out the performance of the distributor, it's clear that the rest of the sales organizations are outperforming previous months by a wide margin.

When downtime isn't an outage (by SLA terms)

If an SLA states that a cloud vendor will be up for 99.999 percent of the time (trailing 365 days), you likely expect them to be down for around 5 minutes over the course of a year (5.256 minutes to be exact). When viewing the many 9s, outages might be far from your mind, but a close reading of your SLA is important in order to understand what an "outage" is under the terms of the SLA. For example, a major cloud vendor was partially down for four days but managed to not breach its SLA. Through an act of good-will, affected customers were compensated, but they did not have recourse under the 99+ percent uptime SLA.

Technical staff should be brought in to consult on SLAs. Simply reviewing these documents on their face and nailing down the terms and conditions to make sure you're compensated when services are not delivered is not sufficient. You must closely read potential SLAs, understand their terms, and know how the resources will be used in your organization. Technical staff should be consulted on vulnerabilities and choke points, and the organization must understand its risk profile as it ventures forward.

Here is a — certainly not exhaustive — list of some occurrences that may lead to downtime without recourse under the SLA:

✔ **Maintenance (both scheduled and emergency):** Think about what kind of notice you expect to receive and whether your cloud provider gives such notice. What is maintenance and more importantly, what is emergency maintenance?

✔ **Attacks by third parties:** Whether the third party is maliciously targeting you, the infrastructure, or another user on the cloud, the SLA may not cover such downtimes. What sort of security does the cloud provider have in effect?

Tip: Also you might want to consider your cloud provider's other customers and whether they're targets for hackers.

✔ **Unavailability due to third-party system failures or services not under the vendor's control:** What third parties does your cloud supplier rely on? Do they have a strong partnership, or are they simply employing fly-by-night companies?

✔ **Force majeure:** These include acts of war, earthquakes, floods, riots, labor strikes, and so on. Think about the actual data center where your cloud services are located. Is it in an area prone to extreme weather or unrest?

What if you take the same approach when you analyze your hybrid cloud environment? We think that is exactly what you will need to do. Of course, some requirements have to be in place; for example, you will need

✔ A catalog that keeps track of performance statistics from each cloud environment

✔ An API that allows those statistics to be visible from the dashboard

✔ Metadata that interprets what each performance measure means from one environment to the next

✔ Tools that allow you to drill down on each element of your hybrid environment

There are indeed tools from many cloud management vendors that are helpful. However, there is still work to do before there are solutions that allow an IT organization to have a comprehensive way to have an overall view of the relationships of all the cloud services a company might be dependent on.

Chapter 18

Standards in a Hybrid World

*S*tandards are established common and repeatable practices that have been agreed to by a business or group. An *open standard* is one which is publically available (typically for free) and has rights surrounding it on how it can be used. Typically, different vendors, groups, and end users collaborate to develop standards based on the broad expertise of a large number of stakeholders. Organizations can leverage these standards as a common foundation and build on top of them.

Broad adoption of open standards throughout an industry or other group is critical in order to yield the benefits. Standards in a hybrid cloud are a work in progress, but they're important because they help you improve quality, reduce cost, and improve choices. Without broadly adopted open standards for the models, formats, and conventions for interacting with cloud capability, the hybrid cloud environment presents significant challenges.

Simply put, without standards, or agreed upon approaches, moving your infrastructure or applications from one cloud provider to another, or from on-premises to a public or private cloud, is a difficult prospect that can slow an organization's development. Integrating your on-premises data center in a hybrid model would be difficult. Standards also help to ensure security and prevent vendor lock-in. All of these issues are key in a hybrid environment.

Evolution of Standards

Standards have generally been established in four ways:

✔ **Multi-national bodies.** These are typically governed by treaties or other similar international legal agreements. These groups generally have long procedures and red tape before agreement is reached. Members might be diplomats instead of technical experts. The International Organization for Standards (ISO) is one such group. It is comprised of representatives from countries all over the world. ISO has developed over 17,500 standards covering many subject areas, and new standards are developed every year.

✔ **Industry consortiums.** Standards are developed when multiple players in an industry come together. Even though the members might be competitors, they know that coming together will help everyone. These groups are often more streamlined and agile than international bodies and often directly engage technical experts in the process. The Open Group, Open Grid Forum, and OASIS are some examples of industry consortiums.

✔ **An ad hoc group.** Ad hoc groups are self-organized and governed. These groups are often built around open source initiatives. They can be a loose body that discusses their matters through an Internet message board, or they might be more formally organized. These groups have even less processes in place than industry consortiums and are therefore able to quickly adapt and change as technology moves. A downside to the lower process overhead is that, when difficult decisions need to be made or problems arise, getting to the correct solution and reaching a consensus might be difficult or impossible.

✔ **De facto standards.** A de facto standard emerges when an approach or product is used so extensively that it becomes a standard. The important distinction is that a de facto standard is not created by a specific body or organization, but instead develops through practice. Often, these de facto standards emerge when industry best practices converge.

According to the National Institute of Standards and Technology (NIST), standards can be categorized based on their level of maturity:

✔ None

✔ Under development

✔ Approved

✔ A reference

✔ Market accepted (in widespread use)

✔ Retired

Some standards organizations require two implementations of a standard before it can be accepted, which, needless to say, takes time and accounts for why de facto standards often become standards. In new technology environments, the philosophy is often to innovate now and standardize later. In fast-paced IT environments, developers may implement nonstandard features to get a job done quickly. They leave the problems of implementing nonstandard components for another day or let somebody else deal with them. Read more about standards bodies in the later section, "Organizations Building Momentum Around Standards."

Categories of Cloud-Related Standards

Cloud standards are still in the process of being developed and implemented. Some are coming along, but watching the development of these standards can be frustrating to many, from cloud providers to cloud consumers. New standard bodies emerge, whereas others seem to flounder. Some of the current challenges in achieving widely adopted hybrid cloud standards include the following:

✔ **The cloud is still undergoing considerable innovation.** The rate and pace of technology innovation is outpacing the rate at which technology can be standardized. Creating standards is difficult if the technology is constantly evolving.

✔ **Hundreds of technology standards organizations are out there.** Many have or are working on creating cloud standards. Some of these groups work together; however, with so many standards bodies, overlapping standards can emerge. Additionally, some lose steam — or more importantly, funding — and simply fizzle out.

✔ **Not all standards are created or established equally.** For a standard to truly succeed, it needs to be

- Broadly adopted by vendors

- Broadly adopted and required by consumers

- Open source (eventually)

If these criteria are not met, a "standard" is far from standard and is instead just a piece of paper.

SDOs versus SSOs

Clearly setting standards can be complex and involves a number of organizations and bodies. Standards Developing Organizations (SDOs) and Standards Setting Organizations (SSOs) can be differentiated by how they create a standard. As the name implies, an SDO comes together to actually create and develop a standard. SSOs only set a standard. An SSO relies on an external body to develop the technical specifications and then subsequently adopts those specifications as a standard. Although SSOs might sound less influential, they can actually be quite successful at setting standards. The World Wide Web Consortium (W3C), for example, has had a long history of developing important standards for the web. These include HTML, CSS, and XML, which have received broad worldwide adoption.

Regardless, establishing hybrid cloud standards is important because standards help improve choice, reduce cost, and improve quality. Standards are being developed in many very specific areas, but broadly, areas where standards are being developed include the following, which we discuss further throughout this section:

- ✔ Interoperability
- ✔ Portability
- ✔ Security

Interoperability

Interoperability is the ability to interoperate between two or more environments. This includes operating between on-premises data centers and public clouds, between public clouds from different vendors, and between a private cloud and an external public cloud. For example, from a tooling or management perspective, with the right broadly stabled standards, one would expect that the application programming interfaces (APIs), the tools used to deploy or manage in the cloud, would be used by multiple providers. This would allow the same tool to be used in multiple cloud environments or in hybrid cloud situations.

Interoperability is especially important in a hybrid environment because your resources must work well with your cloud providers' resources. To reach the goal of interoperability, interfaces are required. In some instances, cloud providers will develop an API that describes how your resources communicate with their resources. APIs may sound like a good solution, but problems can arise. If every cloud provider develops an API, you run into the problem of *API proliferation,* a situation where there are so many APIs that organizations have difficulty managing and using them all. Having so many APIs can lead to vendor lock-in, which means that once you start using a particular vendor, you're committed to them. All of this can also lead to portability issues.

Different approaches have been proposed for cloud interoperability. For example, some groups have proposed a cloud broker model. In this approach, a common unified interface, called a *broker*, is used for all interactions among cloud elements (for example, platforms, systems, networks, applications, data).

Alternatively, companies such as CSC and RightScale have proposed an *orchestration model*. In this model, a single management platform is provided that coordinates (or orchestrates) connections among cloud providers. Recently, NIST documented the concept of functional and management interfaces when discussing interoperability. The interface presented to the functional contents of the cloud is the functional interface. The management interface is the interface used to manage a cloud service. Your management strategy will vary depending on the kind of delivery model utilized (for more on delivery models, see Chapter 1).

Another player in the interoperability space is the Open Services for Lifecycle Collaboration (OSLC). The OSLC is working on the specifications for linked data to be used to federate information and capabilities across cloud services and systems.

NIST has also cataloged existing standards. According to NIST, many existing IT standards can help to contribute to the interoperability among cloud consumer applications and cloud services, and among cloud services themselves. However, only the following two interoperability standards are developed and accepted specifically for the cloud (although others are currently under development and are likely to emerge quite soon):

- ✔ **Open Cloud Computing Interface (OCCI):** A set of standards developed by the Open Grid Forum. OCCI is a protocol and API for all kinds of management tasks and utilizes the REST (Representational State Transfer) approach for interaction. It began its life as a management API for IaaS services. It now supports PaaS and SaaS deployments.

- ✔ **The Cloud Data Management Interface (CDMI):** Developed by the Storage Networking Industry Association (SNIA). It defines the functional interface that applications should use to create, retrieve, update, and delete data elements from the cloud. It also utilizes a RESTful approach.

Some standards currently under development include the Institute of Electrical and Electronics Engineers (IEEE) IEEE P2301, Draft Guide for Cloud Portability and Interoperability Profiles (CPIP); and the IEEE P2302, Draft Standard for Intercloud Interoperability and Federation (SIIF).

Portability

Portability enables you to take applications, data, or instances running on one vendor's system and deploy it on another vendor's implementation. For example, you may want to move your data or application from one cloud environment to another. Or you may want to use the cloud for *cloud bursting* — gaining additional compute power from the cloud during peak demand times or when on-premises resources are otherwise tied up. An example is when you need extra capacity to meet peak demands so you share the load with external cloud providers. Or you may want to move your virtual server from one environment to another.

The goal of obtaining portability is that your components (such as an application or data) can be reused when moved between different vendors. This is regardless of the platform, operating system, location, storage, or anything else in a provider's environment.

One example of a standard that has gained some traction in the cloud environment is the Open Virtualization Format (OVF) developed by the Distributed Management Task Force (DMTF). This standard was developed jointly by the likes of Citrix, Dell, HP, IBM, Microsoft, and VMWare. The idea is to streamline the installation of a virtualized platform. This standard addresses portability and interoperability issues for virtual machines. The multivendor format includes a set of metadata (virtual machine hard drives, information about resource requirements, a digital signature, and so on) that enables virtual machines to be used in multiple environments. This helps with the application portability issue.

On the data side, standard formats and protocols are needed for data to be moved between one environment and another. Most experts believe that data portability is more difficult than applications because there are different kinds of data, with different volumes, and that ultimately the control of that data belongs to the owner of the data. The CDMI standard mentioned previously has been approved to help in data portability. Another standard currently under development by the IEEE is the earlier mentioned IEEE P2301, Draft Guide for Cloud Portability and Interoperability Profiles (CPIP).

Security

Cloud security is such a big concern that we devote Chapter 15 to it. You need to make sure that the right controls, procedures, and technology are in place to protect your corporate assets. Your organization has invested a great deal internally to protect your assets, and it's reasonable to assume that your cloud provider will do the same. A sound security strategy is especially true in a hybrid environment where your private cloud or data center has touchpoints with public cloud services.

Cloud security standards are a set of processes, policies, and best practices that ensure the proper controls are placed over an environment to prevent application, information, identity, and access issues (to name a few).

Numerous standards have already been approved and are currently used widely in the area of security, including standards for the following:

✔ **Authentication and authorization:** A number of standards are in use to verify the identity of a person or computer. These include standards associated with the following keys (see Chapter 15 for more on keys and encryption):

- *IETF RFC 3820:* X.509 Public Key Infrastructure (PKI) Proxy Certificate Profile

- *IETF RFC5280:* Internet X.509 Public Key Infrastructure Certificate and Certificate Revocation List (CRL) Profile

- *ITU-T X.509 | ISO/IEC 9594-8— The Directory: Public Key and attribute certificate frameworks:* Information technology — open systems interconnection

✔ **Security monitoring and incident response:** Some standards have currently been approved to handle security monitoring and incident response. These include the best practices developed by NIST in the NIST SP 800-61 Computer Security Incident Handling Guide.

✔ **Confidentiality, integrity, and availability of data:** We address data issues more fully in Chapter 11. However, a number of standards that have been on the market for some time deal with encryption of data, keys, and data transport. These include the Key Management Interoperability Protocol (KMIP), developed by OASIS; and FIPS 186-3 Digital Signature Standard (DSS), developed by NIST.

✔ **Security policy management:** These standards set forth best practices and procedures for implementing policies around security. FIPS 200: Minimum Security Requirements for Federal Information and Information Systems developed by NIST is an example of this kind of standard.

For a complete list of these standards and gaps in security standards, we encourage you to get a copy of the NIST Cloud Computing Standards Roadmap described in the next section.

Organizations Building Momentum Around Standards

A number of organizations and informal groups are addressing standards issues in the cloud environment. Some of these organizations have been around for years; others are relatively new. *Note:* Some of these standards bodies aren't necessarily looking to create new standards. Instead they are looking to leverage existing best practices and standards such as those used in implementing the web and service oriented architectures (SOA).

Several standards organizations have gotten together to create a cloud standards coordination wiki — a website that uses collaborative software to allow many people to work together to post and edit content. All groups can post their work at one spot: www.cloud-standards.org.

Cloud Security Alliance

We talk a lot about the Cloud Security Alliance (CSA) (www.cloudsecurity.org) in Chapter 15. The CSA formed in late 2008 when cloud security became important in users' minds. Its founding members include Dell, PGP, QualSys, Ascaler, and the Information Systems Audit and Control Association (ISACA). The CSA's goal is to promote a series of best practices to provide security assurance in cloud computing and to provide education. It's important to note that the CSA itself isn't an actual standards body. However, its objectives include promoting understanding between users and providers of cloud computing regarding security requirements and researching best practices for cloud security.

The CSA offers training in three areas:

- ✔ Governance, Risk Management, and Compliance (GRC)
- ✔ Payment Card Industry (PCI) Data Security Standard (DSS) controls in the cloud
- ✔ Cloud Computing Security Knowledge (CCSK)

The CSA also provides a certificate in CCSK via a 50-question timed online test. According to the CSA, the CCSK is meant to augment certifications in information security, audit, and governance, and not to replace them. The CSA recently rolled out its Security, Trust & Assurance Registry (STAR), a free, publically accessible registry that documents the security controls provided by cloud vendors. The registry is a form of self-regulation by cloud providers and is meant to help ensure that CSA best practices become de facto standards.

Recent reports produced by the CSA include version 3 of its Security Guidance for Critical Areas of Focus in Cloud Computing (https://cloudsecurityalliance. org/research/security-guidance/), which we talk more about in Chapter 15.

Distributed Management Task Force (DMTF)

The DMTF (www.dmtf.org) has been around for 20 years and may best be known for its common information model, which is a common view of IT equipment. Its goal is to bring the IT industry together to collaborate on systems management standards.

The DTMF formed the DTMF Cloud Management Working Group. The goal of the group is to develop specifications for architectural semantics to support the interoperable management of primarily IaaS clouds. The group will focus on compute, storage, and network infrastructure.

Its starting point utilizes work already done by the Open Clouds Standards Incubator, which launched in 2009, and focuses on standardizing interactions between different cloud environments by developing cloud resource management protocols, packaging formats, and security mechanisms to facilitate interoperability. The group will also use previous research from its work in the Common Information Model and the Open Virtualization Format (OVF). OVF describes an open, secure, and portable format for packing and distributing software that will be run on virtual machines.

National Institute of Standards and Technology (NIST)

NIST (www.nist.gov) has been in existence since 1901. It's a nonregulatory federal agency that is part of the U.S. Department of Commerce. Its goal is to promote innovation and U.S. competitiveness by advancing standards, measurement science, and technology. NIST has its hands in all kinds of standards, from fire-related standards for your mattress to the auto emissions your car must (not) pass on the road.

NIST formed its cloud computing group to help federal agencies understand cloud computing. However, its reach has gone much further than the federal government. For example, its definition of cloud computing models are widely used across all industries (refer to the NIST special publication 800-545, September 2011).

NIST recently completed its Cloud Computing Standards Roadmap (NIST special publication 500-291, July 2011, www.nist.gov/customcf/get_pdf.cfm?pub_id=909024). The purpose of the document is to assess the state of standards in cloud computing. The document contains an inventory of standards that currently exist to support cloud computing in the areas of security, interoperability, and portability. It also indentifies some of the gaps. We discuss this document in the previous section of this chapter.

Cloud Standards Customer Council (CSCC)

The OMG (Object Management Group; www.omg.org) was formed in 1989 and is an international group focused on developing enterprise integration standards for a wide range of industries, including government, life sciences, and health care. The OMG creates many working groups that focus on issues important to both vendors and customers. One important group within the OMG is called the Cloud Standards Customer Council (CSCC).

The CSCC (www.cloud-council.org) provides modeling standards for software and other processes and has brought together many of the most influential companies in cloud computing. IBM, Computer Associates, Kaavo, Software AG, and Rackspace are the groups founding sponsors. The goal of the CSCC is to establish a set of customer-driven/end-user requirements to ensure cloud users have the same flexibility and openness that they have with traditional IT environments. CSCC will prioritize key interoperability issues in reference architecture, security and compliance, cloud management, and hybrid clouds.

The idea is that this group will work with most of the standards bodies listed here to bring the end-user perspective more fully into the standards discussion.

Open Cloud Consortium (OCC)

The OCC (`www.opencloudconsortium.org`) was formed in 2008. One of its goals is to support the development of standards for cloud computing and frameworks for interoperability among clouds. In fact, it operates cloud infrastructure. It also manages cloud computing infrastructure to support scientific research. Members include Cisco and Yahoo! as well as a number of universities including Johns Hopkins University.

The OCC has a number of working groups. One in particular deals with standards — Malstone is a reference benchmark and standard for dealing with data-intensive computing in the cloud.

The Open Group

The Open Group (`www3.opengroup.org`) is a global consortium with more than 400 member organizations that focuses on achieving business objectives through standards. Its goal is to lead the development of vendor-neutral IT standards and certifications.

In the cloud, the Open Group Cloud Work Group is looking to create a common understanding among various groups about ensuring safe and secure architectures. The group is working with organizations such as the Cloud Security Alliance and the Jericho Forum to make this happen. Incidentally, the Jericho Forum was founded at the Open Group in 2004 and focuses on issues around de-perimeterization.

De-perimeterization is a strategy of securing an organization's IT assets through multiple techniques instead of simply attempting to build a wall around your infrastructure to try and keep out ever varying threats. This is achieved through encryption, inherently-secure computer protocols, inherently-secure computer systems, and data-level authentication. This strategy is clearly important for hybrid clouds because data and applications will likely be on systems that are out of your sole control.

For more on the Jericho Forum and perimeter issues, refer to Chapter 15, which focuses on security.

The Open Grid Forum (OGF)

The OGF (www.ogf.org) is an open community that focuses on driving the adoption and evolution of distributed computing, including everything from distributed high-performance computing resources to horizontally scaled transactional systems supporting SOA, as well as the cloud. The community shares best practices and drives these best practices into standards. It consists of more than 400 companies in 50 countries, including AT&T and eBay.

The OGF is responsible for OCCI, an API for interfacing cloud computing facilities, as previously described.

Storage Networking Industry Association (SNIA)

The SNIA (www.snia.org) has focused for more than ten years on developing storage solution specifications and technologies, global standards, and storage education. This organization's mission, according to the SNIA members is "to promote acceptance, deployment, and confidence in storage related architectures, systems, services, and technologies, across IT and business communities." As part of its 2012–2014 strategic plan, it also intends to promote standards and educational services around information management.

The SNIA is responsible for the Cloud Data Management Interface previously described. This is a functional interface that applications can use "to create, retrieve, update and delete data elements from the Cloud." Clearly, this is an important standard for hybrid cloud environments that deal with data between on-premises and public cloud deployments.

Vertical groups

In addition to the preceding standards groups and discussion groups, *vertical industry* groups — groups comprised of members from a particular industry such as technology and retail — are also beginning to look at cloud standards. Here are two examples:

✔ **TeleManagement Forum (TM Forum):** This large group consists of service providers, cable and network operators, software suppliers, equipment suppliers, and systems integrators. It has provided a standardized operational framework for the creation, delivery, and monetization of digital services. It recently launched its TM Forum Cloud & New Services Initiative that focuses on leveraging these standards into the cloud marketplace. To learn more about the group visit www.tmforum.org.

✔ **Association for Retail Technology Standards (ARTS):** The goal of this group is to create an open environment where retailers and technology vendors can work together to create international retail technology standards. Recently, this group released its Cloud Computing whitepaper (available the ARTS website), which also includes a template of questions for retailers to use when looking at various cloud options. To read more about ARTS or access the whitepaper you can visit www.nrf-arts.org.

The Impact of Standards on the Hybrid Cloud

We think that you will agree that standards, whether developed by SDOs or through the de facto method, play an important role in cloud computing and in a hybrid cloud model. In a hybrid world, there are many interfaces between those that exist at your cloud provider and your applications, data, servers, and so on. This state of affairs means that security is a risk in many places. These can include areas where it's costly to interoperate and where you can get bogged down and limit your options in terms of cloud providers. Standards let you do the following:

✔ **Move your infrastructure or applications from one cloud provider to another.** This means you don't have to rewrite code. In a hybrid world, where you may have part of the resources associated with an application on your own premises and part with a cloud provider, this capability is important because it enables your organization to be more flexible about where your resources might be located.

✔ **Prevent vendor lock-in.** We talk about this earlier in the chapter. Lock-in occurs when you are so entrenched with a particular provider and its interfaces that moving to another provider is too costly. Removing barriers to lock-in improves your choices.

✔ **Integrate applications more easily between your on-premises data center and private and public cloud environments.** Let's face it, integrating your assets across multiple environments can be time-consuming and costly if every cloud provider has a proprietary model. Standards help to make integration easier and eliminate many common barriers.

Open Cloud Manifesto: The notion of an open cloud is so critical to the long-term success of the cloud that more than 200 vendors have already signed on to support a document called the Open Cloud Manifesto (www.opencloud manifesto.org). The group, formed in 2009, realizes that although the cloud presents a great opportunity, a series of challenges must be overcome. These challenges include security, interoperability, portability, management, metering, and governance. The manifesto has a series of statements related to standards.

Part VI
Getting Set for the Hybrid Cloud Journey

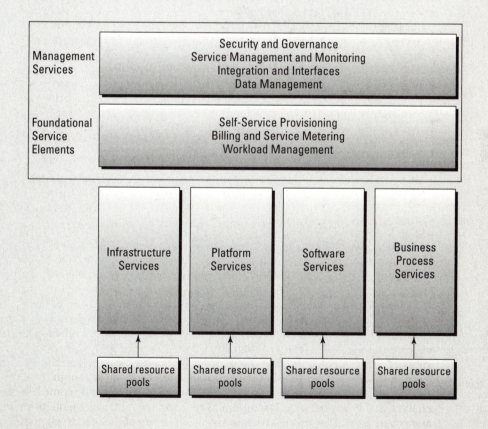

In this part . . .

You have lots of planning to do to create a well-designed hybrid cloud strategy. In this part, we give you some guidelines and best practices to help you get started planning that strategy, as well as preparing for storage and network support.

Chapter 19

Planning Your Hybrid Cloud Strategy

*P*lanning your hybrid cloud strategy is a journey, not a simple set of steps. The right planning strategy is imperative to getting your plan to be operational. So, you need to look at the technical components, the business strategy, and the organizational plan. Remember that cloud computing can offer a dramatic change in the pace and style of computing as well as business strategy. Therefore, although costs will, of course, be imperative, you also need to think about the benefits that may help transform the customer experience. Your overall strategy will include a hybrid of different types and models of computing, so planning will be integral to your path forward. In this chapter, we give you an idea about what to expect as you begin your journey, along with the important issues you need to consider.

Identifying Your Starting Points

With all the discussions around the value of cloud computing, it sometimes can seem overwhelming about how to get started. Do you simply get rid of your data center and turn your future over to a selected cloud provider? Do you do a few small projects leveraging a public cloud just to see what the cloud might be like? Do you simply hire a big consulting firm to create a private cloud? Unfortunately, none of these approaches would get you to the right place.

An overall cloud computing strategy is like any other business strategy — it must be planned within the context of your business goals and objectives. So, before you begin your journey to the hybrid cloud, we suggest that you take the five steps, outlined as stages, described in the following sections.

Stage One: Assess your current IT strategy

Your first step is to assess the current state of your IT strategy and how well it serves the business. IT organizations have typically grown in a relatively unplanned fashion. Although they likely began as well-orchestrated sets of hardware and software, over time they have grown into a collection of various computing silos.

You might think of them as being like a typical two-car garage. In the beginning, the garage held two cars and a few necessities such as yard tools. Over the years, the homeowner began to store lots of different paraphernalia in the garage, ranging from unused pots and pans to an array of old furniture. Suddenly, that well-planned, purpose-built space became crammed with so much stuff that it's hard to use the garage for its initial intent — storing cars!

Today, is your IT infrastructure like that garage, or is it a well-planned and well-orchestrated environment? Does it provide the type of flexibility and manageability that supports new initiatives and business change? Or is it an assortment of different servers, different software products, and a variety of disconnected tools? Most likely your environment is somewhere in between these two extremes.

Your first step is taking an honest assessment — as a joint effort between the business and IT — of your current stage so that you have a good understanding of what works and what doesn't. You should look at what systems are critical to the operations of the business and which applications no longer support changing business needs. You need to consider the flexibility of your existing infrastructure. What happens when the business requires a change in processes? How does the IT organization support partnership initiatives?

Stage Two: Imagine the future

This is the stage where IT has to really spend time not only understanding how the business looks today but also how it might evolve in the next three to five years. What does the future of your business look like? Are you part of an industry that is experiencing dramatic shifts in how you collaborate with suppliers, business partners, and customers? Are there technological approaches that your emerging competitors are starting to implement that you will have to embrace? Are there opportunities to offer new business strategies that are driven by emerging technologies? It may be that your industry is changing, and without new technology approaches you will not be able to sustain a competitive advantage.

This process, which is imperative to planning your hybrid cloud strategy, will also have some unanticipated benefits. It prepares IT to have a deeper understanding of business change and the opportunities that are unfolding. Small and mid-sized companies have extraordinary opportunities to leverage a hybrid cloud environment and some of the new services in the market to gain a level of sophistication that, in the past, were available to only the largest corporations. At the same time, the largest companies can leverage a hybrid cloud strategy to improve their agility and flexibility to respond to new innovations and new business opportunities.

Stage Three: Explore what's out there

Armed with the knowledge of the current state of your business and the supporting IT infrastructure and where it is headed, now is the time to learn and experiment with cloud computing options. Although plenty of organizations will be happy to do all the work for you, it's important that you spend the time understanding the landscape of best practices, as well as different cloud computing options that can help the business.

Spend time with your peers and see what type of cloud strategy they have adopted and the type of dividends it's paying. What are the best practices that have worked well for companies in your industry or of your size? What are the new innovations coming to market from young companies? How can you offer a new approach to business that will allow you to effectively compete with much larger companies in your market?

The wonderful thing about cloud computing capabilities and offerings is that you are free to experiment. Almost every company in the cloud market offers free trials of their technology. There are many open source offerings as well that will give you the opportunity to test out whether different options will serve your business now or in the long run. This education process is critical so that you know what questions to ask. Even if and when you turn to a service provider for help, you will be able to make better decisions about how you approach your cloud strategy.

Stage Four: Create a hybrid cloud strategy plan

At this stage, you're ready to start creating the actual plan. Again, this should be based on a joint effort between the business and IT. If your company has done planning for service orientation to help in creating business services, start by leveraging your earlier work and plans. Also, if you've previously done any strategic planning, leverage it. Always leverage the knowledge and expertise inside your company as a starting point. It's also a good idea to get your most strategic partners involved in the process. Your best partners, suppliers, and customers will help you better understand how they want to collaborate with you in the future. Use all this as the foundation for your hybrid cloud strategy.

At the same time, you need to take into account your security, privacy, and governance policies that your company needs to adhere to. These issues need to become part of how you approach cloud computing in your company. For example, different industries have different regulations that you will have to conform to. Some countries have laws that restrict where and how customer information can be managed and stored. This must be considered for your hybrid cloud strategy.

Stage Five: Plan for implementation

Now you're ready for action. However, it's not practical to try to do everything at once. Most companies will need a *staged implementation* of a hybrid cloud strategy in which they deploy parts of the overall plan in phases. For example, the first phase might be to provide controlled access to a public cloud service for developers prototyping a new application to support an experimental business initiative. Or an initial stage may involve implementing a SaaS application such as customer relationship management that will help streamline the way the sales and marketing teams operate.

Whatever you do, think of your hybrid cloud strategy as a multi-year effort that will include everything from a set of private cloud services to support emerging internal development and deployment needs to a way to leverage public services in conjunction with your data center.

Stages of strategy planning: An overview

Now that we have discussed all five stages of the overall cloud computing strategy, you can take a step back and review the process in terms of the impact each stage will have on your business, as well as the value each stage will bring, as shown in Table 19-1.

You need to think holistically — not just about the most straightforward services such as infrastructure but also about data integration and integrity and cloud management issues. The way you stage these efforts will be directly tied to both the current state of IT and the business strategy for the next several years.

Table 19-1	Evaluating the Impact and Value of the Strategy Planning Stages		
Stage	*Rationale*	*Impact*	*Value*
Assess IT's current state.	You need to understand your level of maturity.	You will better understand how much work is ahead.	You will set the stage for business and IT collaboration.
Map the future.	You need to understand where the business is headed.	You can be better prepared to map your cloud strategy to business change.	It will allow you to make strategy choices based on a different worldview.
Know your cloud computing options.	Understand the choices you have.	Without this knowledge, you will overlook emerging options.	You want to select both tried-and-true and brand-new technologies.
Create the plan.	A road map to plan over time.	This will help you stage your implementation based on business strategy.	You will be ready to execute in an organized way.
Plan for implementation.	Get ready for action.	A coordinated process of implementation and experimentation.	A dynamic approach to moving forward.

Focusing the Plan on Providing Services to Your Constituents

Once you have a concrete understanding of the technical and business considerations, it's time to put the strategy into a technical architectural plan. This technical plan must mirror the requirements and changes in the business strategy. It is helpful to think about what type of customers or consumers you are supporting. It is also important to understand where those services will come from. Your organization may provide some services directly while you will contract with commercial service providers for other services. And you also have to determine how you will create or select those providers who will create services. You need to plan for three different types of services, as we discuss in this section.

Cloud service consumer services

These are the services that touch your employees, your partners, and customers. Although there are sophisticated services underlying these services — for example, business process, cloud-based application, and infrastructure services — they are hidden from the consumer. The consumer wants to see fast performance and security.

Comprehensive cloud provider services

Cloud providers typically offer public cloud services to a range of constituents. In some cases, the services are designed to create a high level of service and security for corporations. Therefore, these companies will offer support for cloud applications ranging from PaaS, BPaaS, SaaS, as well as infrastructure services. They will also create their own service management platform and integration services. These service providers often offer a range of services depending on the level of service required by your company.

Cloud service creation services

Cloud creation services are offered by service provides as a way to create new, innovative business services from a variety of platforms and IP from your industry or company. These runtime services can be designed to create new innovative services that sit on top of a service delivery platform either from a cloud provider or within your private environment. It's common for these creation services to leverage both public and private offerings based on business strategy.

Supporting a Successful Customer Experience

Now that you have a road map for creating a strategy, take a step back and think about how a hybrid approach to cloud computing can transform the customer experience. Everything that you do with this new approach to linking IT and business through the cloud should focus on expanding opportunities. So, think about how you can expand the ability to innovate, satisfy customers, and optimize your environment to efficiently deliver those services. In this section, we focus on the elements that lead to an effective customer experience.

Supporting innovation

Most of the exciting innovations in industries come from creating change that transforms the customer experience. In the days before the Internet became the backbone of business services, companies might have innovated by simply calling customers more frequently or packaging products differently. But in the age where business is conducted online and where communities collaborate and online commerce are the norm, companies are discovering that they must use Internet-driven technologies to support innovation.

Cloud computing offers a much richer set of options to companies. For example, a retailer wanting to provide real-time access to images and videos of products anywhere in the world can select a different public cloud provider in each market it serves, thus reducing latency and improving the customer experience. Likewise, another company may combine these public services with new private, service-oriented clouds that allow intellectual property and highly secure data to be managed in the data center. Other companies are discovering that the private cloud can become an engine to support rapid change.

Each new initiative will be supported by a private cloud environment that allows developers to create new, radical applications that might fail quickly or provide a new model to support a business partnership.

Defining the optimal customer experience

Although most companies will first think about the technology and business model options offered by cloud computing vendors, it's important to put the customer first. The greatest benefit of the hybrid cloud strategy is the way it helps to transform and optimize the customer experience. More and more companies are interacting with their customers online. Customers will judge your company by how well your entire cloud environment performs. Abundant statistics demonstrate that customers who have a poor online experience rarely come back for a second try. Therefore, a hybrid cloud implemented with a strong strategic foundation can help enhance the customer experience.

Optimizing for workloads

Thinking about the depth and breadth of cloud computing offerings can be overwhelming. There are different business models, different platforms, and many different types of services. But at the end of the day, one of the most important considerations is how you handle and manage workloads across your various computing environments. Remember, a *workload* is a unit of work that you execute to complete a task.

So, from a business-strategy perspective, think about every business activity being supported by a computing workload. Using this perspective helps you get a firmer handle on the right cloud service to support each problem. For example, if you're managing a workload that has stringent security requirements, a private cloud environment may be more appropriate. There are also some public clouds that will offer security warranties that you will be able to consider to support security requirements. On the other hand, a temporary workload such as extra storage capacity needed for a day or a month can be supported by a commodity public service. By focusing on the nature of workloads, you're in a better position to create a strategy that matches business requirements.

Supporting a Dynamic Lifecycle

As your cloud computing strategy emerges, you will begin to understand some important differences between the old way of operating and the cloud computing style. In traditional computing environments, it's assumed that different organizations inside and outside of IT will select numerous different tools and technologies to support any given IT initiative. IT then has to do a lot of the hard work of making sure all these disconnected components can communicate or connect to each other so that they act as though they were a single unified environment.

Accomplishing this task has never been easy, but the consequences of failures have become more extreme. For example, several different systems may depend on database configurations, and IT must make sure all of the correct changes are made across the IT operations. If someone forgets to make a change based on the implementation of a new version of a database or tool, the consequences can be serious. Systems can stop working, and customers can be seriously affected.

Abstracting Complexity in the Cloud

In the emerging world of cloud computing, platforms will be much more abstracted. The level of complexity will not be reduced, but the complexity will be managed at an infrastructure level rather than at a tool level. This means that there will be a central way to manage configurations and versions. There will be more centralization of core functions that are leveraged across hybrid environments. Fewer moving parts that are subject to human error will help transform IT into a smoother computing utility in a much more dynamic fashion. These changes will not happen overnight, but looking forward, IT must adopt goals and strategies that promote the automation of the complexity that leads to unintended consequences and errors.

Balancing Costs and Benefits

How you plan your hybrid cloud environment will be driven by economics. You, therefore, need to think in terms of the total costs and whether those expenditures will be worthwhile in the long run. Achieving this balance isn't simple. Many cloud services, including IaaS and SaaS, are offered based on a per-user, per-month, or per-year contract. Some other services are designed for occasional use. Private cloud services can often leverage hardware already existing within a data center. No simple formula will give you the most optimal way to define the total cost of ownership or whether a cloud service will accomplish your long-term goals.

Defining the purpose of your cloud services

Because of the economic impact, you have to look at cost-benefit issues though a different lens than in a traditional data center environment. You need to think about the purpose of each service you are considering and how it will affect the business. For example, a SaaS environment may be more expensive in yearly license fees, but save the company money in terms of hardware, software, maintenance, and support requirements. SaaS also may better support the internal needs of the business. Perhaps the SaaS environment means that your company can be more proactive in addressing customer or employee needs. This SaaS service could result in better internal productivity.

On the other hand, in other situations, a public cloud service won't make economic sense, such as when your company's actual business is a set of cloud services. In this situation, your company is, in reality, a cloud service provider. Therefore, bring these services in-house, because a well-architected cloud service model will provide the most economically viable solution to support the business. If big enough, the company might be able to use its buying power to purchase in a less expensive way than a third-party company could. Likewise, this company can be in a good position to support innovation and optimize the private cloud model so that it produces the right workloads in the right way.

In yet other situations, companies will find that splitting services between public and private is the most optimal financial approach. The company that needs extra storage capacity three times a year will be best served by leveraging a public storage service than by purchasing extra storage capacity.

The bottom line is that there is no one approach to determining total cost of ownership or your return on investment in a hybrid cloud environment. So, part of your planning process is to take into account the financial measures you'll need when moving to the hybrid cloud. What issues will most directly affect your ability to compete? What type of innovation is likely to be important for your long-term strategy for success? Simply looking at all expenses in the same way will not be the best method for determining your strategy. Establishing a set of guidelines for the economics of your cloud strategy will help your decision-making process.

Taking a holistic approach

When you are planning for your movement to a hybrid cloud environment, make sure that you aren't looking though only one lens. Instead, view the hybrid cloud from the perspective of flexibility and agility for your business needs. The hybrid cloud also needs to be understood from a technical implementation strategy so that plans can be put into action in a staged and well-thought-out fashion. Your success with the hybrid cloud will depend not just on how you can justify what you spend and what you save, but also how you affect the bottom line of the business.

Chapter 20

Managing Data Storage in the Hybrid Cloud

Data storage has always been a critical issue in any IT organization. Storage is complex and expensive. This issue does not go away with a cloud environment. In fact, in some ways the movement to cloud computing can complicate data storage because there is a struggle between the need to keep costs in check while at the same time maintaining control over data management. One of the options that many medium-sized and large businesses are investigating is to adopt a hybrid approach to storage that includes many different elements. However, many questions need to be answered. When should you keep data in your private cloud or data center? When is it appropriate to store data in a public cloud environment? How are the storage options going to impact important issues such as latency, availability, security, and governance? In this chapter you explore the evolution of storage requirements leading to the hybrid cloud strategy approach. In addition, you examine how companies can streamline their organization's IT capabilities by leveraging both public and private cloud storage options.

Understanding Cloud Storage Fundamentals

The design of cloud storage is very similar to other cloud architectures in terms of self-service, elasticity, and scalability. Cloud storage is a technique of abstracting storage with a well-defined interface so it can be managed in a self-service manner. In addition, cloud storage needs to support a multi-tenant architecture so that each consumer's cloud data is managed in isolation from other consumer's cloud data. One of the most important characteristics of cloud storage is how it can dynamically interface with other cloud services such as SaaS, PaaS, IaaS, and BPaaS.

It is not new to think about attaching storage to systems — it has been done since the first systems rolled off the assembly line. Today, most storage environments are connected with systems through a standard interface called SCSI (Small Computer Systems Interface). SCSI is a very mature protocol that is widely adopted because of its reliability and performance.

Four key fundamentals of cloud storage — access protocols, usage scenarios, functions, and benefits — are addressed below:

Cloud storage access protocols

One important issue in cloud storage is the speed and ease of accessing the data when it's needed. In order for cloud storage to be a viable alternative to on-premises data storage, you need to be able to access your data at a competitive cost and at a time that is appropriate for the situation. Today, there are four types of cloud storage access methods:

- **Web services application programming interfaces (APIs):** These use RESTful APIs (according to the principals of Representational State Transfer) to integrate with applications.

- **File-based protocols:** These protocols are used to transfer files and provide integration independent of the application being connected. They also provide a faster integration than web service APIs. Different types are

    - Network File System (NFS)

    - Common Internet File System (CIFS)

    - File Transfer Protocol (FTP)

- **Block-based APIs:** These use Internet SCSI to connect a front end to storage middleware that support services such as data replication and data reduction.

- **Web-based Distribution Authoring and Versioning (WebDAV):** This is based on Hypertext Transfer Protocol (HTTP).

Defining the elements of storage

New mobile and digital technologies are among the many market factors that are responsible for an exponential rate of increase in the amount and type of data that companies need to store. Some of this data needs to be readily available and some needs to be stored for five to seven years or longer for compliance purposes. In addition, new technologies like virtualization have helped companies to become more efficient and save money but have also created new and costly storage challenges. For example, some companies found that the savings they expected from consolidating and increasing the utilization of their servers was eaten up by increased spending on storage for a rapidly growing number of virtual machine images. Companies want to find new cost-effective and flexible storage solutions to help meet their evolving storage requirements. So while we expect new methods and innovation in the approach to storage, the following summarizes how large-scale storage is typically managed:

✔ **Direct attached storage (DAS):** In this model, storage is generally done on the local bus. In other words, your storage may be a hard drive that's internal to your machine or an external drive like a USB storage device, or it might be on a server or a shared network resource on a dedicated server. DAS is generally not directly accessible to other servers, although multiple machines may share this storage. In a DAS arrangement, you generally cannot share data unless you explicitly give access to a user or a group of users.

✔ **Storage area network (SAN):** This is a high-speed network of interconnected storage devices. These storage devices might be servers or optical disk drives or other storage media. There can be a large number of them, depending on your company's requirements. The architecture is such that all storage devices are accessible by all devices that are on your company's local area network (LAN) or wide area network (WAN). SANs can require significant configuration and support to install.

✔ **Network addressable storage (NAS):** A NAS is generally constructed as a specialized kind of computer that is connected to a network and that provides file-based storage to other computers. It's generally easier to install and not as high speed as a SAN. The difference between a NAS and a SAN is that a NAS provides a file system, whereas a SAN doesn't.

Here's something else to keep in mind about storage. Traditionally, companies assign the data they need to store into different *tiers*. Tiered storage is the assignment of data to different kinds of media, generally to reduce storage costs. Here are the three kinds of tiers:

✔ **Tier 1:** Refers to data that has been recently accessed or is mission-critical. In other words, you want to have it readily on hand. It's generally stored on high-quality media. Think of your bank account data. It's likely that you want to view the last several months of this data.

✔ **Tier 2:** Refers to data that's rarely accessed. This might be backed up on a periodic basis in a corporate environment. Data stored in databases, for example, is often *mirrored* (copied) by another sever. In a corporate environment, data might be stored this way for three to six months.

✔ **Tier 3:** Data that's almost never accessed. This data may need to be stored for a long period of time for compliance reasons. In the brokerage industry, for example, the Securities and Exchange Commission (SEC) requires that all transactions and e-mails are stored for up to seven years. The amount of tier 3 data can be huge for a large company.

The most common method for accessing cloud storage is by using web service APIs such as REST (Representational State Transfer). Cloud storage vendors implement this technology because it's dynamic and simple to use in the cloud. In addition, because of the use of virtualization in cloud environments, there's a requirement for a more *stateless* (no set location for any code) access protocol. Web service APIs support this requirement for statelessness. This access method is used by Amazon Simple Storage Service (Amazon S3), Windows Azure (Microsoft's Cloud Platform), and others. However, Web service APIs need to be integrated with a specific application when used for cloud storage, which can create some challenges. If you want to avoid the need to integrate with an application, file-based protocols and block-based APIs can be used as alternative access methods. Another connection protocol is WebDAV, a specification designed to create an efficient cloud storage interface.

Delivery options for cloud storage

How will your cloud provider deliver your storage capability? You can use an appliance or connect to a public or remote storage service.

Although latency is a big issue for primary (tier 1) cloud storage, particularly for data used frequently, vendors are currently offering a different class of products called *hybrid cloud storage* solutions that may ultimately address primary storage. (Because we talk about hybrid clouds in general throughout this book, some of the terminology may be confusing, but bear with us.) The idea is to use local and cloud-based resources to address performance issues associated with storage in the cloud. Generally, these offerings consist of two things:

✔ An *appliance* that is a physical or virtual server where the hardware and software are preconfigured so the user doesn't have to understand the details

✔ A connection to a remote storage service

The appliance intelligently handles the movement between the local storage and the cloud; to the end user, all of the data seems to be in one place.

A *cache* is a block of memory for temporary storage on the appliance that provides a high-speed buffer between your client and the cloud service. The cache uses a host of algorithms to keep the most frequently used data on the local, expensive hardware. For read requests, attributes such as the age of the data, time since last accessed, time since last updated, and so on are used. For write requests, the appliance may write the data locally on the machine and then burst it out to the cloud storage provider.

The data is generally encrypted when it's transported. When you request data from the provider, the data is first deduplicated to make it faster to retrieve. Vendors such as Nasuni, StorSimple, CTERA Networks, and others are providing solutions in this space.

Functions of cloud storage

The type of information you need to store and how quickly you need to access data both have an impact on the type of storage you will use. You can use policy-based replication to enable more granular control over how and where data is stored.

Cloud storage can serve multiple purposes:

- ✔ General-purpose storage for day-to-day or periodic use
- ✔ Data protection and continuity, which can include data replication and backup and restore functionality
- ✔ Archive and records management, meaning recoverable long-term data retention to support compliance and regulatory requirements

Benefits of cloud storage

Some of the benefits of cloud storage include:

- ✔ **Agility:** The elastic nature of the cloud enables you to gain potentially unlimited storage in an on-demand model.
- ✔ **Fewer physical devices to purchase and maintain:** When you're storing data in a data center, you have to plan for the servers that will be part of this storage solution. This means you need to plan for purchasing the machines and maintain them during their lifecycle. Additionally, you must make sure that you have enough space and can meet power requirements. In the cloud, you don't have to purchase physical devices or deal with environmental issues. The cloud provider should do this for you (but it pays to do your homework on the services that your provider offers).
- ✔ **Disaster recovery:** The cloud can serve as a good replacement for tape or other backups and can minimize concerns about your own data center capacity to support your backups. Instead of continuing to expand your on-premises storage, your information can be backed up to the cloud. If your systems go down, you can retrieve your data from the cloud.
- ✔ **Cost:** Although DAS is relatively inexpensive, NAS and SAN devices require significant capital expenditures. The cloud storage model is based on usage, so you only pay for what you use. This is similar to how you use your telephone — generally speaking, you pay for what you use.

Amazon's cloud storage model

Perhaps one of the best known cloud storage providers is Amazon. Amazon's S3 is an online storage service. With the service, you store your objects (data), which can be as small as one byte to as large as 5 terabytes of information in what Amazon terms a *bucket*. Each bucket has a unique key. Each bucket can be stored in one of several regions based on how close you want your data or regulatory issues to be. It uses REST and SOAP interfaces as the methods of storing and retrieving data in the Amazon storage cloud. REST and SOAP are standard protocols, and if you choose this method to store and retrieve data, you'll need access to someone with programming skills. Amazon has implemented technology to help give users more control over storage costs. For example, if customers have a redundant copy of the data they are storing or that data can be replicated, they can use Reduced Redundancy Storage (RSS) to minimize costs. RSS replicates data fewer times within the Amazon S3 infrastructure than other options. The cost of cloud storage is an important factor in a customer's decision making about cloud storage. Therefore, there is a lot of market competition on price. In that regard, the prices listed below for Amazon storage are likely to change. In March 2012, posted rates for Amazon standard storage range from $.140 per gigabyte to $.055 per gigabyte per month depending on how much data you're storing. Amazon also charges a setup fee to transfer your data to its cloud. There's no transfer fee once your data is in S3

Other cloud storage vendors include CommVault, IBM, HP, Microsoft, EMC, GoGrid, and Nirvanix.

Of course, no solution comes without drawbacks. Off-premises storage can affect performance, which will now be based on connectivity and latency between your LAN/WAN and your cloud provider. Network connectivity can affect performance (see more on this topic in the next section). Additionally, you need to deal with issues such as the security that your cloud provider puts in place and availability of your cloud provider.

Note: Chapter 11 discusses managing your data; Chapter 15 covers cloud security; and Chapter 17 has more information about service level agreements and managing your cloud provider.

Considerations for Hybrid Cloud Storage

You might consider various scenarios for a storage architecture when you deploy a hybrid cloud. Remember that in a hybrid model, some of your resources and assets will be on-premises and some will live in the cloud. Here are some possible scenarios:

✔ Your applications and data are on-premises, and your tier 2 and 3 data is stored in a public cloud.

✔ Some of your applications are in a public cloud, your data is on-premises, and your storage is in a public cloud.

✔ You have a private cloud within your enterprise, and you're managing a private cloud that's hosted elsewhere.

✔ Some of your applications are in a public cloud along with your data. Some of your applications and data are on-premises. Your storage is both in the cloud and on-premises.

You get the idea. In a hybrid world, there can be multiple permutations in terms of how you architect your applications, data, and storage. So, here's what you need to be thinking about in terms of storage as you deploy a hybrid cloud:

✔ **Interfaces:** To store and retrieve data, your applications need an API that connects your local system to the cloud-based storage system. Users should be able to send data to the cloud storage device and access data from it. You need to ensure that the APIs the cloud provider uses are interoperable with your own, because there are few standards for cloud storage (see Chapter 18 for more on standards). In other words, vendors like to use their own APIs.

According to experts, what users want is a standard like the ubiquitous TCP/IP for the network used across all storage interfaces. However, this may be difficult because each vendor may define its own APIs based on SOAP and REST. So, for the near term, there may be similarities, but vendors won't be completely interoperable.

✔ **Security:** Security is always a concern. Make sure security measures are in place when data is transferred between storage and on-premises locations, as well as access-control measures once the data is stored. Files need to be secure while in storage, too.

✔ **Reliability:** Data integrity is also a piece of the hybrid cloud environment. You need to make sure that your data gets from point A to point B and that it maintains its integrity. Your cloud provider might index your data. Its integrity also needs to remain intact when it's in storage. For example, if indexes are corrupted, you can lose your data. We talk much more about the why and how of security in Chapter 11.

✔ **Business continuity:** Planned and even unplanned downtime can cause problems for your business. Your storage provider needs to include snapshots, mirroring, and backups, as well as rapid recovery so that if the provider's system goes down, you're covered. You also need to make sure that the right service level agreements (SLAs) are in place (for more on SLAs, see Chapter 17).

- ✔ **Reporting and charge-back:** Because cloud storage is a pay-as-you-go model, you need to know what your bill will be at the end of the billing cycle. This will include any transactional charges the provider might charge you as well as storage costs.

- ✔ **Management:** In a hybrid cloud environment, if you choose to store some of your data on-premises and some in the cloud, you'll need to be able to manage the environments together. How will service levels be monitored and managed across these environments? How will you know if there's a problem with your storage provider? It would be nice to be able to manage all of this together, in one spot, in one single "pane of glass." However, the industry is not there yet, because it's continuing to evolve its offerings in this space. See Chapter 4 for more on managing a hybrid cloud environment.

- ✔ **Performance/latency:** Once you put your data in the cloud, you are subject to *latency* (delays that occur when processing data) issues. The questions to ask here are these (which we explore more deeply in the next section):

  - How quickly will your applications need data?

  - What are the risks if data isn't available in a reasonable timeframe?

  - Will your applications experience time-out and thus problems?

  - Does the cloud storage provider match or exceed your network speeds?

  - Are there any bottlenecks?

The reality is that combining internal private cloud storage with external cloud storage to look like one storage is difficult. Different vendors have different approaches.

- ✔ **Open source:** Rackspace offers what it calls Cloud Files as an open source system for standardizing storage between clouds. It's doing so under the umbrella of Openstack.org.

- ✔ **Federation:** EMC provides its Atmos solution as a software-based solution with services loosely coupled and federated to Atmos servers in the cloud. See Chapter 13 for more information on services architectures and federated approaches.

- ✔ **Gateway approaches:** These sit between on-premises storage and cloud storage to translate traditional storage to cloud storage. In many cases, it seems to end users that the storage is a NAS-type storage. We talk more about this in the "Defining the elements of storage" sidebar, earlier in this chapter.

Evaluating the Impact of Hybrid Cloud on Supporting Changing Network Requirements

Once you start moving your data into the cloud, you may need to address latency concerns, depending on the amount of data you're storing there and how often you need to access it. In a hybrid model, you're not just utilizing your LAN or WAN for data access, you're now going across the Internet to access it. So, you really need to think about the kind of data you're willing to store in the cloud based on how often you need to get to it and the network speed that you're dealing with. Although storage may be unlimited (for a price) in the cloud, the network is not. Two issues you need to consider are amount of data and network speed.

Amount of data

Say that you want to store a large amount of tier 3 data in a storage cloud provider. It may not make sense to actually try to transport the data over the Internet. Remember, *the bandwidth of a truck is greater than any existing network*. It might make sense to provide the data to the vendor in another way. Calculate transfer rates based on the amount of data you have and then decide which leads to the next point regarding network speed.

Network speeds

Bandwidth is just one element that contributes to network speed. Latency is another one. Latency refers to a delay in processing data as it moves from one part of a network to another. For example, when a singer's mouth moves on a video but the words don't seem to match, that's because of latency. Low latency is when there's a short delay; high latency is when there's a longer delay. So, although the speed of your network should be fixed according to the bandwidth of the network connection, it doesn't always work that way because of latencies. A number of factors contribute to network latency, including data collisions, contention for bandwidth, encryption, as well as routers and computer hardware delays, to name a few.

A good corporate LAN/WAN is a gigabit network, which means that your internal network might be faster than the Internet. So, after your information gets to the Internet, you may experience a bottleneck as the information moves to your provider. This bottleneck will affect how quickly you can get your data off your premises and, more importantly, *back* to your premises. If you have a petabyte of data in a provider's cloud and want to analyze it on-premises, be aware that it's going to take a while to get the data back. You need to consider this issue when planning your hybrid deployment. For instance, you may decide not to store tier 1 data in the cloud because network speeds may not match your requirements for use.

Planning for Hybrid Resources to Support Growth and Change

Planning for hybrid cloud growth and change involves understanding your data, devising a strategy to deal with the growth, and choosing a provider. We discuss each step in this section.

Understanding your data

In a hybrid cloud environment, as with any environment, you need to understand your rate of data generation. In the hybrid world, of course, this data is being generated both on-premises and in the public cloud.

Devising a growth strategy

The second step is to devise a strategy to determine how you're going to deal with this growth. As part of this strategy, you need to understand how much storage growth you want to support internally and how much you can support outside your corporate walls. You need to do an analysis that compares your investment in corporate infrastructure to a potential cloud strategy. This analysis includes the following:

✔ **What kind of applications and data you're willing to store in the cloud versus what you want to keep on-premises:** This includes data issues associated with regulatory compliance and other risk factors. Although you may be thinking only about archive and backup applications, experts advise considering other applications that may not be mission-critical. However, make sure that your provider can adhere to any regulatory or compliance issues your company has in place. You also need to make sure they are willing to change if something changes in your industry.

✔ **A risk assessment:** Every company has its own tolerance level when it comes to risk. Aside from technology risks, you may also want to consider how your processes might change in the cloud. For example, you need to determine whether there are any people, processes, or cultural issues to consider.

✔ **On-site data storage costs:** Include all costs associated with on-site data storage: hardware, software, maintenance, environmental costs (such as electricity), and so on.

✔ **Cloud storage costs:** Include all costs associated with cloud storage, including data migration costs and storage costs associated with these applications and data.

Choosing a provider

When you've decided that you want some of your applications and data in the cloud, you need to pick your provider with due diligence. Read the fine print in terms of costs associated with the storage and what contract termination looks like. You also want to make sure that the provider puts recovery time objectives (RTOs) in place, in case there's a problem with its service. Also, make sure the vendor you select is viable. For example, what happens to your storage if your service provider goes out of business? Will you be able to recover your assets?

Experts also advise to ensure that an escape clause is in your contract, in case your provider doesn't perform as advertised.

Much of these concerns boils down to trust and doing your homework. Do you trust your vendor and have you put the right contracts in place to protect yourself? Have you done your homework? If you haven't, you need to.

The hybrid cloud storage model offers many advantages to organizations that want to maintain the security of storing their highly confidential data within a private cloud and then selectively store data with fewer confidentiality requirements in the public cloud. Ultimately, the right mix between public and private environments is one that maximizes cost savings while maintaining security and geographic storage requirements.

Part VII
The Part of Tens

The 5th Wave   By Rich Tennant

Now maybe these folks got a decent disaster recovery plan and maybe they don't...

DANGER
WILD RHINOCEROS

In this part . . .

This part is the quintessential *For Dummies* element that consists entirely of lists. We list cloud resources, best practices, a few pointers, and also caveats. We think you'll refer to this part again and again.

Chapter 21

(More Than) Ten Hybrid Cloud Resources

In This Chapter

▶ Seeking standards

▶ Finding open source initiatives

▶ Free resources from your favorite vendors

*Y*ou can find many resources that will help you find out more about the hybrid cloud. There are standards organizations that enjoy wide participation from the most important companies in the cloud market. There are organizations benefiting from the participation of companies on the leading edge of implementing hybrid cloud services within their companies and that are eager to help guide your way. In addition, you can find open source offerings that are very helpful in moving the market forward. Of course, all the vendors in the market have research, papers, and best practices that they're happy to share. In this chapter, we offer you some practical ideas on where to go for resources that can really help.

Hurwitz & Associates

The authors of this book are partners at Hurwitz & Associates. We're happy to help you with your questions about cloud computing. We provide training, strategy guidance, and planning. If you're a cloud vendor, we can help you understand customer requirements so that you can position and offer products that your customers need. We invite you to subscribe to our blogs and to visit our site at www.hurwitz.com.

Standards Organizations

For cloud computing to mature, it needs standards. Luckily, there are a number of important organizations that are working hard at bringing vendors together to help the process evolve. Here are some you should play attention to.

National Institute of Standards and Technology

The National Institute of Standards and Technology (NIST) is a U.S. government agency that focuses on emerging standards efforts. This organization has done a considerable amount of work defining and providing good information on cloud computing. Check out its website at www.nist.gov/itl/cloud/.

OASIS

Creating standards takes a lot of work — often volunteer, financially uncompensated work by dedicated people determined to get things right. People who sit on standards committees deserve the undying gratitude of the rest of us. We thank you, standards committee members.

OASIS, the Organization for the Advancement of Structured Information Standards is a global consortium focused on the creation and adoption of standards for electronic business. The consortium is a nonprofit organization that relies on contributions from its member organizations. OASIS creates topic-specific committees that are beginning to focus on cloud computing. Check out its site at www.oasis-open.org.

Consortiums and Councils

There are important organizations that are not strictly standards bodies. These organizations work closely with vendors and standards groups to move requirements along.

Cloud Standards Customer Council

The Cloud Standards Customer Council is a combination of vendor and large corporate customers. It was established to focus on cloud best practices. Today, the organization includes more than 100 of the world's leading organizations, including Lockheed Martin, Citigroup, State Street, and North Carolina State University. It is operated by the Object Management Group (OMG). Check out its website at www.cloud-council.org.

The Cloud Standards Wiki

This single place gives you access to lots of groups working on cloud standards. Check out its site at http://cloud-standards.org/wiki. The wiki contains information about all the organizations working in the area.

The Open Group

The Open Group is a global consortium that enables the achievement of business objectives through IT standards. With more than 400 member organizations, it has a diverse membership that spans all sectors of the IT community — customers, systems and solutions suppliers, tool vendors, integrators, and consultants, as well as academics and researchers. The group has a cloud working group and has lots of good source material available. Check out its website at www3.opengroup.org.

Open Source Offerings

Open source has become incredibly important, especially as a foundation for cloud computing. There is consistent support, for example, for Linux as the foundation for most of the cloud platforms. Therefore, open source offerings are playing an increasingly important role.

The Linux Foundation

The Linux Foundation is the nonprofit consortium dedicated to fostering the growth of Linux. Founded in 2000, the Linux Foundation sponsors the work of Linux creator Linus Torvalds and is supported by leading technology companies and developers from around the world. The Linux Foundation promotes the platform and works with those vendors and customers that leverage Linux. Check out the Linux Foundation at www.linuxfoundation.org.

The Eclipse Foundation

The Eclipse Foundation is an open-source community focused on providing a vendor-neutral open development platform and application frameworks for building software. It's a nonprofit organization and has widespread participation from developers and corporations around the globe. The Eclipse platform is written in Java and runs on most popular operating systems, including Linux, HP-UX, AIX, Solaris, QNX, Mac OS X, and Windows. Check out the Eclipse Foundation at www.eclipse.org.

Open Cloud Computing Interface

The Open Cloud Computing Interface (OCCI; http://occi-wg.org) is made up of a set of open community-lead specifications delivered through the Open Grid Forum. The group is based on its development of a protocol and API for all types of management tasks.

OCCI was originally initiated to create a remote management API for IaaS-based services, allowing for the development of interoperable tools for common tasks including deployment, autonomic scaling, and monitoring. It has since evolved into a flexible API with a strong focus on integration, portability, interoperability, and innovation, while still offering a high degree of extensibility.

The current release of the Open Cloud Computing Interface is compatible with many other models in addition to IaaS, including, for example, PaaS and SaaS.

Open Cloud Manifesto

Open Cloud Manifesto is a community of more than 250 vendors intended to establish a core set of principles for cloud standards. The group has published several white papers that are worth reading. You can find them by clicking the Blogs, Wikis, and More link at www.opencloudmanifesto.org.

OpenStack

OpenStack is an open source platform originated by Rackspace and NASA for building both public and private clouds. It is supported by more than 150 companies. The organization has hundreds of different initiatives underway. Check out its website at http://openstack.org. The group also has a Wiki which can be found at http://wiki.openstack.org/.

The Cloud Security Alliance

The Cloud Security Alliance (CSA) was established to promote the use of best practices for providing and ensuring security within cloud computing, and to educate people about the uses of cloud computing to help secure all other forms of computing. Check out its website at `https://cloudsecurity alliance.org`.

The Cloud Storage Initiative

The Storage Networking Industry Association (SNIA) is a trade organization focused on the networked storage industry. The cloud storage initiative focuses on the needs for cloud storage standards. Its strategic goal is to lead the storage industry worldwide in developing and promoting standards, technologies, and educational services to empower organizations in the management of information. Check out its website at `www.snia.org`.

Vendor Sites

All the major cloud computing vendors provide great resources online. We recommend checking out vendors such as Google, VMware, EMC, Amazon, Rackspace, IBM, Microsoft, HP, Cisco, and Oracle. This is only a partial list. Hundreds of vendors are in the space, so don't stop with this list; check sites of all the vendors we mention throughout the book. You can find great resources on systems integrators' sites. Take advantage.

Cloud Gatherings

There is no better way to get started learning about the value of cloud computing than to go to conferences and cloud gatherings. Although we don't have room to mention all the organizations and companies that offer conferences and meetings, here are some to give you a starting point.

CloudCamps

Everyone fondly remembers fun times at summer camp. CloudCamps aren't exactly the same, but they *are* great gatherings all over the world that bring together thinkers and doers. Check for a CloudCamp near you at `www.cloudcamp.org`.

Through a series of local CloudCamp (started by Dave Nielson, Reuven Cohen and Sam Charrington. The first CloudCamp was held June 24, 2008 in San Francisco. The organization organizes events, attendees exchange ideas, knowledge, and information in a creative and supporting environment, advancing the current state of cloud computing and related technologies.

Cloud computing conferences

One of the best ways to learn about what is happening in cloud computing is to go to one of the conferences. Because there are so many, we thought we'd give you a link to a calendar. CloudBook is a good resource that includes a calendar of cloud events. Go to its site at www.cloudbook.net/calendar/.

OpenForum Europe

OpenForum Europe (OFE) is a not-for-profit industry organization designed to promote full openness and interoperability of computer systems throughout Europe. It promotes open source software, as well as openness more generally as part of a vision to facilitate open, competitive choice for IT users. Check out its website at www.openforumeurope.org.

CIO.gov

CIO.gov is the website of the U.S. CIO (chief information officer) and the Federal CIO Council, serving as a central resource for information on federal IT. By showcasing examples of innovation, identifying best practices, and providing a forum for federal IT leaders, CIO.gov keeps the public informed about how our government is working to close the technology gap between the private and public sectors. Check out its website at www.cio.gov.

Open Data Center Alliance

The Open Data Center Alliance (ODCA) is an independent organization that is developing a unified vision for cloud requirements — particularly focused on open, interoperable solutions for secure cloud federation, automation of cloud infrastructure, common management, and transparency of cloud service delivery. Check out its website at www.opendatacenteralliance.org.

Chapter 22

Ten Hybrid Cloud Best Practices

In This Chapter
▶ Balancing business objectives with IT requirements
▶ Understanding business processes
▶ Recognizing the importance of governance and security
▶ Identifying the right starting points

*H*ybrid cloud strategies are at an early stage. Companies big and small are beginning to put together a plan to move from disconnected silo systems to pools of resources designed to serve business change. In this chapter, we provide you with some best practices that will help you plan for your journey to the hybrid cloud.

Start with Business Objectives

Although you will have to deal with many technology issues during the planning and implementation of your cloud strategy, you need to think about your business first. Computing has always been about supporting business goals. However, sometimes it's too easy to get caught up in the details of technology options and lose sight of the goals. Hybrid cloud strategies can help your company experiment and innovate in ways that aren't possible with less flexible approaches.

Create a Task Force with Both IT and Business Leaders

One of the best practices in moving ahead with new business and IT strategies is to bring the right players together as a team. By creating this collaborative partnership, all the decision makers come to have a holistic understanding of how business can be affected by innovative and flexible technology. Sometimes knowledge and understanding have a bigger impact than any other approach to strategy.

Understand the Business Process as a Foundation for the Hybrid Cloud

Business processes has always been at the heart of how companies operate internally and with partners, customers, and suppliers. Often business processes have been tightly integrated into packaged applications. However, with the move to a service-oriented approach, there is an effort to separate business processes from application code. The ability to separate processes from services becomes even more important with the emergence of Business Process as a Service (PBaaS). New emerging business models reach across silos. Best practices in the age of the cloud demand that businesses rethink how they create more flexible business process automation.

Think Service Orientation

The companies that are most successful at implementing a hybrid cloud strategy have been transforming their monolithic business applications into a more flexible set of business services. Being armed with a set of clearly built and defined services makes it much easier for companies to create new, innovative business practices and collaborative approaches.

Think Service Management

The same companies that have focused on creating more modular computing resources are also thinking about how to manage a wide range of cloud and on-premises resources. This is not something that most companies know how to do today, but it's important that companies plan for the time when they can have a comprehensive view of all their IaaS, PaaS, and SaaS delivery models, no matter where these models reside or which company owns and manages them.

At the same time, management needs to bring these public cloud resources together with private clouds and data center assets. Doing so will require additional technology, sophisticated business processes, and analytics technologies.

Plan to Manage Multiple Endpoints

Today there are more *endpoints* — traditional desktops, laptops, tablets, smartphones, and even sensors in equipment — than ever in the typical organization. The advent of cloud environments increases the flexibility to allow users to work with the endpoint of their choice. Although this is good for consumers and customers, it puts more burdens on IT to effectively manage endpoints — especially from a security standpoint.

Select Your Partners Carefully

Unlike with a data center, hybrid cloud computing requires that you make careful decisions about with whom you partner and for which services. Companies with a comprehensive plan for a hybrid cloud strategy select a variety of cloud providers depending on the type of job they're trying to do. For example, when companies are managing important data, they will not store that data in a public storage environment that isn't respected and trusted. Likewise, if a company wants to use a SaaS environment to support its sales force, management needs to select a partner that can provide the right level of service and that has a good track record of serving customers.

The benefit derived from selecting SaaS or PaaS delivery models is that a company is able to test a new offering to see whether it can support its business needs. It's important to look under the covers when you're using public cloud service providers. Many providers abstract the complexities of the underlying platform. However, if you're going to rely on these services, find out what's behind the slick interfaces. Do your homework so that you understand the best practices your cloud provider uses to create the value you will come to depend on.

You also need to understand what happens if you are unhappy with a provider. How does the vendor allow you to regain control of your data? What will the vendor charge you for continuing to store that information? If you have built complex business processes using proprietary development tools, you need to plan for disengagement, if necessary. Therefore, when signing on with a public cloud provider, do the groundwork.

Plan Your Strategy Based on Governance and Security

While governance and security are extremely important issues within any data center environment, they take on a new sense of urgency in the cloud. One problem confronting organizations is that when third-party services and platforms are used, management has less control. Larger companies are often subject to governmental reporting requirements that force the companies to prove who has accessed what data at particular times. If that company is using a public cloud resource, it needs to make sure that the provider will be able to support the company's reporting needs. Likewise, many companies are in highly regulated industries, such as financial and healthcare services. These companies need to be able to access the type of reports that will allow them to meet regulations. Some governments require that personal data be stored in the country where individuals live. Therefore, it's the responsibility of management to conduct due diligence to make sure a company is in compliance.

Security in a hybrid world can be complicated. Management needs to have clear policies about what services can be used for which situations. Both a well-understood security policy and the tools and technology to support the policy as it's implemented are required.

Governance and security are not static. Companies must make sure that their selected partners keep up with changing business and governmental requirements. The hybrid cloud requires a well-understood policy across all the players — vendors, partners, suppliers, customers, and employees.

Know Your Starting Points

No two companies have the same level of maturity in terms of their IT and business strategies. You need to have a well-thought-out strategy that allows you to implement your cloud strategy in stages. The best starting points are those that give you good experience with emerging technologies. What does it mean to build an application using a PaaS delivery model? How much training will developers need? What is the impact of this new approach to development on existing projects?

Likewise, if your company is looking at a SaaS delivery model, you need to think about how it will support your existing data resources. How can you integrate data across these sources? You need a plan for this inevitable outcome.

Just as important, you need to understand what it means to use a public cloud for IaaS. Do you use a public cloud service for all your resources? How do you select the right uses of these services? Getting some early experience with a prototype will give you a good understanding about issues you may face in the future.

One important issue that you need to consider is the emerging cloud standards. Some of these standards are available today and are well accepted. Other standards are emerging. Make sure you're watching and participating in the discussions and debates; doing so is part of your journey to the hybrid cloud.

Pay Attention to Detail

Don't just rush in and start building and buying capabilities. You need to have a carefully conceived plan. Talk to peers who have experience. Go to conferences where you can learn from vendors, implementers, and experienced customers.

In Chapter 21, we discuss the many resources, standards organizations, and customer councils that are available to help you on your path forward.

Chapter 23

Ten Hybrid Cloud Do's and Don'ts

*M*any companies that have begun to move into the cloud don't do a lot of planning. Executives in different business units start to use public cloud services out of frustration because of inefficiencies in the IT organization. Many IT departments, responding to rapidly changing business demands, begin implementing various public and private cloud services. However, without a plan and some careful preparation, things can go wrong before you know it. In this chapter, we give you some ideas about what you should do and what you should avoid as you begin your journey to the hybrid cloud.

Do Plan for Data and Services Consistency

Ironically, one of the reasons companies look to cloud computing is to move away from the silos of information, business rules, and business services within organizations. Companies need to have consistent information to manage businesses effectively. Although many tools allow data to be integrated across silos, that data has to have common definitions. Also, companies need to have a set of business services that adhere to business policy. All of the various SaaS applications, business process services, and data sources need to have consistent definitions.

So, do plan for a master data management plan and establish a service catalog that keeps track of common services that are authorized by management. This approach will help you create a well-structured and accurate hybrid cloud environment.

Do Decide Which Cloud Services Can Be Managed in a Public Cloud

Public cloud services offer incredible ease of use and flexibility to add and subtract services as needs change. However, before you begin signing up for a bunch of different public services, do your homework. Because of security and governance, you may need to keep certain services, data, or business processes inside your data center.

You do need to know the difference in requirements and plan a good balance between public and private cloud services.

Do Have a Service Management Plan

In the long term, you will want to have a way to manage all your public, private, and data center resources as though they were a single unified environment. However, as with any business strategy, you can't do everything at once. Do decide what is practical to do right away and what you will do over time as technology matures.

Initially, for example, you need to be able to monitor each service that you use for performance and security. Test new service management products and services as they become available so you're ready when these services are mature enough to support your long-term plan.

Do Plan for Data Portability

Many companies that are using SaaS don't make plans for the future, including what happens if their SaaS vendor goes out of business or becomes too expensive. Another issue to consider for the future is what you'll do if you discover a different SaaS vendor who is better able to meet your needs.

You do need a plan for how you can move your data from one cloud environment to another. Make sure that your selected vendors provide a simple and inexpensive way to move your data. You don't want to be surprised.

Do Execute on an Overall Hybrid Cloud Plan

When you're creating a cloud strategy, it's important to think about an overall plan for the services that will live across the public and private clouds and the data center. Many cloud services will be shared by developers in your company and with contractors. These same services may become product offerings that you provide to partners and customers. It's therefore important that services are well tested, monitored, and catalogued. At the same time, you have to know what your company's IT assets are so that you can create a hybrid environment that's accurate and efficient. Unless you control the quality of your overall environment, your company will be at risk.

Don't Rely on Only a Single Vendor

It's tempting to find a cloud vendor you like and stop. However, that can be a mistake. Do plan to work with more than one cloud vendor so that you're not stuck if something happens. Anything can happen. A vendor can have a catastrophic failure and be out of commission for a few hours or a few days. You'll discover that some cloud vendors are better suited for some tasks than others.

You won't understand these distinctions until you have some experience with cloud computing. This is especially important when you're working in a hybrid cloud environment. You might find that certain cloud services require the capabilities of a high-performance network. Other services may not require this type of sophisticated performance. You need to plan for all the different requirements.

Don't Over Invest in Licenses

Many cloud vendors create packages to make it attractive for their customers to buy in bulk. So, it's tempting to buy more licenses for more years because of price. However, this can be a trap if you over-buy. For example, a vendor might offer you half the list price per user per month if you sign up for 100 users over three years. The price is so attractive that you take the plunge, only to discover that you really are supporting only 25 users. No vendor is going to let you scale down those licenses once you have signed your contract.

Don't Overlook the Need to Manage Infrastructure

One of the reasons companies are attracted to the cloud is that they don't have to worry about the details of managing software and infrastructure. However, don't be fooled. Even if you're using only a couple of public cloud services, you need to keep track of the performance of these vendors. If you're using a customer relationship management SaaS platform and it's unavailable for a couple of days, who is to blame? It's quite likely that the sales and marketing team will blame the IT department, not the vendor. Increasingly, IT will have to provide performance, governance, and security oversight of cloud services.

Don't Leave Your Data Center Alone

It might be a relief to use cloud services to get around some of the inconsistencies and complexities of the existing data center. However, it's dangerous to assume that the data center should be left alone. The data center needs to be transformed as a complement to cloud services. So, don't leave your data center in the dark. Begin to plan a strategy to optimize the data center so that it handles the applications and tasks it's best suited for.

Don't Ignore the Service Level Agreement

All public cloud vendors, including IaaS, PaaS, and SaaS providers, will offer some sort of service level agreement that explains what obligation the vendor assumes and what risks you have to assume. Remember that no vendor will take on obligations it doesn't have to. So, it's up to you to read the fine print and understand exactly what reality looks like. For example, no cloud vendor will reimburse you if you lose business because the service is not operational. They may indeed give you the money back that you spent on a service, but that will be small comfort if you've lost an important customer.

So, you must decide how much risk is acceptable. This information will help you determine which services can reside with a commodity cloud service provider, which ones need to be with a provider that offers a higher level of service, and which services should remain in your private cloud.

Do Move Forward and Don't Look Back

We think that the movement to the hybrid cloud is inevitable. However, it's not a strategy that you should adopt without careful planning. You must deal with issues in the cloud that are very different than those you encounter in a traditional data center. Software license models are different. Vendors take some responsibility for protecting your data and the performance of your services. However, the responsibility will land with your own company. Therefore, you need to move forward armed with the right information and with the right level of caution. However, if you take the right steps, we think that the future can be quite exciting.

Glossary

abstraction: The idea of minimizing the complexity of something by hiding the details and just providing the relevant information. It's about providing a high-level specification rather than going into lots of detail about how something works. In the cloud, for instance, in an IaaS delivery model, the infrastructure is abstracted from the user.

access control: Determining who or what can go where, when, and how.

ACID: An acronym for *atomicity, consistency, isolation,* and *durability,* which are the main requirements for proper transaction processing.

API (application programming interface): A collection of subroutine calls that allows computer programs to use a software system.

application lifecycle: The process of maintaining a piece of code so that it's consistent and predictable as it's changed to support business requirements.

architecture: In information processing, the design approach taken in developing a program or system.

archiving: The process by which database or file data that's seldom used or outdated but that's required for historical or audit reasons is copied to a cheaper form of storage. The storage medium may be online, tape, or optical disc.

asset management: Software that allows organizations to record all information about their hardware and software. Most such applications capture cost information, license information, and so on. Such information belongs in the configuration management database. See also *CMDB.*

audit: A check on the effectiveness of a task or set of tasks, and how the tasks are managed and documented.

audit trail: A trace of a sequence of events in a clerical or computer system. This audit usually identifies the creation or modification of any element in the system, who did it, and (possibly) why it was done.

authentication: The process by which the identity of a person or computer process is verified.

AWS (Amazon Web Services): The set of web services that Amazon offers to help web developers build web applications and use Amazon's cloud computing environment.

Azure: Windows Azure is an operating system for cloud computing from Microsoft. The hosting and management environment are maintained at Microsoft data centers, so there's no need to use internal data center resources when developing applications in Azure.

backup: A utility that copies databases, files, or subsets of databases and files to a storage medium. This copy can be used to restore the data in case of serious failure.

bandwidth: Technically, the range of frequencies over which a device can send or receive signals. The term is also used to denote the maximum data transfer rate, measured in bits per second, that a communications channel can handle.

batch: A noninteractive process that runs in a queue, usually when the system load is lowest, generally used for processing batches of information in a serial and usually efficient manner. Early computers were capable of only batch processing.

best practice: An effective way of doing something. It can relate to anything from writing program code to IT governance.

binding: Making the necessary connections among software components so that they can interact.

biometrics: Using a person's unique physical characteristics to prove his identity to a computer — by employing a fingerprint scanner or voice analyzer, for example.

black box: A component or device with an input and an output whose inner workings need not be understood by or accessible to the user.

BPaaS: See *Business Process as a Service.*

BPEL (Business Process Execution Language): A computer language based on WSDL (Web Services Description Language, an XML format for describing web services) and designed for programming business services. See also *XML.*

BPM (business process management): A technology and methodology for controlling the activities — both automated and manual — needed to make a business function.

broker: In computer programming, a program that accepts requests from one software layer or component and translates them into a form that can be understood by another layer or component.

browser: A program that lets you access information on the Internet. Browsers used to run just on personal computers, but now they are on cellphones and personal digital assistants and soon will appear on refrigerators.

bus: A technology that connects multiple components so they can talk to one another. In essence, a bus is a connection capability. A bus can be software (such as an enterprise service bus) or hardware (such as a memory bus). See also *ESB*.

business process: The codification of rules and practices that constitute a business.

Business Process as a Service (BPaaS): A whole business process is provided as a service involving little more than a software interface, such as a parcel delivery service.

business process modeling: A technique for transforming how business operates into a codified source in code so that it can be translated into software.

business rules: Constraints or actions that refer to the actual commercial world but may need to be encapsulated in service management or business applications.

business service: An individual function or activity that is directly useful to the business.

cache: The storage of data so that future requests for that data can be achieved more quickly.

center of excellence: A group of key people from all areas of the business and operations that focuses on best practices. A center of excellence provides a way for groups within the company to collaborate. This group also becomes a force for change, because it can leverage its growing knowledge to help business units benefit from experience.

change management: The management of change in operational processes and applications.

cloud computing: A computing model that makes IT resources such as servers, middleware, and applications available as services to business organizations in a self-service manner.

cloud ecosystem: Independent software and hardware vendors that partner with cloud providers to create a partnership for selling to customers.

CMDB (configuration management database): In general, a repository of service management data.

COBIT (Control Objectives for Information and Related Technology): An IT framework with a focus on governance and managing technical and business risks.

component: A piece of computer software that can be used as a building block in larger systems. Components can be parts of business applications that have been made accessible through web service–related standards and technologies, such as WSDL, SOAP, and XML. See also *web service*.

compute unit: Within its EC2 service, Amazon uses computer units to measure the infrastructure used by virtual server instances. Currently, one EC2 Compute Unit provides the equivalent CPU capacity of a 1.0–1.2 GHz 2007 Opteron or 2007 Xeon processor. Other IaaS providers also have units for measuring resource usage.

configuration: The complete description of the way in which the constituent elements of a software product or system interrelate, both in functional and physical terms.

configuration management: The management of configurations, normally involving holding configuration data in a database so that the data can be managed and changed where necessary.

container: In computer programming, a data structure or object used to manage collections of other objects in an organized way.

CRM (customer relationship management): Software intended to help you run your sales force and customer support operations.

data cleansing: Software used to identify potential data-quality problems. If a customer is listed multiple times in a customer database because of variations in the spelling of her name, the data-cleansing software makes corrections to help standardize the data.

data fabric: The part of the computer network devoted to transmissions.

data federation: Data access to a variety of data stores, using consistent rules and definitions that enable all the data stores to be treated as a single resource.

data profiling: A technique or process that helps you understand the content, structure, and relationships of your data. This process also helps you validate your data against technical and business rules.

data quality: Characteristics of data such as consistency, accuracy, reliability, completeness, timeliness, reasonableness, and validity. Data-quality software ensures that data elements are represented in a consistent way across different data stores or systems, making the data more trustworthy across the enterprise.

data transformation: A process by which the format of data is changed so it can be used by different applications.

data warehouse: A large data store containing the organization's historical data, which is used primarily for data analysis and data mining.

database: A computer system intended to store large amounts of information reliably and in an organized fashion. Most databases provide users convenient access to the data, along with helpful search capabilities.

dedicated hosting: Dedicated hosting is where the customer is given full control over the server that's hosted in the cloud. This contrasts with managed hosting, where management is the responsibility of the hosting company.

dedicated server: A dedicated server is one the customer doesn't share with other users of the hosting cloud service.

directory: The word is used in both computing and telephony to indicate an organized map of devices, files, or people.

distributed processing: Spreading the work of an information-processing application among several computers.

early binding: Making necessary connections among software components when the software system is first put together or built.

EC2 (Elastic Compute Cloud from Amazon): This is Amazon's commercial Infrastructure as a Service (IaaS) web service that pioneered cloud computing.

elasticity: The ability to expand or shrink a computing resource in real time, based on need.

emulation: When hardware or software, or a combination of both, duplicates the functionality of a computer system in a different, second system. The behavior of the second system will closely resemble the original functionality of the first system. See also *virtualization*.

ERP (enterprise resource planning): A packaged set of business applications that combines business rules, process, and data management into a single integrated environment to support a business.

ESB (enterprise service bus): A distributed middleware software system that allows computer applications to communicate in a standardized way.

eSCM (eSourcing Capability Model): A framework developed at Carnegie Mellon University to provide a best-practices model for improving relationships between customers and suppliers in outsourcing agreements.

ETL (Extract, Transform, Load): Tools for locating and accessing data from a data store (data extraction), changing the structure or format of the data so it can be used by the business application (data transformation), and sending the data to the business application (data load).

eTOM (enhanced Telecom Operations Map): A framework that provides a business process model for the telecommunications industry.

fault tolerance: The ability of a system to provide uninterrupted service despite the failure of one or more of the system's components.

federation: The combination of disparate things so that they can act as one — as in federated states, data, or identity management — and to make sure that all the right rules apply.

framework: A support structure for developing software products.

governance: The ability to ensure that corporate or governmental rules and regulations are conformed with. Governance is combined with compliance and security issues across computing environments.

granularity: An important software design concept, especially in relation to components, referring to the amount of detail or functionality — from fine to coarse — provided in a service component. One software component can do something quite simple, such as calculate a square root; another has a great deal of detail and functionality to represent a complex business rule or workflow. The first component is fine grained, and the second is coarse grained. Developers often aggregate fine-grained services into coarse-grained services to create a business service.

grid computing: A step beyond distributed processing, involving large numbers of networked computers (often geographically dispersed and possibly of different types and capabilities) that are harnessed to solve a common problem. A grid computing model can be used instead of virtualization in situations that require real time where latency is unacceptable.

hardware partitioning: The act of subdividing and isolating elements of a physical server into fractions, each of which can run an operating system or an application.

HIPAA (Health Insurance Portability and Accountability Act of 1996): A set of extensive regulations that healthcare organizations and providers in the United States must follow. One goal of this act is to place controls on the healthcare system to protect patients' rights to privacy regarding information about their health. The policies and regulations place significant demands on technology systems that have anything to do with healthcare.

HTML (Hypertext Markup Language): A data-encoding scheme invented by Tim Berners-Lee in 1991 and the basic way that information is encoded over the World Wide Web.

HTTP (Hypertext Transport Protocol): The basic way that information is linked and transmitted over the World Wide Web. HTTPS is a version of HTTP with encryption for security.

hybrid cloud: A computing environment that includes the use of public and private clouds as well as data center resources in a coordinated fashion.

hypervisor: Hardware that allows multiple operating systems to share a single host. The hypervisor sits at the lowest levels of the hardware environment and uses a thin layer of code in software to enable dynamic resource sharing. The hypervisor makes it seem like each operating system has the resources all to itself.

IaaS: See *Infrastructure as a Service.*

identity management: Keeping track of a single user's (or asset's) identity throughout an engagement with a system or set of systems.

information integration: A process using software to link data sources in various departments or regions of the organization with an overall goal of creating more reliable, consistent, and trusted information.

infrastructure: The fundamental systems necessary for the ordinary operation of anything, be it a country or an IT department. The physical infrastructure that people rely on includes roads, electrical wiring, and water systems. In IT, infrastructure includes basic computer hardware, networks, operating systems, and other software that applications run on top of.

Infrastructure as a Service (Iaas): Infrastructure, including a management interface and associated software, provided to companies from the cloud as a service.

infrastructure services: Services provided by the infrastructure. In IT, these services include all the software needed to make devices talk to one another, for starters.

Internet: A huge computer network linking almost all the computers in the world and enabling them to communicate via standard protocols (TCP/IP) and data formats. See also *SMTP, TCP/IP,* and *XML.*

interoperability: The ability of a product to interface with many other products; usually used in the context of software.

IP (Internet Protocol): A codified technique for communicating data across a packet-switched network. IP can also mean intellectual property such as patents, trademarks, copyrights, and trade secrets. See also *TCP/IP.*

ISO (International Organization for Standardization): An organization that has developed more than 17,000 international standards, including standards for IT service management and corporate governance of information technology.

ITIL (Information Technology Infrastructure Library): A framework and set of standards for IT governance based on best practices.

JCA (J2EE Connector Architecture): A technology that enables Java programs to talk to other software, such as databases and legacy applications.

KPI (key performance indicator): An indicator used to measure the effectiveness of a process.

LAMP (Linux, Apache, MySQL, PHP, Perl, or Python): An increasingly popular open source approach to building web applications. LAMP is a software bundle made up of the *L*inux operating system; the *A*pache web server; a *My*SQL database; and a scripting language such as *P*HP, *P*erl, or *P*ython.

late binding: Deferring the necessary connections among applications to when the connection is first needed. Late binding allows more flexibility for changes than early binding does, but it imposes some cost in processing time.

latency: The amount of time lag that enables a service to execute in an environment. Some applications require less latency and need to respond in near real time, whereas other applications are less time-sensitive.

legacy application: Any application more than a few years old. When applications can't be disposed of and replaced easily, they become legacy applications. The good news is that they're still doing something useful when selected pieces of code can be turned into business services with new standardized interfaces.

Linux: Linux is an open source operating system based upon and similar to Unix. In cloud computing, Linux is the dominant operating system, primarily because it is supported by a large number of vendors and is the predominate cloud operating system.

Linux web hosting: The vast majority of websites run on the Linux operating system managed by a Linux web hosting service using the LAMP (Linux, Apache, MySQL, PHP) software stack.

loose coupling: An approach to distributed software applications in which components interact by passing data and requests to other components in a standardized way that minimizes dependencies among components. The emphasis is on simplicity and autonomy. Each component offers a small range of simple services to other components.

malware: The general term for computer software that intentionally does ill, such as viruses, Trojans, worms, and spyware.

markup language: A way of encoding information that uses plain text containing special tags often delimited by angle brackets (< and >). Specific markup languages are often created, based on XML, to standardize the interchange of information between different computer systems and services. See also *XML*.

mashup: A program (possibly installed on a web page) that combines content from more than one source, such as Google Maps and a real estate listing service.

master-slave: An arrangement in which one system or process is designated as a controller and other participating systems or processes respond to this controller. Should a master fail, the slaves are unable to continue.

metadata: The definitions, mappings, and other characteristics used to describe how to find, access, and use the company's data and software components.

metadata repository: A container of consistent definitions of business data and rules for mapping data to its actual physical locations in the system.

middleware: Multipurpose software that lives at a layer between the operating system and application in distributed computing environments.

mission critical: An application that a business cannot afford to be without at any time.

MOM (Message Oriented Middleware): A precursor to the enterprise service bus. See also *ESB*.

multi-tenancy: This refers to the situation where a single instance of an application runs on a SaaS vendor's servers, but serves multiple client organizations (tenants), keeping all their data separate. In a multi-tenant architecture, a software application partitions its data and configuration so that each customer has a customized virtual application instance.

MySQL: An open source option to SQL.

NAS (Networked Attached Storage): NAS is a disk that includes its own network address rather than being tied to a server.

.NET: Pronounced *dot-net;* a Microsoft programming framework, with heavy emphasis on web services. See also *web service.*

network: The connection of computer systems (nodes) by communications channels and appropriate software.

NoSQL: A set of technologies that created a broad array of database management systems that are distinct from relational database systems. One major difference is that SQL is not used as the primary query language. These database management systems are also designed for distributed data stores.

OASIS (Organization for the Advancement of Structured Information Standards): A consortium promoting e-business and web services standards.

open source: A movement in the software industry that makes programs available along with the source code used to create them so that others can inspect and modify how programs work.

P2P (peer to peer): A networking system in which nodes in a network exchange data directly instead of going through a central server.

PaaS: See *Platform as a Service.*

Perl (Practical Extraction and Report Language): A powerful scripting language in widespread use in system administration, web development, and other activities.

PHP (PHP Hypertext Processor): An open source scripting language (originally designed in Perl) used especially for producing dynamic web pages.

Platform as a Service (PaaS): This is a cloud service that abstracts the computing services including the operating software and the development and deployment and management lifecycle. It sits on top of Infrastructure as a Service.

portal: In computing, a window that contains a means of access, often a menu, to all the applications throughout the whole network that the user is able to run. Often, the window is segmented into smaller windows, or *portlets,* that provide direct access to applications such as stock-market price feeds or e-mail.

private cloud: As opposed to a public cloud, which is generally available, a private cloud is a set of computing resources within the corporation that serves only the corporation, but which is set up to operate in a cloudlike manner as regards its management.

programming in the large: An approach to developing business software that focuses on the various tasks or business processes needed to make the business function — processing an order, for example, or checking product availability — as opposed to more low-level technical tasks such as opening a file.

protocol: A set of rules that computers use to establish and maintain communication among themselves.

provisioning: Making resources available to users and software. A provisioning system makes applications available to users and makes server resources available to applications.

public cloud: A public cloud is a resource that is available to any consumer either on a fee per transaction service or as a free service. It does not have deep security or a well-defined SLA.

real time: A form of processing in which a computer system accepts and updates data at the same time, feeding back immediate results that influence the data source.

real-time event processing: A class of applications that demand timely response to actions that take place out in the world. Typical examples include automated stock trading and RFID. See also *RFID.*

registry: A single source for all the metadata needed to gain access to a web service or software component.

repository: A database for software and components, with an emphasis on revision control and configuration management (where they keep the good stuff, in other words).

resource pool: A set of compute, storage, or data services that are combined to be used across hybrid environments.

response time: The time from the moment at which a transaction is submitted by a user or an application to the moment at which the final result of that transaction is made known to the user or application.

REST (representational state transfer): A software architecture style interface that is commonly used to provide flexible interaction and often stateless interaction in highly distributed environments, including the cloud. REST and SOAP are used in Amazon's S3. See also *SOAP*.

RFID (radio frequency identification): A technology that uses small, inexpensive chips attached to products (or even animals) that then transmit a unique identification number over a short distance to a special radio transmitter/receiver.

RPC (remote procedure call): A way for a program running on one computer to run a subprogram on another computer.

S3 (Simple Storage Service): This distributed storage service, from Amazon, constitutes part of AWS. Amazon provides the capability to read, write, and delete objects (of data) that are up to 5GB in size. This isn't a database capability — just a place to store and access files. See also *AWS*.

SaaS: See *Software as a Service*.

SAML (Security Assertion Markup Language): A standard framework for exchanging authentication and authorization information (that is, credentials) in an XML format called *assertions*.

SAN (storage area network): A high-speed network of interconnected storage devices. These storage devices might be servers, optical disk drives, or other storage media. The difference between a SAN and a NAS is that a SAN runs at a higher speed than a NAS, while a NAS is generally easier to install and provides a file system.

Sarbanes-Oxley: The Public Company Accounting Reform and Investor Protection Act of 2002, a U.S. law enhancing standards for all U.S. public companies' boards of directors, resulting in substantial new requirements for corporate IT.

scalability: As regards to hardware, the ability to go from small to large amounts of processing power with the same architecture. It also applies to software products such as databases, in which case it refers to the consistency of performance per unit of power as hardware resources increase.

scripting language: A computer programming language that is interpreted and has access to all or most operating-system facilities. Common examples include Perl, Python, Ruby, and JavaScript. It is often easier to program in a scripting language, but the resulting programs generally run more slowly than those created in compiled languages such as C and C++.

semantics: In computer programming, what the data means as opposed to formatting rules (syntax).

server farm: A room filled with computer servers, often needed to run large Internet sites.

service: A purposeful activity carried out for the benefit of a known target. Services are often made up of a group of component services, some of which may also have component services. Services always transform something, and they complete by delivering an output.

service catalog: A directory of IT services provided across the enterprise, including information such as service description, access rights, and ownership.

service desk: A single point of contact for IT users and customers to report any issues they may have with the IT service (or, in some cases, with IT's customer service).

SLA (service level agreement): A document that captures the understanding between a service user and a service provider as to quality and timeliness.

service management: Monitoring and optimizing a service to ensure that it meets the critical outcomes that the customer values and the stakeholders want to provide.

servlet: A program that runs on a web server in response to an action taken by the user via a browser.

silo: In IT, an application with a single narrow focus, such as human resources management or inventory control, with no intention or preparation for use by others.

silver bullet: A proposed solution that seems too good to be true and usually is.

Six Sigma: A statistical term meaning six standard deviations from the norm and the name of a quality-improvement program that aims at reducing errors to one in a million.

SMTP (Simple Mail Transfer Protocol): The basic method used to transmit electronic mail (e-mail) over the Internet.

SOA (service oriented architecture): An approach to building applications that implements business processes or services by using a set of loosely coupled black-box components orchestrated to deliver a well-defined level of service.

SOAP (Simple Object Access Protocol): A protocol specification for exchanging data. Along with REST, it is used for storing and retrieving data in the Amazon storage cloud. See also *REST*.

Software as a Service (SaaS): The delivery of computer applications over the Internet.

SQL (Structured Query Language): The most popular computer language for accessing and manipulating databases.

SSL (Secure Sockets Layer): A popular method for making secure connections over the Internet, first introduced by Netscape.

standards: A core set of common, repeatable best practices and protocols that have been agreed on by a business or industry group. Typically, vendors, industry user groups, and end users collaborate to develop standards based on the broad expertise of a large number of stakeholders. Organizations can leverage these standards as a common foundation and innovate on top of them.

subroutine: A piece of computer code that can easily be used (called) by many other programs, as long as they are on the same computer and (usually) are written in the same programming language.

TCP/IP (Transmission Control Protocol/Internet Protocol): The complex stack of communications protocols that underlies the Internet. All data is broken into small packets that are sent independently over the network and reassembled at the final destination.

thin client: Client hardware in the client/server environment that is dependent on the server for loading applications. Most hardware designed for this purpose is similar to a cut-down PC, with no floppy disk drive or hard drive.

throughput: The rate at which transactions are completed in a system.

tiered storage: The assignment of data to different types of media, generally to reduce storage costs. Data is placed into tiers 1, 2, or 3, depending on how often it must be accessed or how critical it is.

TLS (Transport Layer Security): A newer name for SSL. See also *SSL*.

TQM (Total Quality Management): A popular quality-improvement program.

transaction: A computer action that represents a business event, such as debiting an account. When a transaction starts, it must either complete or not happen at all.

UDDI (Universal Description, Discovery, and Integration): A platform-independent, XML-based services registry sponsored by OASIS. See also *OASIS* and *XML*.

utility computing: A metered service that acts like a public service based on payment for use of a measured amount of a component or asset.

virtualization: Virtual memory is the use of a disk to store active areas of memory to make the available memory appear larger. In a virtual environment, one computer runs software that allows it to emulate another machine. This kind of emulation is commonly known as virtualization. See also *emulation*.

VMware: VMware provides the technology, which currently dominates the virtualization of servers. In the cloud, however, the Xen hypervisor is also widely used because it's open source.

VPN (virtual private network): A VPN uses a public telecommunications infrastructure to provide secure access. This is a virtual network dedicated to providing a customer with more security within a cloud environment. Each VPN runs its own operating system, bandwidth, and disk space, and can be individually booted.

W3C: A handy way of referring to the World Wide Web Consortium, an organization that coordinates standards for the World Wide Web.

web service: A software component created with an interface consisting of a WSDL definition, an XML schema definition, and a WS-Policy definition. Collectively, components could be called a service contract — or, alternatively, an API. See also *API, WSDL, WS-Policy,* and *XML*.

workflow: This is a sequence of steps needed to carry out a business process. Workflow technology automates the passage of information between the steps.

World Wide Web: A system built on top of the Internet that displays hyper-linked pages of information that can contain a wide variety of data formats, including multimedia.

WSCI (Web Services Choreography Interface): An XML-based interface description language that describes the flow of messages exchanged by a web service when it participates in choreographed interactions with other services.

WSDL (Web Services Description Language): An XML format for describing Web services.

WS-Policy (Web Services Policy): The Web Services Policy Framework, which provides a means of expressing the capabilities, requirements, and characteristics of software components in a web services system.

WSRP (Web Services for Remote Portlets): A protocol that allows portlets to communicate by using standard web services interfaces.

XML (eXtensible Markup Language): A way of presenting data as plain-text files that has become the lingua franca of SOA. In XML, as in HTML, data is delimited in tags that are enclosed in angle brackets (< and >), although the tags in XML can have many more meanings. See also *SOA*.

XML Schema: A language for defining and describing the structure of XML documents.

XSD (XML Schema Definition): The description of what can be in an XML document.

XSLT (eXtensible Stylesheet Language Transformations): A computer language, based on XML, that specifies how to change one XML document into another. See also *XML*.

Index

• E •

• F •